OLD WORLD ENCOUNTERS

OLD WORLD
ENCOUNTERS

—◆—

Cross-Cultural Contacts and
Exchanges in Pre-Modern Times

JERRY H. BENTLEY

New York   Oxford
OXFORD UNIVERSITY PRESS
1993

Oxford University Press

Oxford   New York   Toronto
Delhi   Bombay   Calcutta   Madras   Karachi
Kuala Lumpur   Singapore   Hong Kong   Tokyo
Nairobi   Dar es Salaam   Cape Town
Melbourne   Auckland

and associated companies in
Berlin   Ibadan

Copyright © 1993 by Oxford University Press, Inc.

Published by Oxford University Press, Inc.,
200 Madison Avenue, New York, New York 10016

Library of Congress Cataloging-in-Publication Data
Bentley, Jerry H., 1949–
Old World encounters : cross-cultural contacts
and exchanges in pre-modern times / Jerry H. Bentley.
p. cm.   Includes bibliographical references and index.
ISBN 0-19-507639-7
ISBN 0-19-507640-0 (pbk.)
1. Intercultural communication — History.
2. World history.
I. Title.
GN345.6.B46   1993   303.48′2 — dc20
92-16378

1 3 5 7 9 8 6 4 2

Printed in the United States of America
on acid-free paper

For Jeani

PREFACE

Christopher Columbus's voyages to the Western Hemisphere mark one of the clearer turning points in world history. Since the year 1492, the cross-cultural contacts inaugurated by Columbus have clearly influenced the experiences of all peoples on earth. As a result, untold numbers of scholars have examined the effects of modern cross-cultural encounters while studying themes such as long-distance trade, transfers of technology, imperial and colonial ventures, mass migrations, exchanges of plants, animals, and diseases, and cross-cultural missionary efforts.

By no means, however, did cross-cultural encounters begin in 1492. Nor have they always come about exclusively at the initiative of European peoples. On the contrary, cross-cultural encounters have been a regular feature of world history since the earliest days of the human species' existence. This book analyzes the dynamics of cross-cultural encounters in pre-modern times. It concentrates attention particularly on the cultural effects of encounters between peoples of different civilizations. In doing so, it seeks to identify and understand the patterns of cross-cultural conversion, conflict, and compromise that came about when peoples of different civilizations and cultural traditions interacted with each other over long periods of time. It makes a special effort to understand the phenomenon of cross-cultural conversion—an extremely complicated process involving the communication of beliefs and negotiation of values across cultural boundary lines, but a process that had the potential to bring about a thorough transformation of an entire society. Finally, the book places cultural developments in the larger context of the political, social, and economic circumstances in which they unfolded.

The book acknowledges that cultural traditions spread over long distances even in ancient times, but it also recognizes that expansive traditions often faced fierce opposition, and it holds further that the notion of cross-cultural conversion is a deeply problematical concept. Indeed, the book argues that religious and cultural traditions rarely won foreign converts except when favored by a powerful set of political, social, or economic incentives. Sometimes the prospect of trade or political alliance drew a people's attention to a foreign cultural tradition. Other times state sponsorship made political and military support available to an expanding cultural tradition. Yet even under the best of circumstances—when strongly favored, for example, by political, social, or economic incentives—expansive cultural traditions rarely attracted large numbers of foreign adherents without the aid of a syncretic process. Syncretism represented an avenue leading to cultural compromise: it provided opportunities for established beliefs, values, and customs to find a place within the framework of a different cultural tradition, and by doing so, it enabled expansive traditions to win popular support in foreign lands. Thus, cross-cultural conversion and the spread of religious and cultural traditions over long distances depended heavily on processes of syncretism that established lines of communication and mediated differences between interacting traditions.

Without the generous aid, advice, and support of many parties, *Old World Encounters* could never have appeared. A Faculty Fellowship from the Center for Arts and Humanities at the University of Hawaii afforded me time to write and revise the book. Special thanks go also to colleagues in many different fields whose counsel and criticism have improved the book. They include Roger T. Ames, Roger B. Beck, David W. Chappell, Alfred W. Crosby, Philip D. Curtin, Elton L. Daniel, Gladys Frantz-Murphy, Karen L. Jolly, Frances Karttunen, David Kopf, Daniel W. Y. Kwok, William H. McNeill, John A. Mears, Jan Nattier, Carla Rahn and William D. Phillips, Allyson Poska, James D. Tracy, and Herbert F. Ziegler. Many thanks to all for their willingness not only to humor me but also to provide thoughtful advice as I sought to become familiar with scholarship in their areas of expertise and to carry out an analysis that trespasses on many scholarly preserves. Finally, thanks go also to my wife, Jeani, who helps me to keep things in perspective.

Honolulu   J.H.B.
March 1992

CONTENTS

MAPS

OLD WORLD ENCOUNTERS

1

Cross-Cultural Contacts and Exchanges

And when the queen of Sheba heard of the fame of Solomon concerning the name of the Lord, she came to prove him with hard questions. And she came to Jerusalem with a very great train, with camels that bare spices, and very much gold, and precious stones. . . . And the navy also of Hiram, that brought gold from Ophir, brought in from Ophir great plenty of almug trees, and precious stones.

1 Kings 10 (Authorized Version)

The anonymous historian of ancient Israel contented himself with a spare, economical description of commercial life at King Solomon's court. His interests revolved around the worship of Yahweh, after all, not the development of complex trading networks and political alliances. Yet he took due pride in the fact that the queen of Sheba herself traveled from southern Arabia to King Solomon's court in order to consult with him and bestow gifts. He drew special pleasure from the lavish temple that Solomon built and decorated with gold, gems, and rare woods from the land of Ophir — probably Yemen or Somaliland, though some scholars have identified it as Mozambique or even Zimbabwe. In a passage following the one cited above, he briefly outlined King Solomon's own commercial interests — his construction of a port and navy at Ezion-geber at the head of the Gulf of Aqaba, his alliance with the Phoenician King Hiram of Tyre, and his control of the trade in horses and chariots between Egypt and Syria.

Solomon's economic and political ventures had cultural repercussions, however, some of them rather disturbing to the pious historian of ancient Israel. Political alliances led Solomon into numerous dynastic marriages, and his harem included the daughter of the Egyptian pharaoh as well as women from all parts of the ancient Middle East. In the interest of harmony and diplomacy, Solomon allowed his wives and concubines to observe their native cults, and he even built shrines and altars for them in Jerusalem. The ancient chronicler reported that

> the Lord was angry with Solomon, because his heart was turned from the Lord God of Israel. . . . Wherefore the Lord said unto Solomon, "Forasmuch as this is done of thee, and thou hast not kept my covenant and my statutes, which I have commanded thee, I will surely rend the kingdom from thee, and will give it to thy servant."   (1 Kings 11:9–11)

Modern historians and biblical scholars have noticed, in fact, that foreign cultural influences extended far beyond Solomon's harem. Phoenician architects designed and built his famous temple, which featured decorative elements suggested by Syrian, Mesopotamian, and Phoenician models. Foreign ideas perhaps also influenced Hebrew thought on the heavenly world and the various orders of angels that populated it. Surviving evidence also shows that cultural influences from abroad helped to transform early Jerusalem into a cosmopolitan city and to encourage development of a remarkable religious syncretism there during Solomon's reign.

The experience of ancient Israel draws attention to a phenomenon of high interest that historians have not yet carefully examined: the establishment of contacts between peoples of different civilizations in pre-modern times. Since the year 1492 C.E., cross-cultural contacts have profoundly influenced the experiences of all peoples on earth, and legions of historians, anthropologists, sociologists, and other scholars have energetically analyzed the dynamics of modern cross-cultural encounters. Their studies—too numerous to mention individually, in spite of their importance for the effort to understand modern world history—focus on themes such as long-distance trade, transfers of technology, imperial and colonial ventures, mass migrations, long-distance exchanges of plants, animals, and diseases, and cross-cultural missionary efforts, all of which have figured as agents of rapid and unsettling change in modern times.

For an earlier period, though, the case is different. Historians have long recognized that a considerable amount of cross-cultural exchange occurred in the pre-modern world: that trade routes collectively known as the silk roads traversed the Eurasian landmass, for example; or that religious faiths like Buddhism, Christianity, and Islam attracted converts far beyond their points of origin; or that the Mongol empire of the thirteenth century underwrote trade and travel throughout Eurasia. Historians have also devoted numerous studies to individual cases or episodes of cross-cultural encounter; indeed, without them, the following book could never have appeared. Only rarely, though, have scholars undertaken large-scale analyses designed to throw light on the patterns of cross-cultural contacts and their effects before modern times.[1]

Even in remote antiquity, as the world's various peoples traveled, migrated, or embarked upon campaigns of conquest, they engaged in cross-cultural encounters that sometimes had momentous results. These encounters naturally occasioned a great deal of conflict, since the parties involved often held different or even contradictory expectations concerning their proper relations and the results of their interaction. Quite apart from inspiring conflict, however, cross-cultural encounters served as remarkably effective agents of change in the pre-modern world. They encouraged the spread of technologies, ideas, beliefs, values, religions, and civilizations themselves. They challenged the cultural identities of all parties engaged in encounter, and sometimes they even resulted in the destruction of established cultural traditions. Yet they also presented opportunities for peoples to reaffirm or redefine their cultural traditions. In all events, by the year 1500 C.E., cross-cultural encounters had played a prominent role—perhaps even the major role—in the shaping of the world's cultural patterns.

Patterns of Cross-Cultural Encounters

This book offers an analysis of pre-modern encounters between peoples of different civilizations and cultural regions. Thus it concentrates attention on the establishment and penetration of cultural boundaries, and it asks a series of questions about the dynamics of cultural frontiers. What conditions — political, social, economic, or cultural — enabled foreign cultural elements to cross cultural boundaries? What human agents served as mediators between indigenous and foreign cultures? What interests encouraged them to represent or even to promote foreign cultural elements? How did they find understandable terms and concepts by which they could translate or communicate foreign ideas, beliefs, and values? How did pre-modern peoples respond to foreign challenges to their inherited cultural traditions? Under what conditions or influences did cross-cultural conversion take place? What conditions or influences encouraged conflicts or syncretism between different cultural traditions? How, in other words, did breaches of cultural barriers lead to new cultural configurations and the drawing of new cultural boundary lines?

Though simple to pose, these questions are difficult to answer in persuasive fashion. One source of difficulty has to do with concepts: historians and other scholars simply have not elaborated a vocabulary or a set of analytical categories appropriate for the study of cross-cultural encounters.[2] This kind of examination calls for terms and concepts that can be applied consistently across the boundary lines of cultures and civilizations. Thus, before embarking on the analysis itself, it will be worthwhile to explain the special vocabulary and categories of analysis that govern this study. The most important of these, discussed in this section, are the various forms of cross-cultural conversion, the process of syncretism that blended indigenous and foreign cultural traditions, and the phenomenon of resistance to foreign cultural challenges.

If cross-cultural encounters took place frequently and systematically even in pre-modern times — something that later chapters will demonstrate in detail — the question naturally arises, to what extent was it possible for beliefs and values to cross cultural boundary lines, win the allegiance of peoples from different civilizations, and attract converts from alien cultural traditions? The notion of cross-cultural conversion is a rather elusive concept. The term *conversion* brings to mind an intense personal experience, a reorientation of the individual soul, a rejection of the old in favor of a new system of values — the sort of profound spiritual transformation experienced by a Buddha, a St. Paul, a St. Augustine, or a Muhammad.[3] Did early cross-cultural encounters commonly lead to conversion experiences of this sort? Or does conversion in this sense refer to a category of spiritual behavior that does not apply outside the realms of certain religious faiths such as Buddhism, Christianity, and Islam?

As it happens, surviving information does not often open windows into the souls of pre-modern individuals—at least not of those who converted from one cultural or religious tradition to another—so that it becomes quite impossible to analyze conversion as a profound spiritual or psychological process. Even when information does survive, it does not always explain conversion experiences to the satisfaction of modern scholars. Take the case of Anselmo Turmeda, a Franciscan from Mallorca who converted to Islam about 1386. According to his autobiography, Turmeda turned to Islam because he became convinced that the New Testament predicted the rise of Muhammad when speaking of the comforter (identified by Christians as the Holy Spirit) who would follow Jesus and inspire his flock. Most commentators have found Turmeda's account of his conversion rather simplistic. They have also discovered some signs that he engaged in political activities against civil and ecclesiastical authorities, and that he came from a Jewish family under suspicion of the Inquisition. These complications do not necessarily call the sincerity of Turmeda's conversion into question: Turmeda accompanied his autobiography with a spirited polemical treatise attacking Christianity and vindicating Islam—a work that inspires confidence in the sincerity of his conversion. Nevertheless, the evidence available does not permit a satisfactory or conclusive analysis of his conversion as a spiritual or psychological process.[4]

It is certainly conceivable, or even probable, that pre-modern individuals often enough accepted alien cultural traditions in a thoroughgoing way and underwent a deep spiritual or psychological conversion experience. It was perhaps more common, though, for pre-modern peoples to adopt or adapt foreign cultural traditions for political, social, or economic purposes. Though not necessarily profound or deeply intentional acts from the viewpoint of the individuals involved, conversions of this sort had cultural consequences as great or even larger than those occasioned by spiritual conversions. Over the long term, they had the potential to bring about large-scale transformations of entire societies, since new cultural traditions introduced new social, educational, and religious institutions, which in turn helped to shape the beliefs and values of individuals born into those societies.[5] Thus it strikes me as reasonable to use the term *social conversion* to signify a process by which pre-modern peoples adopted or adapted foreign cultural traditions. As a practical matter, then, as used in this book, the term *conversion* rarely refers to an individual's spiritual or psychological experience but, rather, to the broader process that resulted in the transformation of whole societies.

Like any process working on a large scale, social conversion was a complicated affair, and it took a very long time for its processes to work their effects. Ultimately, of course, they depended upon the decisions of individuals to adopt new cultural traditions. Yet processes of social conversion also depended upon more than personal decisions. They also presupposed the establishment of institutions to support new cultural alternatives, and these institutions always required a great deal of time to work their effects through the socialization of successive generations of individuals. Processes of social conversion examined in later chapters often took three to five centuries to bring about the cultural transformation of large societies. Yet even though processes of social conversion proceeded quite gradually, they were extremely important for the history of the pre-modern world, because they molded the cultural legacies inherited by many of the world's peoples. Indeed, social conversion ranks among the most important processes that shaped the cultural history of the pre-modern world.

There is no single dynamic that explains this process of large-scale social conversion in pre-modern times. Instead, conversion to foreign beliefs, values, or cultural standards took different forms — followed different patterns — according to the various sets of political, social, and economic influences that governed the processes of conversion. Conversion always took place, after all, in a specific political, social, and economic context, and conversion most often brought something more than just spiritual or cultural advantages for those who adopted a new cultural or religious tradition. As a result, no rigid principle of interpretation nor any single theory of change can account for processes of cross-cultural conversion in general. Thus, rather than a single type of conversion process, the analysis of cross-cultural conversion in its larger social context turns up three patterns that recurred frequently during pre-modern times: conversion through voluntary association; conversion induced by political, social, or economic pressure; and conversion by assimilation.

Of the three modes of conversion, the category of conversion through voluntary association is perhaps the most elusive. Why did individuals abandon a religion or cultural tradition of long standing and replace it with a less familiar alternative? In a world of cultural choices, how and why did individuals decide to discard an inherited tradition and embrace another one that made conflicting claims and demands? After all, conversion to a new religion or cultural tradition often entailed a radical transformation in lifestyle: observance of new laws and rituals, wearing of different clothes, adoption of different relationships with family and friends, dietary changes, and even the use of a different language. What combinations of promises and possibilities persuaded premodern individuals to bring such radical changes voluntarily into their lives?

The most powerful incentives to conversion through voluntary association were prospects for political, economic, or commercial alliance with well-organized foreigners. Indeed, the principal instigators of voluntary conversion in pre-modern times were merchants engaged in long-distance trade. Even in pre-modern times, merchants commonly established diaspora communities in the lands where they traded, and they brought their native cultural traditions with them for their own use in those communities.[6] Over time they brought in cultural authorities such as priests, monks, and *qadis* (Islamic judges), and their diaspora communities often became springboards for the expansion of a religion or cultural tradition.

But why did their hosts voluntarily associate themselves with the traditions of the foreign merchants? After all, merchants can and often have conducted business over cultural boundary lines. In many cases, though, local ruling elites and others who regularly dealt with foreign merchants recognized opportunities to forge alliances with well-organized groups who had the potential to confer political and economic benefits. From a functionalist point of view, their adoption of foreign ways facilitated cross-cultural dealings by ensuring that all parties involved recognized a common code of ethics and values that shaped their expectations of each other. It is clear, too, however, that conversion through voluntary association offered benefits especially to ruling elites who adopted foreign ways. They naturally found opportunities to establish political, military, and economic alliances with foreign powers. More than that, knowledge and recognition from afar often carried great prestige and authority, so that ruling elites gained access to fresh sources of legitimacy in their own societies as well as political support from abroad.[7]

Some of the best illustrations of this process of conversion through voluntary association come from the introduction of Islam into sub-Saharan Africa. Islamic merchants first brought their faith to the kingdoms of west Africa and the cities of the Zanj, the east African region from Mogadishu to Sofala. In both regions they had extensive dealings with the local ruling elites, who controlled trade in their realms. Since trade represented a source of tremendous wealth for the ruling elites, they went to great lengths to accommodate foreign merchants. They allowed the merchants to establish diaspora communities in the principal towns and to bring *qadis* and other religious authorities into their communities. In many cases, local ruling elites themselves began to incline toward the faith of their merchant guests. Islam offered a coherent set of beliefs and values widely observed in the outside world, and adoption of Islam enabled the previously isolated rulers to enter more fully into the political and commercial life of the larger world. Moreover, it brought recognition from Islamic states in north Africa and the Middle East — a powerful reinforcement for local claims to rule — and it established a cultural foundation for political, military, and commercial alliances with other Islamic states. Small wonder, then, that ruling elites voluntarily associated with the Islamic faith of their merchant guests.

From the viewpoint of the individual, it might seem that this category of conversion through voluntary association begs the question of conversion itself. Did such conversions really involve individual transformations warranting the term *conversion*? Or did they, instead, represent ways for local ruling elites to manipulate both their subjects and representatives from the larger world? After all, in many cases, elites did not entirely abandon their inherited traditions, which continued to be useful for many domestic purposes, but, rather, supplemented them with cultural alternatives from abroad. Did this sort of conversion through voluntary association indicate a genuine exchange of cultural commitments or a tactical maneuver intended to attract additional support for a ruling elite?

In the absence of good information on elites' mental states and personal motives, it seems to me quite impossible to offer a definitive answer to this question. In some cases, voluntary conversion certainly resulted in a sense of serious personal commitment: Mansa Musa, the fourteenth-century king of the west African state of Mali, undertook a pilgrimage to Mecca, brought Islamic authorities to Mali, built mosques in his realm, and sent students to Islamic schools in Morocco. Moreover, quite apart from the sincerity of individual conversions, it is quite clear that in the longer run, voluntary conversion of elites and others who participated in the business of the larger world had the potential to lead to the conversion of entire societies. Quite often transformation of the larger society came about only with the application of force, pressure, or state sponsorship for a new cultural alternative. Nevertheless, it strikes me that the notion of conversion through voluntary association remains a useful one for efforts to think about cultural change on the large scale because of its potential to initiate processes of social conversion. As a result, later chapters will make much use of the category of voluntary conversion when examining developments such as the spread of Hindu and Buddhist faiths in southeast Asia, the spread of Buddhism along the silk roads of central Asia, the spread of Manichaeism and Nestorian Christianity across the central Asian steppes as well as the silk roads, and the spread of Islam in southeast Asia and sub-Saharan Africa.

While conversion through voluntary association took place on the trade routes of pre-modern times, some variety of less voluntary conversion often followed from mass migrations of peoples and from campaigns of military conquest. This does not necessarily mean that conquerors forced individuals to accept a foreign faith or system of values. There are of course many recorded cases in which individuals had to choose between the sword on one hand and a conquering faith on the other. Officially, though, neither

Buddhism nor Christianity nor Islam recognized the validity of conversion by coercion—much less nonproselytizing traditions such as Confucianism and Daoism.

Nevertheless, conquerors had ways to encourage large-scale social conversion without resorting to threats against individuals. Though it required a great deal of time to bring about a more or less thorough conversion of an entire society, conquerors commonly relied on several means to encourage or hasten the process. Their tactics included differential taxation, diversion of financial resources from established institutions to those associated with a new cultural alternative, preference of adherents to a particular tradition when recruiting military and political officials, limitation of access to religious services or rituals, and the closure or destruction of temples, churches, and shrines. Because they focused pressure especially on the institutions that preserved and transmitted a society's cultural traditions, these methods were far more effective means to bring about large-scale social transformation than was the direct coercion of individuals. None of these methods absolutely guaranteed conversion, and this book will document many cases of remarkable persistence and cultural resilience in the face of sometimes vicious pressure to change. But over the long term— sometimes as long as four or five centuries—consistent pressure had the potential to bring about near-total conversion of a society from one religion or cultural system to another.

In some cases, conversions induced by political, social, and economic pressures have taken place when states chose as a matter of policy to support one cultural or religious alternative at the expense of another. After the conversion of Constantine, for example, the Roman imperial government increasingly favored Christianity, while placing the pagan cults under progressively tighter restrictions. Not surprisingly, the numbers of Christians grew rapidly, while the pagan cults withered. Historically speaking, however, conversions induced by pressures have most often followed from mass migrations of peoples or from campaigns of conquest. When the new faith of Islam spread to the Middle East, Persia, and north Africa, for example, it benefitted enormously from the sponsorship of a dynamic and expansive state. It is well known that Muslims have mostly tolerated adherents of other religions and permitted them to maintain their traditions. Yet they levied special taxes on non-Muslims, and sometimes they also imposed discriminatory restrictions that required non-Muslims to wear a certain style of dress or to reside in a certain quarter. Meanwhile, they favored Muslim candidates for important positions and diverted the financial resources of established religious institutions to Islamic uses. In various combinations, these policies gradually induced large majorities of non-Arab populations to convert to Islam, and they helped to bring about a thorough social and cultural transformation of the Middle East, Persia, and north Africa.

Like the concept of conversion through voluntary association, the notion of conversion induced by pressure might seem to beg the question of conversion itself, at least when considered from the viewpoint of an individual. How can one distinguish, for example, between outward conformity and genuine acceptance of a new cultural tradition? Campaigns of conversion by pressure resulted in a good many cases of faked conversion: external observance of a new cultural tradition in order to escape persecution or to take advantage of political, social, or economic opportunities. Over the long term, though, it seems to me that this problem resolves itself. When external conformity persisted over several generations, or even centuries, it had the potential to result in a social transformation that not even a St. Paul or a Muhammad could improve upon. As new generations became educated in new beliefs and socialized according to new sets of values, a religious or cultural tradition that once was alien came to seem quite natural indeed. Thus, like the concept of conversion through voluntary association, that of conversion induced by political, social, or economic pressures remains useful for the effort to think about cultural change on the large scale, and it will make frequent appearances in this book.

A third type of social conversion also merits mention here: conversion by assimilation, a process by which a minority group adapted to the cultural standards of the majority and eventually adopted its beliefs and values. In some cases, minority peoples actively and enthusiastically sought assimilation into a foreign culture, so that they could take better advantage of political, social, or economic opportunities. Thus, when the Visigoths and other Germanic peoples entered the Roman empire and sought participation in its political, social, and economic life, they also adopted Christianity: their entry into Roman society naturally inclined them toward a faith quite foreign to their own cultural traditions, but one that was becoming increasingly prominent throughout the Roman empire.

In other cases, assimilation brought about the conversion of people who were perhaps unaware quite what was happening to them. If they lost regular communications with cultural authorities of their native traditions, merchants, migrants, and even missionaries sometimes fell into the orbit of foreign cultural traditions. Over time, as individuals used new languages, took foreign spouses, and produced offspring who became socialized according to different norms, whole groups of people could become absorbed into larger societies. Something like this seems to have happened to Nestorian Christians and Manichaeans who migrated to central Asia and China. They could not maintain close communications with their fellow faithful in western lands, nor could they attract large numbers of converts and establish permanent communities in Asia. Gradually, they gravitated toward the communities of Buddhists and Daoists, who ultimately absorbed them altogether.

Like the other modes of conversion, so also conversion by assimilation takes on a different aspect when examined from the viewpoint of an individual rather than a society. An individual in course of conversion by assimilation might well represent a case of cultural drift or alienation more than thorough conversion. Having abandoned or lost contact with the native cultural tradition, yet socialized at best to a limited extent in the new alternative, the individual would be truly at home in neither the native nor the adopted tradition. Even in cases where individuals consciously and energetically sought assimilation, signs of their original cultural orientations would inevitably persist. Again, though, as in the other varieties of conversion, this problem resolves itself over time by way of social conversion. Even if individuals rarely or never became thoroughly converted, later generations took new ways as their native traditions. Once again, then, individual conversions of an incomplete or problematic character nonetheless served as a foundation for social conversion on a large scale.

Conversion through voluntary association, conversion induced by pressure, and conversion by assimilation thus represent three avenues by which cultural traditions spread their influences in premodern times. The three modes of conversion obviously reflected

their broader political, social, and economic contexts, and in particular they had a great deal to do with the relative strengths of the
parties involved in cross-cultural encounters. Small numbers of
individuals could not very well bring about conversion of another
people by political, social, or economic pressure. But if they were
well organized and tightly integrated into long-range networks of
trade and communication—and if they brought an ostensibly powerful or attractive cultural alternative to a foreign site—their hosts
might well associate themselves voluntarily with the new tradition.
On the other hand, large numbers and great relative strength could
enable a people to bring about the conversion of an entire society
by pressure when they conquered others or migrated to foreign
lands. Meanwhile, small numbers of individuals became liable to
conversion by assimilation if they fell out of communication with
cultural authorities or could not maintain their traditions in more
or less regular and systematic fashion. Whether at home or abroad,
they became especially vulnerable to conversion by assimilation
when overwhelmed by large numbers of people observing an alternate cultural tradition.

The three modes of conversion thus served as roads penetrating
cultural boundaries and enabling cultural traditions to spread their
influences to new peoples. How did it happen, though, that a foreign cultural tradition found widespread acceptance among peoples
who used different languages, observed different customs, held
different values, and recognized different relationships between the
cultural and the political, social, and economic dimensions of their
lives? Mass appeal of foreign cultural traditions is difficult or even
impossible to explain in the absence of syncretism. Though analyti-
cally distinguished from conversion, syncretism often figured in
pre-modern times as the principal agent that facilitated the large-
scale conversion of whole societies to new cultural traditions. Syncretism blended elements from different cultural traditions in such
a way that a foreign tradition could become intelligible, meaningful, and even attractive in a land far from its origin.[8] Ultimately, it
had the potential to produce altogether new cultural configurations.

Actually, the simple effort to communicate beliefs and values
across cultural boundary lines almost inevitably entailed a certain
amount of syncretism, since the explanation of foreign concepts

required some degree of comparison and assimilation to familiar ideas. Thus, when Buddhist missionaries introduced their faith to China, they borrowed liberally from the language and concepts of the native Chinese Daoists. When Manichaeans and Nestorian Christians sought converts in China, they appropriated the vocabularies of both the Buddhists and the Daoists.

Quite apart from the problem of basic communication, the conversion of an entire society to a foreign cultural tradition entailed a thoroughgoing process of syncretism. Foreign traditions always arrived in pieces — wrenched from the political, social, and economic context in which they had originally developed — and converts always selected certain elements that they adopted, adapted, emphasized, or otherwise appropriated for their own purposes. In communicating and explaining an alien cultural tradition, they fractured its original elements, restated them in new terms, endowed them with different meaning, and assembled them in a new way that made sense and significance from their own cultural point of view. In doing so, consciously or not, converts also retained elements of their inherited traditions and incorporated them into the alternative from abroad. Furthermore, they integrated the foreign cultural alternative in their own ways into their larger political, social, and economic orders. Thus, large-scale social conversion always involved some degree of syncretism rather than wholesale acceptance of an alien system of beliefs and values: social conversion depended upon some form of compromise between the demands of an inherited cultural tradition and the promises of a foreign alternative. If the three modes of conversion represented avenues by which foreign traditions could penetrate cultural boundaries, syncretism represented the drawing of new cultural boundary lines reflecting the relative strengths and attractions of several traditions engaged in cross-cultural encounter.

The cases of early Christianity in the Roman empire and early Buddhism in China illustrate this general point. Christianity posed a serious challenge to the pagan cults of the Roman empire, but the new faith also reflected the culture and accommodated the interests of the pagans. Christians observed several rituals quite similar to those of the pagan cults — a ceremony of initiation to the faith, a community meal for the initiates, and worship services featuring ritualized liturgies. Meanwhile, Christians also made room in their faith for pagan values. They associated the qualities of pagan heroes with Christian saints, and they observed their holy days at precisely the times established by tradition for the reverence of pagan deities. St. Paul himself implicitly blessed this syncretic practice when he declared to his disciples in Corinth that "I am made all things to all men, that I might by all means save some" (1 Cor. 9:22).

Buddhists in China had an even more difficult task than the early Christians, who at least shared much of the larger culture of the Roman empire. By contrast, the political, social, and moral values of the original Indian Buddhists differed profoundly from those held in China. To mention only a single point of difference, the monastic celibacy esteemed by Buddhists clashed directly with the Chinese interest in producing large families so that later generations could honor their ancestors. Buddhists accommodated this interest by embracing the traditional Chinese virtue of filial piety — something the Buddha himself would hardly have understood — and by persuading Chinese that one son in the monastery would bring the salvation of ten generations of his kin. As in the case of early Christianity, then, the Buddhists' willingness to accommodate foreign values resulted in a syncretic blend of traditions, which in turn enabled an alien faith to attract converts in a land far removed from its origin.

Though outlined here as if they were ideal types clearly distinguished from one another that operated quite autonomously, it perhaps bears mention that the three modes of cross-cultural conversion and syncretism rarely worked their effects in isolation but, rather, combined in various ways. Conversion through voluntary association, for example, has often established a foundation for the conversion of a society by political, social, or economic pressure, since ruling elites have often used their cultural preferences as ideological symbols or sources of legitimacy when attempting to tighten their grips on the levers of power. Both voluntary conversion and conversion by pressure required the aid of syncretism in order to bring about the thorough conversion of entire societies. Meanwhile, enslavement of foreigners historically has been an extremely efficient means of bringing both pressure and assimilation to bear on the process of conversion.

By no means, however, did cultural traditions and their representatives proceed unchallenged as they sought to expand their spheres of influence. To the contrary, in almost every recorded case they encountered tremendous resistance from established cultural traditions: indeed, arrival of a new cultural tradition often enough inspired a backlash that served to strengthen commitment to an established but threatened tradition. Thus conversion to the standards of a new cultural tradition did not represent the only possible result of cross-cultural encounters in pre-modern times. Alongside conversion and syncretism, resistance stood among the most prominent responses of pre-modern peoples to foreign cultural challenges and opportunities.[9]

Like conversion and syncretism, cultural resistance took several forms in pre-modern times. Sometimes, peoples resisted rather passively by simply persisting in their traditions and more or less ignoring foreign cultural alternatives that became known to them. Other times, they aggressively attacked representatives of an alternate cultural tradition. On occasion, resistance led to dramatic and spectacular conflict, as when individuals sacrificed themselves in spirited resistance to a foreign cultural challenge, or when institutionalized political and cultural authorities organized large-scale campaigns of repression or persecution, sometimes quite brutal.

Resistance to foreign cultural traditions had the potential to inspire rebellion: for thirty years the pagan Saxons battled Charlemagne as he sought to extend Christianity and Frankish rule to Germany; likewise, the early Islamic conquerors faced persistent rebellion and rejection of their faith in Egypt, north Africa, and other lands as well. But cultural resistance could also inspire flight: large communities of Manichaeans and Zoroastrians fled their homes in Mesopotamia and Persia in order to escape the growing political and cultural empire of Islam; the Manichaeans went to central Asia and China, the Zoroastrians to India, where their descendants survive even today as the Parsis. The ultimate form of resistance, however, was suicide or self-martyrdom. Perhaps the best-documented episode examined in this book took place in the mid-ninth century at Córdoba in Spain. During a ten-year period, at least forty-eight Christians deliberately and publicly insulted the prophet Muhammad and his Islamic faith, thus provoking the Muslim authorities of Córdoba to execute the offenders. In all cases, whatever the precise form it took, resistance represented an effort to establish barriers that could defend cultural boundary lines and limit the spread of cultural traditions from abroad.

The prominence of syncretism and the high incidence of resistance to foreign cultural challenges suggest some caveats for notions of diffusion widely held by world historians and global analysts. It is certainly true that the various peoples of the world have never lived in isolated, self-contained civilizations or cultural groups. From the earliest days of the human experience, impulses to trade, migration, empire-building, evangelization, and other activities brought about cross-cultural encounters and challenges. Where they had the will, the world's peoples easily overcame both geographical obstacles (deserts, mountains, and oceans) and human barriers (linguistic, cultural, and political differences) in the interests of cross-cultural commerce. Even in pre-modern times peoples of different civilizations and cultural groups exchanged goods and technologies with remarkably little resistance. Many studies have shown that disease, technology, weapons, and material products diffused easily and rapidly across cultural as well as geographical boundaries.

Beliefs and values, however, crossed these boundaries much more gradually and with much greater difficulty. Cultural diffusion takes place in complex fashion, and its understanding entails subtle contextual analysis. After all, cross-cultural encounters take place in specific political, social, and economic contexts, and it stands to reason that those contexts would help to shape local cultural development. Generally speaking, so this book argues, large-scale conversion to foreign cultural standards occurred only when powerful political, social, or economic incentives encouraged it — and even then it led universally to syncretism rather than to outright, wholesale adoption of a foreign cultural tradition. In the absence of powerful incentives, a kind of stubborn cultural conservatism stoutly resisted foreign cultural imports.

And yet the diffusionist vision survives in some form. Breaches of cultural boundaries did not result in a cultural cloning process whereby belief and value systems replicated themselves in new settings. But they did bring about an enormous amount of cultural change. Sometimes that change took the form of strengthened commitment to existing cultural identities. Other times foreign cultural elements attracted interest and won at least partial acceptance by new adherents. Yet other times they provoked suspicion and met hostile resistance and even violence. In any case, though, they brought about responses and reactions that had consequences of some moment for the cultural identities of all parties involved in cross-cultural transactions. Absent cross-cultural encounters, it is impossible to understand the cultural history and development of the world's various peoples.

Principal Eras of Cross-Cultural Encounter in Pre-Modern Times

Where does the study of cross-cultural encounters begin? Human groups embarked on long-distance travels almost as soon as *Homo sapiens* emerged as a species some 40,000 years ago. By about 15,000 B.C.E., humans had spread to most of the earth's habitable regions, and their travels no doubt led them into cross-cultural encounters even in prehistoric times. Analyses of language families, blood types, and material remains have enabled scholars to trace the movements of at least some prehistoric peoples with remarkable precision.[10] In no case, however, does information survive to illuminate the dynamics or the processes of cross-cultural encounters in prehistoric times. Language families and material remains reflect the ultimate results of prehistoric encounters, but evidence of this type does not shed light on human reactions to cross-cultural challenges.

Beginning in the late fourth millennium B.C.E., several developments in the technology of transportation quickened the tempo of cross-cultural contact and exchange. Sometime around 3200 B.C.E., central Asian nomads brought the horse under domestication. Not long thereafter — probably between 3000 and 2500 B.C.E. — Arabian peoples domesticated the camel. About that same time, Egyptians developed sailing craft that enabled them not only to travel up and down the Nile but also to traverse the Red Sea and carry on trade in incense with the land they called Punt — probably Yemen or Somaliland, though some scholars have placed it as far south as Mozambique. Over time, these and similar developments underwrote the rapid development of long-distance trade. A large amount of archeological and documentary evidence survives to show that already in the third millennium B.C.E., trade passed regularly between Mesopotamia and the Harappan civilization of the Indus River valley. By the twentieth century B.C.E., well-established donkey caravans linked Mesopotamia and Asia Minor.[11] The establishment of roads, sea routes, and communication networks obviously figures as a precondition for intense cross-cultural contacts. The work of merchants and traders in opening highways and arranging accommodations along these routes quite literally paved the way for the encounters examined in this book.

As in the case of prehistoric contacts, though, lack of information precludes thorough analysis of the human dimensions of these ancient cross-cultural encounters. Scarcity of information has not prevented the emergence of several theories concerning the diffusion of culture and civilization in remote antiquity. Thor Heyerdahl, for example, holds that Phoenicians or other voyagers from the Mediterranean crossed the Atlantic and introduced civilization to the peoples of Mesoamerica; later travelers would have carried Eurasian cultural elements into the Andean regions and the Pacific islands.[12] Joseph Needham agrees that Eurasian traditions influenced cultural developments in the Western Hemisphere, but he locates the source of inspiration in China rather than the Mediterranean: from about 1000 B.C.E., he argues, Chinese fishermen and traders intermittently crossed the Pacific Ocean and introduced into the Americas a wide range of Asian technologies and cultural elements, including metallurgy, sailing rafts, paper production, religious art, music, and folklore, among other things.[13]

The travel envisioned in these extreme diffusionist arguments was not inherently impossible; in both cases, it fell within the range of technology available in ancient times, albeit barely so. Yet neither of the positions outlined above — nor any other similar suggestions of wholesale cultural diffusion between hemispheres in ancient times — has won widespread endorsement. When faced with cultural and technological similarities between ancient Eurasian and American civilizations, most scholars prefer independent invention as an explanation involving fewer difficulties than intercontinental diffusion of culture on a large scale.

The lack of solid, substantial information will make it impossible, probably forever, to develop definitive proofs either for or against theories of intercontinental diffusion. While it might have been possible to complete some transoceanic voyages in ancient times, it seems most unlikely that contacts between Eurasia and the Americas led to any significant cultural encounters before modern times. This caveat aside, it seems to me entirely possible to identify three important intracontinental developments brought about by cross-cultural encounters in ancient times. In none of the three cases does information survive to illuminate the human dimensions or the precise social dynamics of cross-cultural encounters. Yet all of them rank as developments of large significance for this book, for two reasons: first, because they helped to promote a strong sense of cultural identity among the peoples they touched; and second, because they helped to establish cultural structures that guided the courses of cross-cultural encounters in later centuries.

The first and most fundamental of these three developments was the emergence and expansion of those complex, city-based social orders that we call civilizations. Like states, churches, trading networks, and other human creations, civilizations have the capacity to expand and contract. In the interests of maintaining stability and ensuring adequate supplies of food and other necessary resources, early civilizations sought to extend their political authority and establish economic relationships with other peoples in everwidening spheres of interest. This point holds true for all early civilizations: Mesopotamian, Egyptian, Indian, Chinese, and Mesoamerican. Rulers and traders from the central regions of these early civilizations naturally carried a great deal of cultural baggage on their adventures, and they deposited some of it in the hinterlands that they visited. As a result, neighboring peoples became increasingly linked — first politically and economically, later culturally and socially as well — to early civilizations.

In some cases, in fact, individual cultural elements spread far beyond the effective political boundaries of early civilizations. Perhaps the most dramatic example of this process of early cultural diffusion comes from the experience of the ancient Phoenicians. A Semitic people who settled in Canaan (modern Lebanon and Syria), the Phoenicians were energetic seafarers who dominated trade in the Mediterranean from about 1100 to 800 B.C.E. They even ventured into the Atlantic Ocean in order to carry on trade with tin-producing regions of southern England, and some evidence suggests that one of their navigators circumnavigated Africa. They drew their beliefs and values largely from Mesopotamian and Egyptian sources, but they spread Middle Eastern culture far more broadly and efficiently than the Mesopotamians or Egyptians themselves. Most notable of all their disseminations was the alphabet, which like most of their culture they borrowed from others. The Greeks appropriated it and adapted it to their own needs, and the Romans later introduced yet other alterations. Despite many later modifications, all western script stands on the foundation of the Phoenician alphabet.[14] The Phoenician legacy to western cultures and civilizations thus looms rather large, since elaborate cultural development and identity would have been nearly inconceivable in the absence of a technology of writing. Even in the days of remote antiquity, then, the spread of civilizations and subsequent cross-cultural contacts yielded results of long-term cultural significance.

A second result of ancient encounters between different peoples also survived over a long term and helped to structure the courses and consequences of future encounters. This was the development of the notion of barbarism. In Greek usage, the term *barbarian* originally was a linguistic rather than social or cultural category: it referred to an individual who did not speak Greek. After Greeks became prominent in Mediterranean trade and began to develop an increasingly sophisticated civilization, about the eighth century B.C.E., the term *barbarian* took on strong connotations of cultural inferiority. The presence in Greek city-states of increasing numbers of foreign slaves—barbarians by definition—reinforced this semantic shift. Over time, the association of barbarism with inferiority encouraged settled, civilized peoples to adopt an aggressive and sometimes violent policy toward their nomadic or less urbanized neighbors. Roman foreign policy beyond the Alps perhaps best illustrates this point, so far as early western civilizations are concerned.

By no means, though, was the notion of barbarism an exclusively western concept. Owen Lattimore has shown how early Chinese agriculturalists and steppe nomads progressively differentiated themselves, largely as a result of the almost inexorable enlargement by Chinese of the zone dedicated to agriculture. Already in prehistoric times, cultivators using stone tools flourished in the valley of the Huang He (Yellow River) with its well-watered, easily worked loess soil. As they enlarged the agricultural zone, they encountered mixed agriculturalists and herding peoples, whom they either absorbed into their own ranks or pushed into steppe regions beyond the point where settled agriculture was a practical activity. The first group assimilated into Chinese agricultural society; the second developed into steppe nomads. Political, social, and cultural differentiation followed naturally from the radically different economic and environmental conditions of agricultural and steppe societies. Chinese soon came to regard nomadic steppe peoples as barbarians and to place relations with them under close supervision.[15] Once again, as in the western case, ancient encounters led to progressive cultural differentiation and to the designation of less settled, less agricultural peoples as barbarians. Once again, too, the distinction took on heavy cultural significance and influenced relations between settled and mobile peoples for millennia to come.

Military developments in the nomadic societies of the steppes played a large role in bringing about the third general result of ancient cross-cultural encounters. Perhaps as early as 900 B.C.E., steppe peoples began to experiment with cavalry formations and to develop tactics for mounted conflict. It is possible that Assyrians had first recognized the potential of cavalry formations. But access to abundant grazing lands constituted a considerable natural advantage for steppe dwellers, who quickly eclipsed all other peoples with respect to equestrian skills in general and mounted warfare in particular. Thus nomadic peoples became a serious threat to the settled civilizations of Eurasia, all of which suffered repeatedly from the unpredictable raids and incursions of swiftly moving cavalry units.

Karl Jaspers once argued that the nomadic threat to settled societies helped to account for the so-called axial age — the period about 800 to 200 B.C.E. when ethical and reflective thought flourished independently in China, India, the Middle East, and Greece. Axial thinkers included Confucius, Laozi, the authors of the Upanishads, the Buddha, Zarathustra, the Hebrew prophets, Socrates, and Plato, among others. Their works all manifest deep concern for political and social stability, for ethics and personal morality, for the recognition of standards that would regularize human relationships and place them on rational, predictable courses. The various cultural traditions that flowed from axial thought — Confucianism,

Daoism, Hinduism, Buddhism, Zoroastrianism, Judaism, and Greek rational thought — decisively influenced the development of civilizations in all parts of Eurasia.[16] Jaspers's argument is not the sort that is susceptible to definitive confirmation or rejection. But it certainly is conceivable that axial thought, especially its ethical and political facets, represented a cultural response to the political, social, and economic disruption of settled lands by nomadic invaders. To the extent that nomads' adventures did encourage such a cultural reaction, axial thought represents an enormously important result of early encounters across cultural boundary lines.

Despite their significance over the long term, cross-cultural encounters that resulted in the early spread of civilizations, the emergence of the category of the barbarian, and axial thought do not lend themselves to deep analysis, since very few materials survive to illuminate the processes that drove them. It would be fascinating to have sources illuminating cross-cultural encounters generated by Mesopotamian and Harappan trade or by the migrations of Indo-European and Bantu peoples. But the ancient historical record does not often accommodate contemporary fantasies.

In the case of the Americas, for example, lack of information precludes a sustained analysis of cross-cultural encounters between the various native American peoples in pre-Columbian times. It seems certain that long before Europeans arrived in the Americas, cross-cultural encounters took place there with results similar to those occurring in Eurasia. Indeed, Miguel León-Portilla has analyzed one such encounter between the nomadic Chichimec hunters, who inhabited the plains of northern Mexico, and the settled, urbanized Toltecs. Beginning about the eleventh century C.E., some Chichimecs moved south into central Mexico, and many of them settled in Texcoco, near modern Mexico City. They gradually adopted Toltec ways of eating and dressing; they began to grow maize; and they intermarried with their sedentary hosts. Offspring of mixed parentage received a Toltec education, and a series of chieftains of mixed parentage encouraged further Chichimec adaptation to Toltec civilization. By the fourteenth century, Chichimecs in central Mexico had adopted Toltec beliefs, religion, culture, and even their Nahuatl language; they had become a settled people who lived in cities, appreciated Toltec music and poetry, and preserved Toltec values in Texcoco. These Chichimecs in central Mexico thus underwent conversion by assimilation to the cultural standards of a dominant majority people. But these developments did not unfold without resistance: some of the migratory Chichimecs fought against adaptation to Toltec standards and for the preservation of nomadic culture; other Chichimecs chose not to migrate at all but remained in the northern plains and retained their independence until long after the Spanish conquest of the Aztecs.[17] Whether it led to adaptation and development of a new cultural identity or to resistance and reinforcement of a traditional identity, the process of cross-cultural encounter plainly influenced the cultural experiences of the Chichimecs and Toltecs.

Cross-cultural encounters no doubt shaped the experiences of other peoples throughout the pre-Columbian Americas. Given the lack of information about them, however, the analysis of cross-cultural encounters as historical phenomena must concentrate on the experiences of Eurasia and Africa. In the interests of gaining some insight into the processes and dynamics of cross-cultural encounters, the remainder of this book will concentrate on four periods that generated especially intense and even systematic interactions across cultural boundary lines.

For practical purposes, sustained analysis of cross-cultural encounters can begin only about the time of the Roman and Han empires. The era of the ancient silk roads—roughly 200 B.C.E. to 400 C.E.—thus figures as the first major period of cross-cultural encounter examined here. The consolidation of large imperial states pacified enough of Eurasia that trading networks could safely link the extreme ends of the landmass. Nomadic peoples played an especially prominent role in the economy of the silk roads, since they both consumed the finished products of settled lands and transported them to other customers. So long as the silk roads remained active, they facilitated not only the exchange of trade goods but also the communication of cultural and religious traditions throughout much of the Eastern Hemisphere. This era came to an end, though, with the collapse of the Roman and Han empires, which had anchored and sustained much of the interregional commerce in goods and ideas, and with the outbreak of devastating epidemic diseases that disrupted societies and economies throughout Eurasia.

Beginning about the sixth century, however, a revival of long-distance trade underwrote a second round of intense cross-cultural encounters. The revival of cross-cultural dealings depended again on the foundation of large imperial states, such as the Tang, Abbasid, and Carolingian empires, which pacified vast stretches of Eurasia, and on the cooperation of nomadic peoples who provided transportation links between settled regions. But long-distance trade in the sixth century benefitted also from much more frequent use of sea lanes across the Indian Ocean. Merchants once again linked the Eurasian landmass, while impressive numbers of missionaries and pilgrims traveled in their company. In an era often labeled a dark age—quite inappropriately—literacy and religions of salvation extended their influence to most parts of Eurasia.

This second period did not so much come to an end as it blended into a new era—roughly 1000 to 1350—when cross-cultural encounters proceeded according to a different set of historical dynamics. Long-distance trade over both land and sea increased dramatically during this period and continued to bring peoples from different civilizations in contact with each other. The distinctive feature of this era, however, had to do with the remarkable military and political expansion of nomadic peoples, principally Turks and Mongols, who established vast transregional empires and sponsored regular and systematic interactions between peoples of different cultural traditions. Indeed, the intensity and systematic nature of cross-cultural encounters in this period had much to do with its end. Mongol hegemony in Eurasia facilitated the efficient spread not only of trade goods and cultural traditions but also of communicable disease. The bubonic plague spread with such devastating effect in the later fourteenth century that it disrupted economy, society, trade, and communications throughout Eurasia. Cross-cultural encounter became temporarily a much less prominent feature of the Eurasian experience.

Recovery from the plague began already in the fifteenth century, and the peoples of Eurasia ventured again to distant lands. With technologies ever more refined, they sought to reconstitute networks of trade and communication, and western Europeans in particular discovered that they possessed the capacity to bring sustained power to bear in their dealings with many of the peoples they encountered. This fourth era of cross-cultural encounters thus represents the early stage of the vast expansion of European power and influence throughout the world during the period from 1500 to 1900. It will require another volume to analyze that expansion, which proceeded according to dynamics quite different from those that governed cross-cultural encounters in pre-modern times. But this book examines fifteenth-century encounters at least briefly in order to locate early European expansion securely in the larger context of cross-cultural encounters in pre-modern times.

Thanks largely to political, military, and economic developments, these four periods all witnessed sustained and systematic cross-cultural encounters of high intensity. Equally important for purposes of this book, the four periods also generated source materials that illuminate some of these encounters. Sources do not survive in the quantity and quality that historians might altogether desire. They are sufficient, however, at least for experiences of Eurasians and some African peoples, to serve as the foundation for a meaningful analysis of cross-cultural encounters, which begins in earnest with the analysis of cross-cultural communication and exchange over the ancient silk roads.

2

The Era of the
Ancient Silk Roads

After the Han had sent its envoy to open up communications
with the state of [Bactria], all the barbarians of the distant
west craned their necks to the east and longed to catch a
glimpse of China.

Sima Qian, *Records of the Grand Historian of China*

Deserts, mountains, and oceans have rarely figured as much more
than temporary obstacles to human travel and communication.
Well before 3000 B.C.E., Mesopotamians had begun to organize
long-distance trading ventures, and during the next millennium
commercial networks progressively linked the Middle East, Egypt,
Persia, and even northwestern India. Given the right combination
of incentive, will, and transportation technologies, geographical
inconveniences became roads and highways rather than barriers to
interregional communication and exchange.

In the most remote days of antiquity, these roads and highways
were fragile links, liable to sudden and unpredictable disruption
because of political instability, banditry, or piracy. During the latter part of the first millennium B.C.E., however, as large states and
empires took form in several regions of Eurasia, long-distance
travel and trade became a less risky proposition. The Qin dynasty
unified China (221–207 B.C.E.), and the Han (206 B.C.E.–220 C.E.)
provided a framework for centralized imperial rule there over the
long term. The Maurya dynasty (320–183 B.C.E.) brought at least
temporary imperial unity to India. Following the death of Alexander the Great (323 B.C.E.) and the collapse of his vast personal

29

MAP 1. The world of the ancient silk roads.

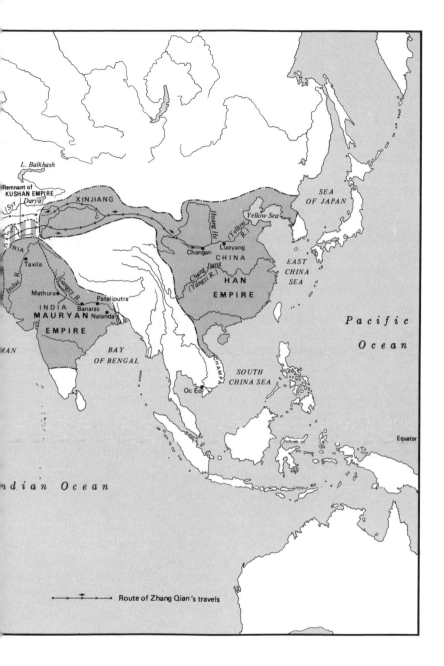

L. Balkhash

Remnant of
KUSHAN EMPIRE

(Syr Darya)

XINJIANG

BACTRIA

Indus R.

Taxila

Ganges R.

Mathura

INDIA

MAURYAN

Banaras

Pataliputra

Nalanda

EMPIRE

MAN

BAY
OF BENGAL

Huang He

(Yellow R.)

Yellow Sea

Changan

Luoyang

CHINA

Chang Jiang
(Yangzi R.)

HAN

EMPIRE

SEA
OF JAPAN

EAST
CHINA
SEA

Pacific

Ocean

CHAMPA

Oc Eo

SOUTH
CHINA SEA

Equator

Indian Ocean

×———×———×———×———→ Route of Zhang Qian's travels

empire, the Parthian and Roman states provided stable political order in western lands.

These states and empires generated systematic cross-cultural encounters in two ways. In the first place, campaigns of imperial expansion placed empire builders—along with their soldiers, administrators, diplomats, and the merchants who followed them—in direct contact with foreign peoples. Even during times of tense relations, frontier territories were sites of constant dealings between peoples from different cultural traditions. In the second place, these states and empires secured roads and markets over large stretches of Eurasia and thus laid a crucial political foundation for increased travel and trade over long distances. Indeed, they served as political and economic anchors for the extensive network of long-distance commerce and communication.

Also important for cross-cultural trade and communication in ancient times was the growing political and economic prominence of "barbarian" peoples. Contacts between settled, agricultural peoples and their more mobile, nomadic neighbors led to increasingly large volumes of trade. This in turn offered opportunities that ambitious chieftains found difficult to resist. Control of trade with settled peoples could provide chieftains with enormous economic and political leverage—enough in some cases to enable them to build states capable of governing nomadic peoples over large areas. Increased stability of the regions between settled civilizations encouraged further development of trading relationships, and nomadic peoples themselves generally served as middlemen and carriers in exchanges conducted over long distances. Without the various political and economic services of nomadic peoples—barbarians, from the viewpoint of settled, agricultural peoples—it would have been impossible for ancient civilizations to sustain long-distance trade on the scale actually experienced.

The result of political and economic collaboration between settled and nomadic peoples was a complex network of trade routes known collectively as the silk roads. At the eastern end lay Chang-an, capital of the Han dynasty. From there the road went west through Mongolia and Turkestan (modern Xinjiang). When it arrived at the dangerous and forbidding Taklimakan desert, the road split into northern and southern branches that skirted the desert and passed through the numerous oasis towns on its fringes. The road continued through Ferghana to Transoxiana – the wealthy region between the Oxus and Jaxartes rivers (today called the Amu Darya and Syr Darya) – where a branch led to northwestern India by way of the Khyber Pass. The principal road continued west, however, leading through Persia to the Caspian Sea, Mesopotamia, Egypt, the Levant, Asia Minor, and the Roman empire.

Quite apart from these land routes, sea lanes in the Indian Ocean also came into use during the era of the ancient silk roads. Though not so well developed or widely used as the land routes, by the first century B.C.E. the sea lanes already linked ports in southeast Asia, India, Persia, Arabia, Egypt, and east Africa. An impressive variety of products traveled the silk roads even in ancient times. Silk and lacquerware went west from China; southeast Asia and India exported coral and pearls; western lands traded horses, wool, linen, aromatics, glass, and precious stones.[1]

Opportunities for trade thus tempted Eurasian peoples into regular cross-cultural encounters during the era of the ancient silk roads, approximately 200 B.C.E. to 400 C.E. It soon became apparent that beliefs, values, and cultural traditions could travel the silk roads alongside the merchants and ambassadors who opened them. Yet during this first period of intense cross-cultural interaction, cultural traditions rarely won the allegiance of the popular masses in lands very far removed from their origins. The era of the ancient silk roads witnessed instead a threefold pattern of cultural development. In the first place, throughout Eurasia, peoples in all areas of settled agricultural civilization – China, India, the Middle East, and the Mediterranean region – elaborated systems of beliefs and values that helped to lend coherence to their civilizations. These cultural traditions were not necessarily new; indeed, in all cases, at least some of their most important elements trace back to the axial age mentioned in the previous chapter. During the era of the silk roads, though, they first became prominent in such widespread fashion that they could help to integrate entire civilizations. In the second place, when securely established within the precincts of their respective civilizations, these traditions offered cultural alternatives to neighboring peoples. Frontier regions and large, cosmopolitan cities provided venues where peoples mingled and became acquainted with different cultural traditions. Inevitably, a certain amount of cultural exchange took place, even if there were few

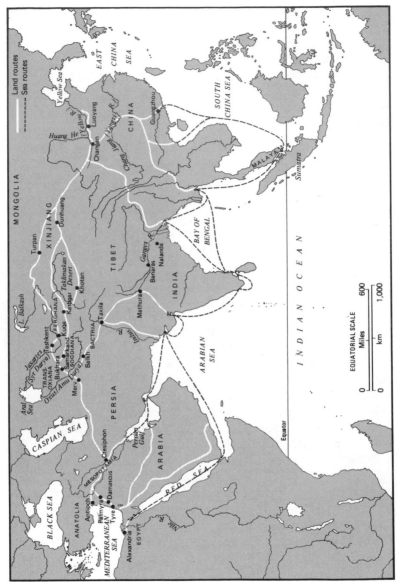

Land routes
Sea routes

MONGOLIA

Yellow Sea

EAST
CHINA
SEA

Huang He Luoyang
Changan
Huang (Yellow) R.

CHINA

Guangzhou

SOUTH
CHINA SEA

Yellow R.

XINJIANG

Turpan

Dunhuang

Chang (Yangzi) R.

MALAYA

Sumatra

Taklimakan
Desert

Khotan

Kashgar
Kuqa
FERGHANA

L. Balkhash

TIBET

Ganges
Benares
Mathura
Nalanda

BAY OF
BENGAL

Jaxartes
Syr Darya Tashkent
TRANS-
OXIANA
Bukhara Samarkand
SOGDIANA
Oxus Merv *Amu Darya*

Taxila

Indus R.

INDIA

I N D I A N   O C E A N

Aral
Sea

Balkh BACTRIA

PERSIA

ARABIAN
SEA

CASPIAN SEA

Ctesiphon

Persian Gulf

ARABIA

EQUATORIAL SCALE
Miles
600
1,000
km
0   0

Antioch
Palmyra
Damascus
Tyre

MESOPOTAMIA

RED SEA

Equator

BLACK SEA

ANATOLIA

MEDITERRANEAN
SEA

Alexandria

EGYPT

Nile R.

MAP 2. The silk roads.

34

cases of mass social conversion to new cultural alternatives. In the third place, perhaps most important, merchants brought their native cultural traditions with them to diaspora communities. In at least a few cases, their traditions attracted the serious interest of local elites, who adopted the merchants' traditions in processes of conversion through voluntary association. Mass conversion of entire societies of course did not come right away, and in some cases not at all, but the voluntary conversion of local elites during the era of the silk roads laid a foundation for social conversion over a longer term.

Confucians and Xiongnu

The teachings of Confucius have about them an air of moderation and good sense that have long appealed to intellectual elites. Like most codes of political and social ethics, the Confucian tradition places high value on order, stability, and regularity. It deeply honors literature and formal education, and it emphasizes especially strongly the point that a conscientious, highly educated class of men ought to play the principal role in government. During the Han dynasty (206 B.C.E. to 220 C.E.), the Chinese state sponsored the development of a formal educational system based on Confucian texts and values to produce administrators and bureaucrats. This policy significantly advanced the cultural integration of the settled, agricultural regions of the Han empire.

Toward the margins of agricultural society, however, Confucian values encountered spirited resistance. In their efforts to consolidate Han authority in south China, for example, Confucian governors and military officers faced numerous political, social, economic, and cultural obstacles. Tribal and clan loyalties, confusing marriage and family relationships, hunting-and-gathering or mixed agricultural economies, the authority of shamanistic leaders, and a wide variety of local superstitions — all hindered the extension of Chinese civilization into the valley of the Chang Jiang (Yangzi River) and beyond. Nevertheless, over the long term, a variety of policies brought the south securely into the orbit of Chinese civilization. These policies included promotion of settled agriculture, institution of patriarchal family relationships, education of local notables in Confucian values and Chinese ritual, and even the promotion of Chinese dress.[2] By the eighth or ninth century C.E., aided by large-scale migration and centuries of Chinese presence, these policies had effectively sinicized the southern regions of China.

In other regions, Chinese culture did not take hold on such a scale. Han statesmen and state builders encountered far more difficulties with their western and northern than with their immediate southern neighbors. At least since the time of the Shang dynasty (1766–1122 B.C.E.), Chinese states had experienced tense relations with the nomadic peoples of the steppes. Chinese wealth, agricultural surpluses, and finely produced goods such as silk all attracted the nomads' interest. When they could not acquire the products they sought by way of peaceful exchange, they rarely hesitated to mount their horses and organize raids into Chinese territories.[3] To a certain extent, the development of large, centralized states during the Qin and Han dynasties posed a threat to nomadic raiders, since Chinese could mobilize larger and more effective defenses against the nomads' incursions, and could even mount a powerful offensive in steppe regions. But centralized rule brought opportunity as well as challenge for nomads, since it enabled Chinese to produce even more wealth, agricultural surplus, and finished goods than they had in earlier times.

Most prominent of the nomads bordering the Han empire were the Xiongnu, a Turkish-speaking people from the Mongolian steppes.[4] Soon after the founding of the Han dynasty, Maodun (reigned 209 to 174 B.C.E.), organized the Xiongnu into a vast confederacy that extended from the Aral Sea in the west to eastern Mongolia and the Yellow Sea. During the early, vulnerable years of the Han dynasty, Xiongnu raided Chinese territory almost with impunity, causing enormous instability in frontier regions. Indeed, Liu Bang, founder of the Han, almost lost his army, his throne, and his life under Xiongnu siege in the year 200 B.C.E.

Han diplomats and strategists tried several policies in their efforts to regularize relations with the Xiongnu. First they arranged dynastic marriages, sending Han princesses to wed Xiongnu leaders. At the same time they sent the Xiongnu valuable gifts — essentially tribute — in exchange for token gifts and cessation of border hostilities. Later they established a series of border markets where

Xiongnu could trade for the Chinese goods that they desired. None of these policies worked very well. In spite of marital links, tribute, and officially sponsored markets, Xiongnu continued to carry out border raids that destabilized frontier regions. Meanwhile, Chinese policy and reactions to the Xiongnu also contributed to instability. Han law prohibited the sale of iron, crossbows, and other weaponry to barbarians, so that Xiongnu could not legally acquire some of the products that they most desired. (Imperial writ did not always run very far, however, and Xiongnu easily found adventurous traders willing to supply their needs; in 121 B.C.E., the emperor Han Wudi ordered the execution of five hundred merchants who had traded in contraband materials with the Xiongnu.) Furthermore, Chinese forces sometimes mounted surprise attacks on Xiongnu who had gathered in large numbers at border markets for purposes of peaceful trade.

The long term of tension ultimately led to outright war between Han Chinese and the Xiongnu. The "Martial Emperor," Han Wudi (140–87 B.C.E.), mounted a series of aggressive campaigns designed to stabilize the steppes and bring the Xiongnu into a tributary relationship with the Han empire. Chinese armies captured one Xiongnu stronghold after another and pacified a large central Asian corridor from Mongolia to Turkestan. In an effort to consolidate their hold, they established agricultural colonies in places where the local environment allowed Chinese-style cultivation. Most of the colonies eventually withered; they proved to be painfully expensive to maintain, and economic policies designed to support them became the subject of fierce debate among Han advisers and ministers.[5] Nevertheless, the powerful Chinese military presence encouraged the growth of internal dissension among the Xiongnu. By the late first century C.E., the Xiongnu had become politically disorganized, and they never again posed a serious, large-scale military threat to China.

Meanwhile, Chinese efforts to bring the Xiongnu under control led to cross-cultural encounters of high interest and significance. A large and varied number of individuals served as agents who transmitted ideas, values, and techniques across cultural boundary lines. They included traders, ambassadors, hostages, prisoners, slaves, partners in cross-cultural marriages, and the offspring of these unions. Their encounters led to a fair amount of adaptation on both sides of the cultural frontier. Some Xiongnu adopted Chinese agricultural techniques, for example, although they preferred to avoid excessive toil by using captives and prisoners of war as heavy laborers. Xiongnu also wore silk, ate with chopsticks, and lived in houses of Chinese style. Some even decided to cast their lots with China and to a large extent developed a new cultural identity: they took Chinese names and played important roles in Chinese political and military affairs. At the same time, the material culture of the Xiongnu and other nomads left clear signs of its influence across the frontier. Already about 300 B.C.E., even before the founding of the Han dynasty, King Wu Ling of Zhao forced his reluctant army to develop the "barbarian" skills of horsemanship and mounted archery, the better to resist incursions of nomadic raiders. (For the next two thousand years, their interest in good horseflesh strongly influenced the policies of Chinese rulers toward peoples of the steppes.) Toward the end of the Han dynasty, Emperor Ling and many aristocrats went so far as to adopt barbarian dress and to promote performances of the nomads' music and dance.[6]

Perhaps the most unexpected result of encounters between Chinese and Xiongnu was the defection of Chinese in sensitive positions to barbarian society. Chinese military forces sometimes went over to the Xiongnu en masse when they feared that failure to defeat the enemy would place them at risk of punishment. Chinese commanders on the frontier often had lengthy experience trading with the Xiongnu, whom they knew well. Political, social, or economic opportunity tempted more than a few of them to cross the cultural frontier. A popular saying of the Han frontier summarized their attitude in succinct fashion: "Northward we can flee to the Hsiung-nu [that is, Xiongnu] and southward to the Yüeh."[7]

The experience of Zhonghang Yue illustrates in remarkable fashion the sort of cross-cultural influence that such defectors had the potential to wield. Zhonghang served as tutor to a Han imperial princess who was sent to the court of Jizhu, Maodun's successor as leader of the Xiongnu. Zhonghang attempted to avoid the transfer, saying that his mission would bring misery to the Han, but he received orders to make the journey in spite of his prediction. Jizhu showed favor to Zhonghang and soon won his loyalty. Zhonghang then performed many and various services for his new patron. In the first place, he offered advice on the maintenance of Xiongnu independence. He told the Xiongnu that they should avoid Chinese luxuries and cultivate their own customs. Felt or leather clothing would serve them much better than silk, he said, when they rode their horses through briars and brambles. Quite apart from its practical value, though, native dress would help the Xiongnu to maintain their distinctiveness and resist absorption by the much larger population of China. In the second place, Zhonghang instructed Jizhu in Chinese techniques of administration and diplomacy. He taught his patron how to take a census of the Xiongnu people and to keep inventories of their animal stocks. He also showed him how to respond to Chinese diplomatic communications in such a way as to embarrass the Chinese and place them on the defensive. Finally, he defended Xiongnu customs and values against Chinese critics. He praised the Xiongnu for their strong sense of family and clan loyalty and charged that Chinese frequently became so estranged from their families as to murder their own kin. Zhonghang did not shrink from lecturing Han diplomats on the decadence and moral decay of China, nor even from an occasional intemperate tirade: "Pooh! You people in your mud huts—you talk too much! Enough of this blabbering and mouthing! Just because you wear hats, what does that make you?" Han envoys should resist the temptation to instruct the Xiongnu, he said, but simply deliver Chinese tribute in timely fashion—or face punitive raids.[8]

It is difficult to know exactly how to interpret the experience of Zhonghang Yue. One problem concerns the motives of Sima Qian, who reported Zhonghang's mission in his history of the Han dynasty. Sima favored policies that would promote stability between Chinese and Xiongnu, but he opposed Han efforts to pacify the distant steppes. At the end of his long account of the Xiongnu, he conveyed clearly enough to his readers the point that he had employed "subtle and guarded language" when dealing with sensitive current affairs.[9] Sima certainly did not invent the story of Zhonghang Yue in order to criticize Han policies toward the Xiongnu. But it is entirely possible that he related it in such a way as to call those policies into question. His emphasis on differences between Chinese and Xiongnu culture especially looks like a critique of Han Wudi's expansion into the steppes and subsequent efforts to tame the Xiongnu.

Quite apart from the problem of Sima Qian's motives, the qual-

ity of the information he provided also complicates the interpretation of Zhonghang Yue. There is no evidence that Zhonghang
adopted Xiongnu culture. Indeed, his importance stemmed directly
from his role as cultural mediator — as one who bridged settled and
nomadic cultures, not as one who abandoned an inherited cultural
tradition in favor of an alternative. As a mediator, Zhonghang
advised the Xiongnu and instructed them in Chinese administrative
and diplomatic techniques. But the question arises: Did these techniques represent an expansion of Chinese civilization, or simply
tools that could strengthen the hand of the Xiongnu against the
Chinese? And what about Chinese beliefs and values? If Sima Qian's account is basically reliable, it looks as though Zhonghang not
only did not promote Chinese civilization but sought actively to
reinforce Xiongnu culture and to enable it to resist a serious Chinese threat. Finally, what motives can account for Zhonghang's
transfer of political allegiance to the Xiongnu? Did he benefit fi-
nancially? Did he gain opportunities to wield power and influence?
Did he simply find more personal satisfaction working for Xiongnu, who presumably appreciated his skills, rather than the Chinese
who had sent him out to the steppes?

Sima Qian's account obviously does not address all the questions
that Zhonghang's case raises. It is clear that mediators transferred
specific cultural elements across cultural frontiers, where different
peoples employed them for their own purposes. Yet there was no
mass conversion of either Chinese or Xiongnu society. Individuals
and small groups from both societies pursued opportunities across
the cultural frontier. Chinese experience with the Xiongnu thus
differed entirely from their encounter with the native peoples of
south China. Massive immigration and imperial sponsorship
brought about social conversion by assimilation south of the Chang
Jiang, where Chinese-style agriculture was ecologically possible.
The steppes, however, would support neither intensive agriculture
nor large populations. Meanwhile, their immensity precluded the
possibility that Chinese might have induced nomads to adopt new
cultural traditions by means of political, military, or economic
pressure. Thus geography reinforced political, social, economic,
and cultural differences between Chinese and Xiongnu, and it
positively discouraged any large-scale cultural transformations of
either society. As a result, nomadic resistance successfully pre-

2

vented the permanent establishment of Chinese cultural traditions in the steppes.

Although it did not bring about any large-scale social conversion, the encounter between Chinese and Xiongnu led to one further development of long-term significance for all kinds of cross-cultural exchange in Eurasia: the opening of roads and trade routes across central Asia. Both Xiongnu and Chinese played roles in this development. The Xiongnu received silk and other fine goods from their trade and tributary dealings with the Han dynasty. They redistributed these products throughout their realm, which helped to create a demand for Chinese goods in central Asia. Eventually, Chinese products found their ways to India, the Middle East, and the Roman empire, which led to accelerated demand for silk in particular. Xiongnu and other nomads served as the most important transporters and distributors of Chinese goods in central Asia and thus helped to establish reliable networks for the exchange of trade goods.[10]

Meanwhile, Chinese efforts to outflank the Xiongnu and pacify the steppes also led to the organization of roads and the exchange of trade goods over extraordinarily long distances. The central figure in this development was Zhang Qian, a Han ambassador who twice traveled as far as Bactria and Ferghana in search of allies against the Xiongnu.[11] (See map 1 for the route that he traveled.) During his first trip, which began in 139 B.C.E., he spent more than ten years in Xiongnu captivity. He lived in nomadic society — he even took a Xiongnu wife, by whom he had one son — and developed military and political intelligence of great use to Han policymakers. While in Bactria, about 128 B.C.E., Zhang Qian had noticed Chinese bamboo and textiles offered for sale. Upon inquiry, he learned that they had come from southwest China by way of Bengal. From his observation, Zhang Qian deduced the possibility of establishing safe roads from China through India to Bactria — roads that would not expose ambassadors or merchants to the Xiongnu or other unfriendly peoples in central Asia. Zhang Qian won special praise also for discovering a source of large and powerful horseflesh. In a campaign of 102 to 98 B.C.E., Han Wudi sent an expedition of some thirty thousand soldiers to obtain the so-called blood-sweating horses that Zhang Qian had reported seeing in Ferghana.[12]

Western demand for Chinese silk and other fine products combined with Chinese interest in western horses to produce a powerful commercial dynamic throughout Eurasia. As Sima Qian noted in the passage quoted at the head of this chapter, Zhang Qian's travels alerted central Asian peoples to the economic opportunities that Chinese trade made available, and they quickly moved to establish commercial relationships with Chinese producers and to serve as carriers of Chinese products to points west. Especially after about 200 C.E., the roads traveled by material goods figured also as routes serving long-range cultural as well as commercial exchange.

The Early Spread of Indian Cultural Traditions

Envoys and traders opened the roads across Eurasia with political and commercial considerations in mind, but missionaries, pilgrims, and other cultural mediators soon began to make use of them for their own, quite different purposes. By the first century C.E., at the latest — probably in the first century B.C.E. — Buddhist teachings had found their way to the heart of China. This sort of cultural migration has led one recent scholar to a perhaps unexpected conclusion: "The real significance of the silk road was cultural rather than commercial. Its true sponsors were Hellenism, Chinese curiosity, Buddhism and Christianity."[13]

During the era of the ancient silk roads, Indian cultural traditions took best advantage of the new avenues of transportation and communication. In India as in China, this period witnessed the elaboration of an influential cultural tradition and its secure establishment within its own society, followed by an early and somewhat tentative spread into neighboring regions. Indian cultural traditions, however, sparked a good deal more interest in foreign lands than did the Chinese even in early times. They did not attract enough support to bring about social conversion on a large scale, but in two regions local elites underwent voluntary conversions to Indian cultural traditions, and in both cases conversion through voluntary association served as a foundation for long-term cultural influence and eventually for large-scale social conversion. This section will begin by examining the establishment of

Buddhism in India and its tentative influence in neighboring regions to the north and west. It will continue by analyzing the early spread of Buddhism into central Asia and China and the spread of both Buddhism and Hinduism into southeast Asia, concentrating on processes by which local elites of central and southeast Asia voluntarily associated with foreign merchants and converted to Indian religious traditions.

Many clouds and legends obscure the remote history of Buddhism, but certain general features of its early development stand out with reasonable clarity. Three of them are especially important for present purposes. In the first place, Buddhism arose at a time of great change in the social and economic order of ancient India. During the sixth and fifth centuries B.C.E., commerce and cash became increasingly important in an economy previously dominated by self-sufficient production and bartered exchange. Merchants found Buddhist moral and ethical teachings an attractive alternative to the esoteric rituals of the traditional brahmin priesthood, which seemed to cater exclusively to brahmin interests while ignoring those of the new and emerging social classes. Natural allies, Buddhists and merchants soon developed a mutually beneficial, even symbiotic relationship. Merchants generously supported Buddhist monasteries and other foundations. Meanwhile, Buddhists established their communities along trade routes linking important political and economic centers, where they could provide hospitality for merchants and other travelers.[14] As a result of this relationship, the Buddhist faith was well positioned to spread dramatically whenever Indian merchants expanded the geographical range of their commercial activity.

This point directs attention to a second feature of early Buddhism that also helps to explain its widespread dissemination: the importance that early Buddhists attached to monastic communities and missionary activities. The two in fact go hand in hand. Monks provided many social and spiritual services but did not contribute directly to agricultural or industrial production. For their subsistence they relied instead on alms and gifts donated by lay followers. Maintenance of a monastic tradition thus entailed the attraction of a large laity to Buddhist values and allegiance. Further development of the monastic tradition—the better to serve the interests of the faith and the needs of the faithful—entailed the recruitment of even more lay supporters. Because of its organization and institutional structure, then, Buddhism became a missionary religion already in the earliest days of its existence.

Finally, Buddhism benefitted from its doctrinal flexibility. Almost as soon as the Buddha died (about 486 B.C.E.) it became clear that the new faith had great potential to adapt to various needs, interests, and circumstances. The basic doctrine of Buddhism was quite simple, and Buddhist scriptures required several centuries to acquire canonical status. In the meantime, disciples of the Buddha emphasized various elements of his teaching that appealed to them. This development raised the possibility that schism would divide or weaken or even destroy the fledgling faith. Indeed, early Buddhists probably held two councils—one immediately following the Buddha's death and another about a century thereafter—in a relatively unsuccessful effort to determine the elements of orthodox Buddhist belief and practice. From one point of view, then, variety in early Buddhist values posed a threat to a religion that had not yet securely established itself. Over the long term, however, its relatively simple doctrine enabled Buddhism to respond flexibly to the challenges of different cultural traditions. Its adaptability certainly helps to account for the spread of Buddhism from its north Indian homeland to other cultural regions.

By the third century B.C.E., Buddhism had established a solid presence in northern India, where it offered a practical and ethical alternative to the cults of the brahmins. It had also spread along the trade routes into southern India—presumably by a process of voluntary conversion—where it increasingly attracted the allegiance of merchants engaged in trade with the north. Then, during the middle decades of the third century, King Asoka (reigned 269–232 B.C.E.) promoted Buddhism energetically and supported it morally, materially, and legally. As a result, Buddhism became consolidated as a major religion throughout India, and it even began to spread tentatively beyond the subcontinent.

Asoka converted gradually to Buddhism, beginning about 263 B.C.E. at the latest.[15] By his own testimony, he did not develop a deep sense of piety in the years immediately following his profession of the faith. About 260, though, he waged a bitterly destructive war against the state of Kalinga (modern Orissa). The death and suffering of Kalingans deeply affected Asoka, and he began to heed the moral and ethical teachings of Buddhism much more seriously than before. For the remainder of his long reign he sought to implement a policy of *dhamma*: virtue, benevolence, and humanity.

Some elements of this policy had nothing specifically to do with Buddhism. Asoka's avoidance of war, maintenance of roads, and provision of comforts for travelers on Indian highways signal a sense of enlightened self-interest as much as Buddhist piety. But other elements of the policy of *dhamma* — such as increasingly strict prohibitions against slaughter and sacrifice of animals — reflect Buddhist values clearly enough. Indeed, in many ways Asoka promoted specifically Buddhist interests. He made pilgrimages to holy Buddhist sites and built numerous temples and monasteries. He protected the integrity of Buddhist doctrine and ordered the expulsion of schismatics from their monasteries. He dispatched ambassadors of goodwill and missionaries to all parts of India and to neighboring lands. It is possible that he presided over a council of Buddhist leaders held at his capital of Pataliputra about 250 B.C.E. This council also sent out missions — some to central and southern India, others to Burma, Ceylon, the Himalayan region, and even to Greek-speaking lands, probably the Greek states in Bactria.

To a large extent, Asoka's policy of *dhamma* reflected his personal values, which Buddhism had of course deeply influenced. The language of his rock and pillar edicts leaves no doubt about Asoka's conviction that his policies proceeded from a sense of moral imperative. In his famous thirteenth rock edict, for example, Asoka reflected on the war in Kalinga, which reportedly had resulted in more than 100,000 deaths and 150,000 deportations:

> On conquering Kalinga, the Beloved of the Gods [that is, Asoka] felt remorse, for, when an independent country is conquered the slaughter, death, and deportation of the people is extremely grievous to the Beloved of the Gods and weighs heavily on his mind. What is even more deplorable to the Beloved of the Gods, is that those who dwell there . . . all suffer violence, murder, and separation from their loved ones. Even those who are fortunate to have escaped . . . suffer from the misfortunes of their friends, acquaintances, colleagues, and relatives. This participation of all men in suffering, weighs heavily on the mind of the Beloved of the Gods.[16]

The weight on his mind led Asoka then to develop and to announce in this same edict his policy of *dhamma*: henceforth he would seek conquest by virtue, benevolence, and humanity rather than arms.

Quite apart from his sincere personal conviction, though, sound political interests and instincts underlay Asoka's promotion of Buddhism. His grandfather Candragupta had established the Mauryan empire less than forty years before Asoka's coronation in 269 B.C.E. In Asoka's time it remained a polyglot realm of enormous cultural diversity. It seems reasonably clear that Asoka regarded Buddhism as a doctrine that could serve as a cultural foundation for political unity. Buddhist ethics replaced locally or ethnically based value systems with a universal standard of morality. Furthermore, Buddhism was prominent in communities of merchants, who found it well suited to their needs and who increasingly established commercial links throughout the Mauryan empire. Asoka perhaps did not think about Buddhism in the analytical fashion of the twentieth century, but he could not have failed to recognize its usefulness for his task of maintaining the political integrity of his empire.

As a result of intensive cross-cultural encounters during the late centuries B.C.E., however, the influence of Buddhism and Indian culture in general carried well beyond the boundaries of Asoka's realm. To the north and west, interest in Indian culture developed in the wake of the eastern campaigns of Alexander the Great, whose conquest of Bactria brought Greeks, Persians, Indians, and others into close relationships. Greeks immediately became intrigued by Indian culture and civilization. An early Greek ambassador, Megasthenes, composed a work entitled the *Indika*, which described Indian geography, society, customs, and culture; though now lost, its deep influence is apparent from many other ancient Greek works that cited it or quoted from it.[17]

Indian culture also established a presence in Persia, although it did not appeal strongly to the native population there. At least by the first century C.E., Buddhist communities had become established in the eastern part of the Parthian empire. Buddhism undoubtedly spread to this region through the diaspora communities of foreign merchants. Buddhist communities occurred in merchant towns such as Merv, and Parthian traders were especially prominent among the early Buddhists in central Asia and China. Buddhism did not attract many converts in Persia and never became a popular faith there. Zoroastrian and other indigenous traditions continued to satisfy the cultural needs of the region during the early centuries of Buddhist presence in Persia. Later on, the Sassanian kings did not tolerate any religion except the officially approved Zoroastrianism, and eventually the establishment of Islam precluded any further possibility that Buddhism might bring about social conversion in Persia.[18]

Given the widespread western interest in India, scholars have often considered the possibility that Buddhism influenced the early development of Christianity. They have drawn attention to many parallels concerning the births, lives, doctrines, and deaths of the Buddha and Jesus, as recorded in their respective traditions of scripture and legend. Nineteenth-century scholars often emphasized these parallels and concluded that Christianity reflected deep influence of Buddhist stories and values. More recently, however, scholars have placed less emphasis on parallels than on the profound differences between Buddhism and Christianity. While acknowledging the possibility or even the likelihood that Buddhism influenced certain, individual, specific stories or practices of early Christianity — also that Christianity influenced the development in later centuries of the Mahayana school of Buddhism — they generally find no reason to suspect foreign influence on the formation of the essential doctrines of the two faiths.[19] Only in the case of Manichaeism, discussed in the next section, is there clear evidence that Buddhist beliefs and values decisively influenced the development of religious doctrines in lands west of Bactria.

To the east and south, however, the case is quite different. Buddhism traveled the silk roads and established its presence in the diaspora communities of foreign merchants in central Asia and China. Meanwhile, Buddhism and Hinduism both sailed the Indian Ocean and attracted the strong interest of southeast Asian elites, who voluntarily associated with Indian traders and converted to the Indian faiths. Each of these developments bears some discussion and analysis.

Buddhism benefitted enormously from the commercial traffic that crossed the silk roads. Once it arrived on the trade routes, Buddhism found its way very quickly indeed to distant lands. Merchants proved to be an efficient vector of the Buddhist faith, as they established diaspora communities in the string of oasis towns—Merv, Bukhara, Samarkand, Kashgar, Khotan, Kuqa, Turpan, Dunhuang—that served as lifeline of the silk roads through central Asia. The oases depended heavily on trade for their economic survival, and they quickly accommodated the needs and interests of the merchants whom they hosted. They became centers of high literacy and culture; they organized markets and arranged for lodging, care of animals, and storage of merchandise; and they allowed their guests to build monasteries and bring large contingents of Buddhist monks and copyists into their communities. Before too long—perhaps as early as the first or even the second century B.C.E.—the oasis dwellers themselves converted to Buddhism.[20]

Thus a process of conversion through voluntary association with well-organized foreigners underwrote the first major expansion of Buddhism outside India. Buddhist merchants linked the oases to a large and cosmopolitan world, and the oases became enormously wealthy by providing useful services for the merchants. It is not at all surprising that inhabitants of the small oasis communities would gradually incline toward the beliefs and values of the numerous Buddhist merchants who traveled the silk roads and enriched the oases.

Once established in oasis communities, Buddhism had the potential to spread both to nomadic peoples on the steppes of central Asia and even to China, a land of long-settled civilization with its own long-established cultural traditions. Buddhism realized this potential only partially, however, and only in gradual fashion. As a faith foreign to China and generally despised by Chinese during its early centuries there, Buddhism had a certain attraction for nomadic peoples who themselves had quite difficult relations with Chinese. In other words, Buddhism exercised a kind of countercultural appeal to nomads who loathed the Chinese, but who also desired and even depended upon trade with China. Yet many nomadic peoples found it difficult to accept Buddhism; they did not have traditions of literacy to accommodate Buddhist moral and theological teachings, and their mobility made it impossible to maintain fixed monastic communities. As a result, many nomadic peoples held to their native shamanist cults, and others turned to Manichaeism or Nestorian Christianity. Meanwhile, some of those who adopted Buddhism did so at a very late date. Among the Mongols, for example, Buddhism did not become a popular faith until the sixteenth century. When nomadic peoples became involved in commerce, however, or when they established themselves as rulers of settled lands that they conquered, they frequently adopted Buddhism through a process of conversion through voluntary association. These patterns were quite prominent in central Asia and northern China during the era of the ancient silk roads.

The career of the monk and missionary Fotudeng especially helps to illuminate the voluntary conversion of nomadic peoples to Buddhism.[21] Fotudeng probably came from Kuqa, an oasis town on the silk road in modern Xinjiang. He became a priest at an early age, traveled through central Asia, visited Kashmir, and set out to do missionary work in northern China during the early fourth century. He went to Dunhuang in order to improve his Chinese, then continued on to Luoyang about the year 310. There he caught the attention of Shi Le, the ruler of the nomadic Jie people (western allies of the Xiongnu), who controlled most of northern China during the fourth century. Fotudeng realized early on that he would not get very far with Shi Le by lecturing him on fine points of Buddhist philosophy, but he had a reputation for working miracles, which he used to the advantage of his mission. He dazzled Shi Le by producing bright blue lotus blossoms from his monk's begging bowl and by looking into his palm to see the reflection of distant events. Among his more utilitarian talents were rainmaking, healing, and prophecy. Fotudeng helped Shi Le plan military campaigns by foreseeing the outcome and devising clever strategies to ensure success. As a result of his miraculous talents, Fotudeng won widespread fame, and people from distant regions worshipped him. When he died about the year 345, he reportedly had ten thousand disciples and the erection of 893 temples to his credit.

Thus did a process of voluntary conversion help to establish Buddhism in northern China. The nomadic Jie settled in northern China and became deeply engaged in the political and economic affairs of a large and complex world. Fotudeng represented the culture of that larger world and brought talents useful for Jie rulers as they entered its life. He parlayed his personal relationship with Shi Le into official approval for his efforts to spread Buddhist values and even to found Buddhist institutions in northern China.

Hence, his work not only illuminates the voluntary conversion of nomadic peoples but also helps to explain the early presence of the Buddhist faith in China.

The establishment of Buddhism in China was an even more difficult and gradual affair than its spread among nomadic peoples. Indeed, it required half a millennium for Buddhism to attract a large popular following in China.[22] There as in Persia, the foreign faith could not immediately attract many followers away from indigenous cultural traditions, in this case principally Confucianism and Daoism. Even in its early years in China, Buddhism encountered determined resistance from Confucian and Daoist quarters. Representatives of the native Chinese traditions charged that Buddhism detracted from the authority of the state, that monasteries were unproductive and useless drags on the economy, that Buddhism itself was a barbarian faith inferior to Chinese traditions, and that the monastic life violated the natural order of society and disrupted family life. Not surprisingly, then, during its early centuries in China, Buddhism remained largely the faith of foreigners: merchants, ambassadors, refugees, hostages, and missionaries. During the second century C.E., for example, the Buddhist monastery at Luoyang included among its inhabitants two Parthians, two Sogdians, three Indians, and three Scythians, but no known Chinese. During its early years in China, then, Buddhism seems to have served principally as a cultural resource for trade diaspora communities.

As an alien cultural tradition that did not resonate in China, Buddhism could easily have experienced the same fate there that it did in Persia: it could have survived in the quarters inhabited by foreign merchants as an expatriate faith, perhaps even for centuries, without attracting much interest from the larger host community. The explanation for Buddhism's remarkable spread as a popular faith in east Asia begins with the voluntary conversion of elites, which enabled the foreign tradition to gain a foothold in Chinese society. In the north, where Buddhism first established its presence in China, voluntary conversion reflected the political interests of ruling elites. In most cases they were nomads, such as the Jie whom Fotudeng served so well, or the Toba rulers of the Northern Wei dynasty (386–534). After an initial period of tension and uncertain relations, it dawned on both Buddhists and rulers that an alliance could serve the interests of both parties. Buddhist monasteries provided ideological and economic support for established ruling houses: they recognized the legitimacy of Jie and Toba rule; they facilitated long-distance trade, which figured prominently in the local economy; and they served as a conduit for the importation of exotic and luxury goods that symbolized the special status of the ruling elites. Meanwhile, the dynasties patronized the Buddhists in return, participated in their rituals, and protected the interests of their monasteries.

Like the oasis dwellers of central Asia, then, the ruling elites of northern China made common cause with representatives of a foreign cultural tradition who had extensive political and commercial links in the larger world. This sort of voluntary conversion was the only way by which Buddhism could find a place in Chinese society. Buddhists entered China in numbers too small to bring about a massive social transformation by way of pressure or assimilation. Only by winning the favor and protection of elites could the early Buddhists ensure their survival in China. As it happened, when missionaries found ways to communicate their message effectively to native Chinese and thus to bring a process of syncretism to their aid, their faith brought about a large-scale social conversion in China—but this development took place well after the era of the ancient silk roads and so comes up for analysis in the next chapter.

Meanwhile, as Buddhism found tentative footing in China, both Buddhism and Hinduism attracted the attention of elites and won converts in southeast Asia. As in China, the carriers of Indian cultural traditions were mostly merchants. During the late centuries B.C.E., Indian traders began to sail the seas and visit the coastal towns of southeast Asia. Even during those remote centuries, there was considerable incentive for merchants to embark upon long and often dangerous voyages. According to an ancient Gujarati story, for example, men who went to Java never returned—but if by chance they did return, they brought with them wealth enough to provide for seven generations. By the early centuries C.E., southeast Asian mariners themselves traveled to India as well as to other southeast Asian sites. The resulting networks of trade and communication invigorated not only the economic but also the political and cultural life of southeast Asia.[23]

Among the principal beneficiaries of early trade between India and southeast Asia were the political and cultural traditions of India. Merchants from the subcontinent established diaspora communities, into which they invited Hindu and Buddhist authorities. Local chiefs controlled commerce at the trading sites they ruled, and they quickly became introduced to the larger world of the Indian Ocean. The ruler of an important trading site was no longer a "frog under a coconut shell," as the Malay proverb has it, but, rather, a cultural and commercial broker of some moment.[24] Trade and external alliances enabled local rulers to organize states on a larger scale than ever before in southeast Asia. The first of these well represented in historical sources—though by no means the only early state in southeast Asia—was Funan, founded along the Mekong River in the first century C.E. Through its main port, Oc Eo, Funan carried on trade with China, Malaya, Indonesia, India, Persia, and indirectly with Mediterranean lands. By the end of the second century, similar trading states had appeared in the Malay peninsula and Champa (southern Vietnam).

Indian influence ran so deep in these states that they and their successors for a millennium and more are commonly referred to as the "Indianized states of southeast Asia." Indian traditions manifested their influence in many different ways. In a land previously governed by charismatic individuals of great personal influence, for example, rulers adopted Indian notions of divine kingship. They associated themselves with the cults of Siva, Visnu, or the Buddha, and they claimed both foreign and divine authority to legitimize their rule. They built walled cities with temples at the center, and they introduced Indian music and ceremonies into court rituals. They brought in Hindu and Buddhist advisers, who reinforced the sense of divinely sanctioned rule. They took Sanskrit names and titles for themselves, and they used Sanskrit as the language of law and bureaucracy. Indian influence was so extensive, in fact, that an earlier generation of historians suggested that vast armadas of Indians had colonized southeast Asia—a view now regarded as complete fiction. More recent explanations of the Indianization process place more emphasis on southeast Asian elites who for their own purposes associated themselves as closely as possible with the Hindu and Buddhist traditions. They certainly found no lack of willing and talented tutors; the quality of Sanskrit literature produced in southeast Asia argues for the presence there of many sophisticated and well-educated representatives of Indian cultural traditions. But high interest in foreign traditions on the part of southeast Asian elites drove the process of Indianization.

By no means did indigenous cultures fade away or disappear. During the early years after their arrival in southeast Asia, Indian traditions worked their influence mostly at the courts of ruling elites, and not much beyond. Over a longer term, however, Indian and native traditions combined to fashion syncretic cultural configurations and to bring about social conversion on a large scale — processes discussed in the next two chapters. In any case, though, the voluntary conversion of local elites to Hinduism and Buddhism decisively shaped the cultural development of southeast Asia.

Missionary Religions in the Middle East and Mediterranean

On the western as on the eastern end of the Eurasian landmass, imperial expansion brought about intensive intermingling of peoples from different civilizations and cultural traditions. During the late fourth century B.C.E., Alexander the Great had toppled the Persian empire of the Achaemenids, explored northwestern India, and established Greek states as far east as Bactria. After Alexander's early death, his Seleucid successors governed the region from Anatolia to Bactria, which included by far the largest portion of Alexander's realm. The Seleucid state thus coordinated the dealings of Greeks, Phoenicians, Babylonians, Persians, and Indians, among other peoples. Alexander had shattered national and ethnic boundaries, and the Seleucids ruled over an enormous, cosmopolitan, polyglot empire.

These fundamentally political developments had large cultural implications. Peoples from different civilizations met and mingled especially in Bactria and the north Indian kingdom of Gandhara, where western cultural traditions left their mark on Indian civilization. The most graphic evidence of this cultural exchange comes from the Gandharan school of Buddhist art, which clearly reflected the influence of Mediterranean styles of painting and sculpture. The earliest Buddhist artists had considered it improper to depict the Buddha himself in human form. They represented him instead

by means of an appropriate symbol: a pipal tree (under which
he had gained enlightenment), a footprint (which suggested his
peregrinations), an empty throne (which he had abandoned in favor of enlightenment), or the wheel of the law (which he had set
in motion). As Greeks established diaspora trade communities in
Bactria and Gandhara, they brought works of art in Mediterranean
styles, and they perhaps even brought western artists and craftsmen
into their communities. By the first century C.E., the Gandharan
school reflected the influence of western styles. Not only did the
Gandharan artists portray the Buddha in human form; they also
dressed him in Mediterranean garments and depicted him in poses
commonly found in western art. During the following centuries,
artists departed from the Mediterranean style and provided the
Buddha with more characteristically Indian features. In the meantime, however, western styles quite plainly influenced the image of
the Buddha in the land of his birth.[25]

Meanwhile, Hellenistic culture itself also reflected the post-
Alexandrian political environment and adjusted to the realities of
the large and cosmopolitan world in which it developed. On the
level of popular culture, this adjustment quite commonly took the
form of a remarkable religious syncretism.[26] As traders, soldiers,
administrators, slaves, and other travelers moved from one part of
the vast Hellenistic world to another, they naturally carried their
beliefs, values, and faiths along with them. The awareness that
many and various deities had the same or similar functions led to
the conflation of cults—those of Zeus and Amon, for example—
and sometimes even to a search for a single, universal deity who
oversaw the affairs of all nations and races from a heavenly van-
tage point, as Alexander and his Seleucid successors governed them
on earth. The moral philosophers who represented the tradition of
elite culture often did not object to this religious syncretism, but
they concentrated their efforts less on the conflation of deities than
on the search for moral and ethical standards of universal validity.
Most notable of all these efforts was the ethical thought of the
Stoics. Their prime political ideal was a well-governed, cosmopolitan, universal state. Their conviction in the essential equality of all
humankind followed from this vision, which did not provide for
superior and inferior, dominant and subordinate relations between
states. From the ideal of equality there followed the Stoics' emphasis on virtue, conscience, duty, and absolute personal integrity.

The Hellenistic empires did not survive intact over a long term; as early as 250 B.C.E., the Parthians carved an independent state from the Seleucid empire, and soon thereafter the Romans progressively extended their hegemony over the Mediterranean basin. Nevertheless, Hellenistic culture continued to develop along the lines established in the third century. The Parthian and the Roman empires both posed cultural challenges similar to those that arose during Alexandrian and Seleucid times. Both empires — especially the Roman — organized vast territories and placed peoples of different civilizations and cultural traditions in touch with one another. In both realms, there arose powerful missionary religions that addressed the needs of individuals living in cosmopolitan society. Both Manichaeism and Christianity promised personal salvation while also establishing a universal framework that informed individuals' experiences, obliged them to observe high moral and ethical standards, and provided meaning for their existence.

The establishment of the Parthian empire brought a renewal of state support and patronage for Zoroastrianism, the traditional religion of Persia from a very early date.[27] The Achaemenid kings had already promoted Zoroastrianism as a national religion. Its dualism harmonized well with their political interests and their need to legitimize their rule. In one notable inscription, for example, Darius I attributed his success to the will and work of Ahura Mazda, the Zoroastrian Lord of Wisdom, and associated rebels with the principle of evil. Meanwhile, Zoroastrian doctrine promised personal salvation and eternal life to individuals who observed the commandments to think good thoughts, speak good words, and perform good acts.

Zoroastrianism was more a national or ethnic faith than a missionary religion. Even without benefit of active proselytization, though, Zoroastrian beliefs and values exercised a remarkably wide influence. Postexilic Jews adopted and adapted many elements of Zoroastrian belief — including notions that a savior would arrive and aid mortal humans in their struggle against evil; that individual souls would survive death, experience resurrection, and face judgment and assignment to heaven or hell; and that the end of time would bring a monumental struggle between the supreme creator god and the forces of evil, culminating in the establishment of the kingdom of god on earth and the entry of the righteous into paradise. Many of these elements appear clearly in the Book of Daniel, composed about the middle of the second century B.C.E., and they all influenced the thought of the Jewish Pharisees. Indeed, in its original usage, the term *Pharisee* very likely meant "Persian" — that is, a Jew of the sect most open to Persian influence. It goes without saying that early Christians also reflected the influence of these same Zoroastrian beliefs. Some scholars hold that Zoroastrian appeal extended even into India, where the notion of personal salvation would have influenced the early development of the Mahayana school of Buddhism.

Closer to home, Zoroastrian beliefs and values helped to shape the moral and intellectual structure of Manichaeism, one of the most explosive missionary religions of the ancient world. Manichaeism is especially interesting also because of the variety of cultural influences that inspired it. The prophet Mani (216–272 C.E.) came from a Zoroastrian family in Babylonia, but he drew most of his inspiration from the ascetic tradition of Christianity that thrived in Mesopotamia. He also became acquainted with Hindu and Buddhist thought during a sojourn in northwestern India. He regarded Zarathustra as the prophet of the Persians, Buddha as the prophet of the Indians, and Jesus as the prophet of the westerners. Himself he regarded as the heir of all three — as a prophet for the entire world. He did not so much attempt to fuse the elements of various faiths into a syncretic religion as he sought to promote his own, peculiar vision of Christianity and spread it universally. As Mani himself explained:

> He who has his Church in the West, he and his Church have not reached the East: the choice of him who has chosen his Church in the East has not come to the West. . . . But my hope, mine will go towards the West, and she will go also towards the East. And they shall hear the voice of her message in all languages, and shall proclaim her in all cities. My Church is superior in this first point to previous churches, for these previous churches were chosen in particular countries and in particular cities. My Church, mine shall spread in all cities and my Gospel shall touch every country.[28]

Mani's teaching proved to have enormous appeal for several reasons. In the first place, its intellectual coherence was a powerful attraction for sophisticated residents of cosmopolitan cities. It examined faith in the light of critical reason, and its dualism offered a persuasive explanation for the presence of both good and evil in the world. Before his conversion to Christianity, Augustine of Hippo found the faith so appealing that he spent nine years in the company of Manichaeans. In the second place, Manichaeism exercised a strong personal and psychological appeal that made a place for individuals and placed their existence in meaningful perspective. It held out hope of individual salvation for sincere believers, and the cordiality and companionship that marked Manichaean cells contributed to a powerful sense of community. Even its severe asceticism represented an attractive alternative for sensitive souls repelled by the materialism of late antiquity. Finally, Manichaeism appealed across cultural boundary lines because missionaries took a remarkably flexible attitude toward foreign cultural traditions. They consistently retained a few core elements — cosmic dualism, strict asceticism, and high moral standards — when seeking to establish their faith in foreign communities. But they willingly adapted local deities and demons to the framework of Manichaean doctrine. Indeed, the specifically Zoroastrian and Buddhist elements that scholars have identified in Manichaeism entered the faith largely as missionaries sought ways to communicate their message to peoples from different cultural traditions.

As a result of its manifold appeal, Manichaeism quickly became a world religion. Mani took St. Paul, the Christians' apostle to the gentiles, as a model for himself. He made numerous trips, corresponded widely, and sent disciples on missions to foreign lands. Even during his life, missionaries carried the Manichaean message beyond Mesopotamia to all parts of the Sassanian empire, northern India, and the eastern regions of the Roman empire. Meanwhile, Manichaeism was an urban faith — its adherents mistrusted agriculture but positively encouraged commerce — so that it spread also through the work of merchants. By the late third century, Manichaeism had become well established throughout the Mediterranean: cells of the faithful thrived in the trading centers of Syria, Anatolia, Egypt, Greece, Italy, Gaul, Spain, and north Africa.

The successful spread of Manichaeism and its establishment as a world religion is the more remarkable because it took place in the face of violent persecution. Mani himself died in prison under severe duress. The Sassanian kings took the advice of their Zoroastrian advisers and attacked his movement as a threat to public order and to their own rule. The Islamic conquests later put an end to Manichaeism in the Middle East. Meanwhile, in the Roman empire, Manichaeism ironically suffered from its association with Persia, eastern nemesis of Roman expansionists since the second century B.C.E. Following the legalization of Christianity in the early fourth century, the Roman Catholic church joined forces with the Roman state. Especially during the fifth and sixth centuries, cultural and political authorities mounted vicious campaigns of repression in both Byzantine and western regions of the empire. Indeed, the persecution was so intense that it effectively exterminated Manichaeism in the Mediterranean world. (Later dualist movements in the Mediterranean, such as those of the Bogomils and Cathari, had little or no relation to the ancient Manichaean tradition.)

And yet Manichaeism survived. The next chapter will show that the Manichaeans' doctrinal flexibility enabled them to find a home in central Asia and China. By assimilating their teachings to those of Buddhism and Daoism, Manichaeans spread their faith among Uighur Turks and even native Chinese. Indeed, in the commercial region of Fujian in south China, Manichaean communities maintained a distinctive existence until the sixteenth century.

Meanwhile, in the Roman empire as in the Parthian and Sassanian realms, cross-cultural dealings decisively shaped the experiences of ancient peoples. The Roman experience closely resembled that of China, as two forces—imperial expansion and long-distance trade—drove the process of cross-cultural encounter. The sheer size of the Roman empire guaranteed the mingling of peoples from different cultural traditions, especially considering the Roman practice of dispatching administrators and soldiers to distant parts of the realm. Their movements help to explain the spectacular diffusion of mystery religions throughout the Mediterranean basin during the early centuries C.E. Meanwhile, imperial expansion also brought Romans into regular and sustained dealings with peoples beyond the frontiers who recognized different values and observed different cultural traditions. Roman prosperity attracted the attention of nomadic peoples and others less politically organized than the Romans. Trade with Rome provided opportunities for Germanic "barbarian" chieftains to build states, which in turn enabled them to increase their military capacities, sometimes to the point that they could menace the empire and extract tribute from the Romans. Some nomadic peoples settled on the imperial frontiers, entered Roman service as border guards or mercenaries, and in varying degrees adopted Roman culture. But cultural influence also ran in the other direction. In Rome as in China, imperial expansion created a cultural frontier, which in turn offered opportunities to talented individuals on both sides of the divide. Roman administrators and soldiers posted on the frontier became familiar with their counterparts across the border. In more than a few cases they defected in order to pursue opportunities across the cultural frontier.

Long-distance trade worked alongside imperial expansion to ensure that a variety of foreign cultural traditions came together and won a hearing in the Roman empire. Palmyra in Syria served as entry point for trade coming overland from central Asia and China. Most notable among the products traded was silk, which came into great demand among the fashionable women of Rome during the first century C.E. Meanwhile, Romans also carried on direct trade with India by way of sea routes. About the second century B.C.E., western sailors became aware of the monsoon rhythms that governed travel on the Indian Ocean. By the first century C.E., Roman demand for pepper and other spices had stimulated a flourishing trade between ports in southern India and the Mediterranean. Roman trading communities such as the one at Arikamedu in southern India conducted especially brisk business in the pepper and spice trade. Products from afar of course required distribution within the Roman empire, and merchants obliged by establishing trading networks that linked all parts of the Mediterranean basin.[29]

Administrators, soldiers, merchants, and others who traveled throughout the Roman empire served as effective agents of cultural diffusion. One development that illustrates especially well their capacity to spread cultural traditions was the spectacular diffusion of the cult of Mithra in the Roman empire. Mithra's remote origins trace back to Indo-Aryan mythology and Zoroastrianism, where he was a deity associated with sun and light. Scholars once thought that the Roman cult of Mithra represented a case of a Persian cultural tradition extending its influence to the Mediterranean world. For the most part, however, contemporary analysts believe that the Roman cult preserved few if any distinctively Persian elements beyond the name of Mithra. Its values and mythology reflect Hellenistic and Roman rather than Persian traditions. Nonetheless, its remarkable spread — largely by way of administrators, soldiers, and merchants — demonstrates the potential of long-distance communications to disseminate cultural traditions even in ancient times. During the first century C.E., Mithraic altars, temples, and sculpture appeared in all corners of the Mediterranean basin, and they were especially prominent in military and commercial centers. Other deities — such as the Greek Orpheus, Egyptian Isis, and Syrian Baal — accompanied Mithra as traveling companions on his peregrinations throughout the Roman empire.[30]

Manichaeism, Mithraism, and other mystery cults clearly demonstrated the potential for cultural traditions to spread quickly throughout the tightly integrated Mediterranean world. Of all the religions that established themselves in the Roman empire, however, none succeeded on such a large scale or over such a long term as Christianity. Its early experience thus calls for some discussion.

Christianity had many things in common with other religions that became widely popular in the Roman empire. It offered an explanation of the world and the cosmic order, one that endowed history with a sense of purpose and human life with meaning. It addressed the needs and interests of individuals by holding out the prospect of personal immortality, salvation, and perpetual enjoyment of a paradisiacal existence. It established high standards of ethics and morality, well suited to the needs of a complex, interdependent, and cosmopolitan world where peoples of different races and religions intermingled on a systematic basis. It was a religion of the cities, efficiently disseminated throughout the empire along established routes of trade and communication. It welcomed into its ranks the untutored and unsophisticated as well as the more privileged classes. It even shared with the other religions several of its ritual elements, such as baptism and the community meal. In many ways, then, early Christianity reflected the larger cultural world of the early Roman empire.

During its first three centuries, Christianity developed under a serious political handicap. The earliest Christians were associated with parties of rebellious Jews who resisted Roman administration in Palestine. Later Christians, even gentiles, refused to honor the Roman emperor and state in the fashion deemed appropriate by imperial authorities. As a result, Christians endured not only social contempt and scorn but also organized campaigns of persecution. Meanwhile, the Roman state generously patronized many of the empire's pagan cults: in exchange for public honor and recognition, the emperors and other important political figures provided financial sponsorship for rituals, festivals, and other pagan activities.

Nevertheless, Christianity benefitted from the work of zealous missionaries who were able to persuade individuals and small groups that the Christians' god possessed awesome and unique powers. They communicated this message most effectively among the popular masses by acquiring a reputation for the working of miracles — healing illnesses, casting out demons, bestowing blessings on the faithful — that demonstrated the powers at their god's disposal. Ramsay MacMullen has recently argued, in fact, that fear of pain and punishment, desire for blessings, and belief in miracles were the principal inducements that attracted pagans to Christianity in the period before the conversion of Constantine about the year 312 C.E.[31]

A bit of information survives on one of the more effective of the early Christian missionaries, Gregory the Wonderworker, and it illustrates the importance of miracles for the building of the early Christian community.[32] Gregory had studied with the great Origen, and he wrote several formal theological treatises. For present purposes, though, his significance arises from his work in the Roman province of Pontus (north central Anatolia) during the 240s. Early accounts of his mission record one miracle after another. Gregory's prayers prevented a pagan deity from exercising his powers, but upon request Gregory summoned the deity to his pagan temple, thus demonstrating his superior authority; as a result, the caretaker of the temple converted to Christianity. On several occasions individuals interrupted Gregory's public teaching; each time, Gregory exorcized a demon from the offensive party, provoking widespread amazement and winning converts in the process. Gregory moved boulders, diverted a river in flood, and dried up an inconveniently located lake. By the end of his campaign, Gregory had brought almost every soul of the town of Neocaesarea into the ranks of the

Christians, and surrounding communities soon joined the band-wagon. As in the case of Fotudeng in north China, Gregory's repu-tation as a miracle worker seized the attention of his audiences and helped him to promote his faith among pagans.

Did the conversions brought about by Christian miracle workers represent cases of conversion through voluntary association? To some extent, this interpretation seems plausible, in that converts voluntarily adopted Christianity as the cultural alternative that best reflected the realities of the larger world — for example by offering access to powers not available to others. A reputation for the abil-ity to work miracles helped missionaries to dramatize the benefits and blessings that Christianity promised to individuals and sug-gested that Christianity possessed an unusually effective capacity to explain and control the world. In other ways, however, the winning of early Christian converts differed from the more com-mon pattern of conversion through voluntary association. Con-verts came from all ranks of society, not just those of merchants, rulers, and others who had extensive dealings with representatives from the larger world. Moreover, until the conversion of the em-peror Constantine and the legalization of Christianity, there were some powerful disincentives to conversion, so that potential con-verts to the new faith had to weigh heavy political, social, and economic risks against the personal and spiritual benefits offered by Christianity.

On balance, then, it seems to me that the category of conversion through voluntary association helps at least in a limited way to explain the early spread of Christianity in the Mediterranean basin. From the viewpoint of Roman society as a whole, however, rather than that of individual citizens, early conversion to Christianity benefitted especially from two additional developments that ac-companied the process of conversion through voluntary associa-tion. In the first place, until the fourth century, Christianity spread largely through a process of syncretism. In the second place, fol-lowing the conversion of Constantine, Christianity gained state sponsorship, and a process of conversion by political, social, and economic pressure consolidated the new faith as a securely institu-tionalized church. Both of these developments warrant some atten-tion.

The decline of long-established pagan cults afforded an opportunity for Christianity to extend its influence by way of syncretism.[33] Beginning in the third century, the pagan cults suffered progressively more difficult financial problems as the Roman economy went into serious decline. The Roman state could no longer afford to support the cults on the generous basis of centuries past. Wealthy individuals continued to provide a great deal of aid, but their sponsorship was more erratic and precarious than that of the state.

As the pagan cults failed to provide for the needs and interests of their followers, Christianity offered a meaningful alternative that was the more acceptable for its resemblance to the cults. In their rituals and their assumptions about the natural world, the early Christians very much reflected the larger culture of the late Roman empire. Like devotees of the pagan cults, they offered their sacraments as great mysteries, and there were pagan analogues to many of their rituals, such as the intonation of divine language, the use of special garments and paraphernalia, and even the observance of ceremonies like baptism and a community meal open only to initiates. Christians appropriated the power and authority associated with pagan heroes by emphasizing the virtues of a saint or martyr with similar attributes. Eventually, Christians even baptized pagan philosophy and festivals, which served as new links between pagan and Christian cultures: St. Augustine transformed Neoplatonism into a powerful Christian philosophy, and the birthdate of the unconquered pagan sun god became Christmas, the birthdate also of Jesus. Thus from a very early date, Christianity appealed to Mediterranean peoples partly because of its syncretic capacity: it came in familiar dress, and it dealt with many of the same concerns addressed by the pagan cults.

The conversion of Constantine amplified the effects of syncretism by inaugurating a process of officially sponsored conversion that ultimately resulted in the cultural transformation of the entire Roman empire. Constantine favored Christians from the moment that he consolidated his hold on the imperial throne. In the year 313 he issued his famous edict of toleration, which for the first time recognized Christianity as a legal religion in the Roman empire. At some indeterminate point, Constantine himself converted to Christianity. Constantine's personal example of course did not lead to immediate Christianization of the Roman empire, or even of the army that the emperor directly supervised. In several ways, though, it brought long-term changes that favored the Christians' efforts. It brought immediate material benefits, as Constantine and his successors underwrote the construction of churches and showered Christians with financial support. It also brought an intangible but nonetheless important social benefit: Christianity gained more public respect than it had ever previously enjoyed. As a result, ambitious and reputable individuals of increasing prominence joined Christian ranks — especially because Christians received preferential consideration for high imperial posts. Finally, the legalization of their religion allowed Christians to promote their faith more publicly and more aggressively than ever before. From its earliest days, the Christian community had produced combative and confrontational spokesmen. After Constantine's edict of toleration allowed Christians to promote their faith publicly, they relentlessly attacked the pagan cults, sometimes sparking episodes of personal violence, forcible conversion of individuals, and destruction of pagan temples and images.[34]

State sponsorship provided Christianity with the material and political support required to bring about social conversion on a large scale. Christianity quickly became the official and only legally tolerated religion of the Roman empire: already by the late fourth century, the emperors had begun to prohibit observance of pagan cults. By no means, however, did the various pagan religions forfeit their claims to cultural allegiance. Pagan spokesmen resisted efforts to destroy their cults, and thanks to syncretism, their values and rituals to some extent survived in Christian dress. Nevertheless, by the late fourth century, Christianity had won a cultural and institutional initiative over paganism that it would never relinquish.

The Falling of Empires

The consolidation of the Roman and Han empires deeply influenced the dynamics of world history. Most obviously, the two empires both organized vast territories into orderly and coherent polities, enabling their subjects to carry on trade and to seek prosperity under conditions of relative stability. By virtue of these achievements, the two empires left legacies that shaped political ambitions and ideals in their respective regions for two millennia and more. But the Roman and Han empires also influenced developments far beyond their frontiers. Military and diplomatic expeditions brought their power to bear on distant lands. More important, by anchoring the ends of the Eurasian landmass and bringing stability to their realms, the two empires created an environment favorable to the establishment of long-distance trade and exchange networks.

These political, military, and economic developments had cultural implications of large significance. In China, India, and the Mediterranean world, traders and travelers contributed to the development of an increasingly cosmopolitan atmosphere. As peoples of different races and cultures intermingled, it became desirable or even necessary for them to observe some common standards of ethics and morality. The establishment of a Confucian political order helped to maintain cultural order in regions dominated by Chinese arms and agriculture. In the Indian and Mediterranean worlds, the Buddhist and Christian faiths promoted ethical and moral values that were calculated to preserve harmony in diverse, cosmopolitan societies. During the era of the silk roads, Confucian, Buddhist, and Christian cultures became solidly established in their homelands, and they began to expand tentatively beyond their places of origin. In a later period, Buddhism and Christianity would cross cultural frontiers in especially dramatic fashion and establish themselves in lands distant and vastly different from those of their origin.

That further round of cross-cultural influence did not take place immediately, however, because of instability and severe political and social disruption in Eurasia. Long-distance trade served as a conduit for the spread of virulent diseases as well as for the distribution of goods and the dissemination of religious and cultural traditions. During the second and third centuries, population declined precipitously in the Mediterranean and China, and probably in other parts of Eurasia as well. Epidemics of measles, smallpox, and bubonic plague took ferocious human tolls on peoples previously unexposed to their pathogens.[35] Demographic collapse aggravated social and economic difficulties, which resulted in a shrinking of the markets that long-distance trade depended on. Combined with increasing instability and insecurity along the trade routes, this weakening of the international markets led to a sharp cutback in the volume of long-distance trade. Long-distance travel did not come to a complete halt, but it became far less common than during the era of the ancient silk roads. Eventually, too, the Roman and Han empires, twin anchors of the Eurasian networks of cross-cultural exchange, both succumbed to nomadic invaders.

The fifth and sixth centuries C.E. thus did not offer conditions that favored long-distance trade or cultural exchanges. The trade routes remained, however, and retained their potential to bear beliefs and values as well as trade goods on their journeys from one civilization or cultural region to another. The restoration of order and stability in the seventh century helped to transform that potential into historical reality.

3

Missionaries, Pilgrims, and the Spread of the World Religions

Verily this your order is one order, and I am your Lord; so worship Me. . . . Verily there is a message in this for people who are devout. We have sent you as a benevolence to the creatures of the world. Say: "This is what has been revealed to me: 'Your God is one and only God.' So will you bow in homage to Him?"   Qur'an 21:92, 106–7

The weakening of international markets, political disintegration, and the spread of disease all worked to undermine the networks of trade and exchange that had linked distant parts of Eurasia in ancient times. Between the late fourth and the late sixth century, turmoil and disorder afflicted most parts of Eurasia. The Roman and Han empires both collapsed, and barbarian successor states fought to establish themselves in large portions of their former realms. The Xiongnu confederation likewise fell apart, opening central Asia to fierce competition between various nomadic peoples, including the Toba, Ruanruan, White Huns, and Avars, among others. The Byzantine and Sassanian empires survived, but both experienced severe pressure on frontier regions and lost territories to mounted nomadic warriors. India enjoyed relative stability during the reign of the Gupta dynasty (320–550 C.E.), but there too nomadic incursions ultimately destroyed central authority and enabled competing princes to pursue their ambitions. As a result of general instability throughout Eurasia, long-distance trade, travel, and communication became risky undertakings.

Yet by no means did imperial states and cross-cultural dealings permanently disappear. Beginning in the late sixth century, large-scale political organization returned to several regions of Eurasia. The Sui dynasty (589–618) restored imperial unity to China, and the Tang (618–907) maintained it over a long term. Meanwhile, the central Asian steppelands fell under the domination of Turkish peoples, most notably the Uighurs. The rapid emergence and explosive spread of Islam resulted in two early dynasties, the Umayyad (661–750) and even more important the Abbasid (750–1258), that organized and pacified the Middle East. Even the western end of Eurasia experienced an important, though short-lived restoration of large-scale political organization as the Carolingian empire (751–987) brought some semblance of order to much of Europe from Saxony to northern Spain.

Because the architects of these new imperial structures did not build on foundations laid by their classical predecessors — certainly not in any direct fashion — they could not justify their rule by asserting that they were continuing political legacies of long standing. In seeking to legitimize their rule, they allied with a religious or cultural tradition, which they generously supported. Under this state sponsorship, Buddhism, Christianity, and Islam all spread widely and became popular religions through processes of conversion induced by political, social, and economic pressures. These material considerations of course did not preclude the possibility — or even the likelihood — that many individuals adopted new traditions for spiritual reasons and in good conscience. And processes of syncretism naturally helped to make foreign traditions comprehensible and meaningful to new audiences. But the sponsorship of these faiths by expanding imperial regimes certainly helps to explain the large-scale conversion of entire societies to new cultural traditions.

Meanwhile, as in ancient times, processes of imperial expansion generated entirely new encounters between peoples of different civilizations. As political order returned to Eurasia, merchants quickly moved to take advantage of fresh opportunities to carry on trade at long distances and with relative security. Chinese vessels plied the waters of southeast Asia, and by about the year 1000 they regularly traveled as far west as India. Meanwhile, Persian and Arab sailors visited ports in all parts of the Indian Ocean — from east Africa to India and beyond to southeast Asia — and even ventured into the South China Sea. Land as well as sea routes linked the various regions of Eurasia. Camels bore heavy burdens over long distances at minimal expense, and caravans dominated transportation in north Africa, the Middle East, and central Asia well into modern times. In some cases, individual merchants themselves traveled over vast expanses of Eurasia in carrying on their business. By the mid-ninth century, large diaspora communities of Persian and Arab merchants had become established as far away from home as Guangzhou. Even more dramatic was the network of the Radanite Jews, who perhaps came from the Rhone valley. According to Ibn Kurdadhbeh, a ninth-century Persian geographer and postal official, the Radanites' network stretched from the Mediterranean to China, and they made use of both land and sea routes in conducting their business. They commanded Persian and Arabic as well as western and Slavic languages, and they traded in a wide variety of commodities, such as silk, furs, swords, aromatics, spices, eunuchs, and slaves.[1]

The volume of long-distance exchange during the period 600 to 1000 C.E. easily eclipsed trade conducted over the ancient silk roads. The tempo of cross-cultural encounters consequently quickened, and Eurasia's various cultural traditions began to exercise their influences over longer distances than ever before. This period—sometimes called a dark age—saw among other developments widespread conversion to Buddhism in central Asia, China, and Japan; the extension of Confucian values into southeast Asia; the spread of Islam to north Africa, the Middle East, and central Asia; the conversion of northern Europe to Christianity; and the promotion of literacy and education in much of Eurasia.[2] During this period, then, the twin dynamic of imperial expansion and long-distance trade worked even more effectively than during ancient times as inducements to cross-cultural encounters. The results of these encounters shaped the cultural experiences of almost all Eurasian peoples well into modern times.

Conversion to Buddhism throughout Asia

Already during the era of the ancient silk roads, merchants disseminated Buddhism throughout east, southeast, and central Asia. Not until a later period, though, did Buddhism win a large number of

MAP 3. The post-classical world.

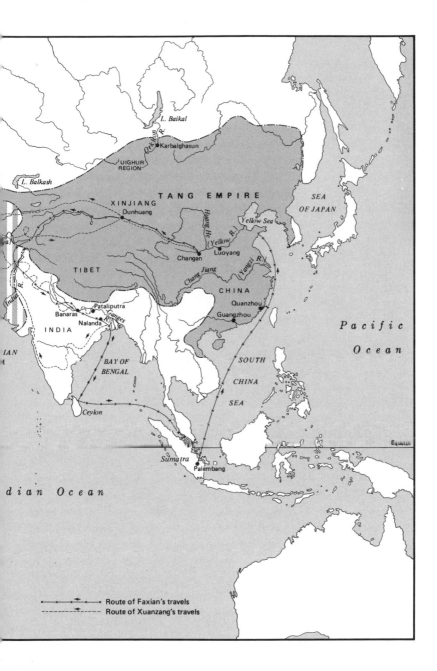

L. Baikal

Orkhon R.

Karbalghasun

UIGHUR
REGION

L. Balkash

TANG EMPIRE

SEA
OF JAPAN

XINJIANG

Dunhuang

Huang He

Yellow R.

Yellow Sea

TIBET

Changan

Luoyang

Chang Jiang

Yangzi R.

Indus R.

CHINA

Pataliputra

Banaras

Ganges R.

Nalanda

INDIA

IAN
M

Quanzhou

Guangzhou

Pacific

Ocean

BAY OF
BENGAL

SOUTH

CHINA

SEA

Ceylon

Equator

Sumatra

Palembang

dian Ocean

×—×—× Route of Faxian's travels
------+------ Route of Xuanzang's travels

converts and bring about large-scale social conversion beyond India. The crucial era for the permanent establishment of Buddhism
as a popular religion was the period 600 to 1000 C.E., when large
states and long-distance trade helped the faith to spread throughout
Asia. This section will briefly examine the fortunes of Buddhism in
southeast Asia and central Asia, then will discuss in more detail
the consolidation of Buddhism as a popular religion in China.

In southeast Asia, Buddhism began to flourish as the declining
kingdom of Funan gave way before island empires that controlled
the sea trade between India and China. Most important of these
empires was Srivijaya, centered on Palembang in southeastern Sumatra, which dominated the region's seas from the late seventh to
the thirteenth century. The kings of Srivijaya viewed Buddhism in
utilitarian fashion as a cultural support lending luster, authority,
and a sense of legitimacy to their rule. But their patronage helped
Buddhism to develop into much more than a courtly adornment in
southeast Asia. They encouraged Buddhist establishments in Java,
Malaya, and other lands that they conquered. The eighth century
in particular witnessed an impressive expansion of Mahayana Buddhism throughout the mainland as well as the islands of southeast
Asia, just as Srivijayan commercial and political weight spread
over the region.

Perhaps more important, Buddhism became an increasingly popular faith during the Srivijayan period. The Chinese pilgrim Yijing
testified to its importance as early as the year 671. He spent six
months at Palembang en route to India, and he found more than
one thousand Buddhist monks living there. He reported that they
studied the same subjects and observed the same practices as Indian
Buddhists, and he even advised future Chinese pilgrims to spend a
year or two in Palembang before continuing on to India. Yijing
himself later returned to Srivijaya for a ten-year sojourn (685–695),
and he even recruited other Chinese Buddhists who accompanied
him there.[3] The size and sophistication of the Buddhist community
in Srivijaya points up the potential for a process of conversion
through voluntary association to serve as a foundation for large-
scale cultural change. Originally cultivated by ruling elites and merchants, Buddhism thrived as the Srivijayan thalassocracy expanded. As commerce progressively dominated the Srivijayan
economy, ever-larger numbers of people converted to Buddhism

and supported the development of an impressive institutional structure.

Yijing and his fellow monks perhaps cultivated a rather pure and sophisticated version of the faith, but it is clear that in many ways Buddhism accommodated the interests of other cultural traditions in southeast Asia. In courtly circles it had to make room also for the cults of Siva and Visnu; Hindu values appealed strongly to ruling classes because of their emphasis on a hierarchical social order. Meanwhile, indigenous values honoring beneficent deities and spirits — such as those associated with sun, soil, and water — not only survived but also blended with Indian cultural imports to form new syncretic cultural configurations. Southeast Asians did not simply discard their indigenous traditions and replace them with a foreign alternative but, rather, expressed the foreign tradition in terms that made sense from a local point of view. This process inevitably entailed syncretism rather than pure conversion to alien cultural standards. Thus local deities found their ways into Indian pantheons. A seventh-century inscription from Cambodia provides a case in point, for it shows that the spirit of a sacred local tree joined the ranks of Siva, Visnu, and other imported deities.[4]

As Buddhism increased its presence in southeast Asia, it positively flourished in the oasis communities of central Asia. Temples, monasteries, and officially sponsored copyists appeared in all the major oases. Translators also worked there, rendering Buddhist sutras from Sanskrit or Prakrit into the various central Asian languages and Chinese. The most spectacular surviving evidence of all this activity comes from Dunhuang, where the northern and southern branches of the silk roads came together and entered China.[5] During the early twentieth century, scholarly expeditions of Aurel Stein, Paul Pelliot, and others brought to light stunning collections of manuscripts and art works produced at Dunhuang. Thousands of manuscripts represent the observance of Buddhism at Dunhuang, while at least a few survive to illuminate the fortunes of Manichaeans and Nestorian Christians in central Asia. Most spectacular of all the remains, though, are the paintings and statuary that adorn the cave-temples that Buddhist monks carved into the hills around Dunhuang. Scholars have identified 492 such cave-temples in the vicinity of Dunhuang, many of them lavishly illustrated with murals depicting scenes from the Buddha's life and experiences of the various boddhisatvas recognized in the Mahayana Buddhist tradition. The construction and illumination of these caves stretched over the millennium from the fourth to the fourteenth century, but the vast majority were built during the period 600 to 1000, clearly reflecting the growing popularity of Buddhism stimulated by the revival of long-distance trade and travel.

Indeed, the revival of imperial expansion and long-distance trade helped Buddhism to make the great leap from oasis communities to the steppes of central Asia. Already during the days of the ancient silk roads, Buddhism had found a home in the oases frequented by merchants traveling between China and points west. But in those early times, nomadic peoples from the steppes showed interest in Buddhism only when they conquered agricultural lands, gave up the mobile lifestyle, and settled in to govern their new territories. Beginning about the seventh century, however, the reestablishment of large imperial states and the revival of long-distance trade worked in combination, as a powerful historical dynamic, to draw steppe dwellers more directly into the political and commercial life of Eurasia. Their potential for bringing about cultural change became most clear in the case of the Uighur Turks.

The Uighurs had lived for several centuries under the domination of various nomadic peoples in Mongolia.[6] About the middle of the seventh century, as the Tang empire extended its influence in central Asia, they fell under Chinese protection. From an early date, the Uighurs allied with the Chinese against other nomadic peoples, and they eventually emerged as the dominant people of the steppes. Their power waxed so strong, in fact, that on several occasions they helped the Tang state to overcome threats mounted by other, less friendly nomads. Most notably, they helped Tang authorities put down the serious rebellion of An Lushan, a maverick Tang general. In the year 757 they recaptured the capital cities of Chang-an and Luoyang, which themselves had fallen into the rebels' hands. Uighur support came at a steep price: in exchange for saving the Tang dynasty, the nomadic warriors looted and pillaged Luoyang for three days. And over the long run the Uighurs constituted a serious drain on the Chinese economy. They demanded commerce in exchange for peace, and because of their military prowess they were able to negotiate favorable terms of trade. During the mid-eighth century, they received forty rolls of silk for each of the old, broken-down horses that they herded to Changan. (On the steppes, by contrast, a horse was generally worth a single roll of silk.) These extortions helped to fuel the economy of Eurasia; the Uighurs obtained silk from China, and their western cousins and allies traded it in Persia and the Byzantine empire. For a century and more, the Uighurs served as the economic and political linchpin of Eurasia.

In light of their rather abrupt entry into a large and cosmopolitan world, it is not surprising that the Uighurs voluntarily associated themselves with the cultural traditions of peoples already well situated in that world. As they entered into systematic dealings with Chinese, Persians, Byzantines, and inhabitants of the oasis communities in central Asia, the Uighurs encountered Buddhism, Manichaeism, and Nestorian Christianity. Large numbers of Uighurs opted for each of the three faiths. Most significant for the Uighurs' cultural development was the Manichaean tradition, discussed in a later section. But Buddhism also benefitted from the Uighurs' attention. Manuscripts from Dunhuang show that Uighurs supported a large Buddhist community alongside the Manichaean and Nestorian, even as many Uighurs continued to observe their traditional shamanist cults. More important, the Uighurs' mobility and widespread commercial dealings served as a conduit for Buddhist influence throughout central Asia. Through the Uighurs' agency, Buddhism first established a foothold in the steppes.[7]

Thus, in both southeast Asia and central Asia, Buddhism demonstrated its capacity to continue attracting adherents through a process of voluntary conversion. In China it demonstrated even more potential as it parlayed the voluntary conversion of merchants and ruling elites into a large-scale conversion of Chinese society as a whole. During its early centuries in China, Buddhism had served basically as a cultural resource for trade diaspora communities. The earliest Buddhists in China were foreign merchants, who supported communities of monks and preachers, who were also foreigners. They all faced resistance from native Chinese who considered their values too alien for comfort. But they also won patronage and protection from ruling elites, particularly nomads who conquered northern China, voluntarily associated with foreign merchants, and adopted their Buddhist faith. When the volume of

long-distance trade began to grow in the sixth century, Buddhists
in China were well positioned to take advantage of the situation.
Indeed, as their numbers swelled, Buddhists themselves stimulated
a sizeable portion of the long-distance trade that supported their
communities: incense, ivory, statues, gems, and paraphernalia of
religious significance flowed into China because of their role in
Buddhist ritual and the desire of the faithful to provide fitting
decoration for their temples and monasteries.[8]

How did Buddhism pass beyond the precinct of the foreigners'
trade diaspora and develop a following among Chinese? This question has long challenged the ingenuity of historians and religious
scholars. The reason is that the cultural traditions of India and
China differed in many ways—linguistic, psychological, moral, political, and social—and it is difficult to understand why Chinese
would find any attractions in an alien faith that espoused strange
ideas in an unfamiliar language. It is hardly a surprise that during
its first few centuries abroad, Buddhism won few converts from
the ranks of native Chinese. Gradually, though, Buddhist monks
and missionaries found ways to communicate their faith so that its
appeal crossed the cultural frontier and attracted Chinese allegiance on a large scale through a process of syncretism that brought
about a thorough social conversion.

Part of the explanation for the appeal of Buddhism in China has
to do with a development internal to Buddhism itself. During its
earliest days, Buddhism had taught a rather severe doctrine: it
offered personal salvation, but only to those who followed a strict
code of ethics and behavior. During the early centuries C.E., however, Buddhists in northern India elaborated a more accessible doctrine. They held that certain Buddhists had merited nirvana but
delayed their entry in order to aid their fellow mortals seeking
salvation. They came to be known as boddhisatvas—Buddhas-to-
be—and like Christian saints, they had the power to intervene in
worldly affairs, help less accomplished Buddhists to merit salvation, and even perform worthy acts on behalf of individuals. This
school of thought came to be known as the Mahayana ("the greater
vehicle"), since it envisioned the salvation of much larger numbers
of individuals in a much shorter period of time than the earliest
Buddhists had thought possible. Mahayana Buddhists sometimes
referred to other schools by the unflattering term Hinayana ("the

lesser vehicle"), since they restricted salvation to smaller numbers of especially devout individuals. Particularly after the collapse of the Han dynasty, when nomadic incursions and political maneuvering unsettled Chinese society, the offer of personal salvation on relatively easy terms held a certain appeal for the popular masses in China.

When seeking to communicate unfamiliar beliefs and values in China, Buddhists found Daoism the most important bridge between Indian and Chinese cultures. Daoist and Buddhist doctrines differed in many fundamental respects, and over the long term there developed a spirit of competition and even hostility between the two traditions. During their early days in China, though, Buddhists frequently situated their communities close to Daoist temples, and they allowed Chinese to worship the Buddha as a god alongside Daoist deities. Furthermore, Daoism provided a vocabulary by which missionaries and translators could express Buddhist concepts in language familiar to Chinese. Early translators of Buddhist texts represented the concept of *dharma* (the basic doctrine of Buddhism) with the Chinese term *dao* ("the way," as understood in its Daoist sense—that is, as the principle of universal order). The Buddhist notion of *nirvana* (state of ultimate bliss) appeared in Chinese as *wuwei* (the Daoist social ethic of quietude and noncompetition). The Confucian and other Chinese traditions also supplied terminology for early translators of Buddhist works—the Sanskrit term *sila* (ethics or morality) was translated as *xiaoxun* (Confucian concept of filial piety)—but its Daoist associations were so many and so strong that Chinese sometimes mistook Buddhism as a sect of Daoism.[9]

On the popular level, Buddhism exercised an appeal similar to that of Christianity in the Roman empire. Buddhist missionaries impressed their audiences with displays of magic and the performance of miracles. They ostensibly had access to supernatural powers, which lent credibility to their message about the blessings and benefits that flowed from Buddhism. Exemplary miracles abound in early accounts of Buddhism in China: good works bring health, social status, and salvation; gifts to monasteries bring relief from supernatural torments. Some miracles had political implications but nonetheless served to increase the prestige of Buddhism among common people. In Luoyang, for example, statues of the

Buddha often indicated the onset of political turmoil by spontane-
ously shedding tears, moving about, or even departing from their
posts altogether.[10] It is not difficult to see that widely reported
incidents of this sort could impress a restive populace—especially
in the period before the Sui and Tang dynasties restored political
order in China.

Buddhism also had the capacity to appeal to Chinese intellectual and political elites. Especially in the southern regions, well-
educated aristocrats developed the so-called gentry Buddhism as an
alternative to Confucianism and Daoism. They did not necessarily
abandon their native Chinese traditions. Indeed, until the late
fourth or fifth century, they mostly emphasized aspects of Buddhism that ran parallel to Confucian and Daoist interests. Their
emphasis on morality and ritual appealed to Confucians, for example, while their desire to cultivate inner wisdom or insight was a
concept familiar to Daoists. In some ways gentry Buddhism was a
superficial and artificial construct: the early gentry Buddhists ex-
celled in the witty repartee popular in courtly circles and salon
society, but most had little interest in Buddhist doctrine and none
in the broad dissemination of their faith. Gradually, though, gentry
Buddhism attracted courtly and even imperial support, and by the
early fifth century it had become securely established in south
China.[11]

Meanwhile, political elites also discovered an interest in Buddhism. Especially important in this connection were the Toba, a
Mongol or possibly Turkish people who ruled northern China during the Northern Wei dynasty (386–534). The Toba emperors did
not abandon their traditional shamanistic cults but added Buddhism as a religious alternative in their realm. They closely supervised the Buddhist establishment, though, and had themselves worshipped as incarnations of the Buddha. Their capitals at Pingcheng
and Luoyang were the sites where Buddhism first became established as a state institution in China. Thus Toba emperors lavishly
patronized Buddhism by building temples and monasteries, award-
ing land grants, and leading popular rituals and festivals, all in
exchange for religious endorsement and legitimization of their
rule.[12]

The Sui and early Tang emperors largely continued the Toba
policy of patronizing Buddhism in return for political support.

Indeed, several of these emperors were enthusiastic devotees of Buddhism. They did not give Buddhism free rein to develop institutions and policies on an independent basis but, rather, established bureaucracies to oversee religious affairs and ensure that Buddhists as well as adherents of all other faiths properly supported the dynasty. But Buddhists in many ways received especially favorable treatment from the late sixth to the mid-eighth century. They received vast landholdings in gift from the Sui and Tang emperors. They held important advisory positions at the imperial court. They benefitted from thousands of building projects that the emperors either directly sponsored or indirectly encouraged. They received support also in numerous ways of smaller moment: the Sui and Tang emperors organized feasts on behalf of Buddhist monks; they supported the copying and distribution of Buddhist texts; they encouraged princes and courtiers to take vows as lay Buddhists; they introduced Buddhist rituals into court ceremonies and state observances. As a result of this official attention and patronage, Buddhism became something very like a state religion in China during the Sui and early Tang dynasties.[13]

By no means was support for Buddhism limited to the imperial court. Official policy of the Sui and Tang dynasties had its counterpart in an enthusiastic popular response to Buddhism — a response, however, that represented not so much a conversion to an Indian faith as an adaptation of Buddhism and appropriation of it for Chinese purposes. Popular support came partly because of the significant role Buddhism played in Chinese society. When Buddhists obtained land grants, they quickly moved to build monastic communities and to organize the agricultural economy of the vicinity. Eventually, they gained control over vast tracts of land, as well as the grain produced and its distribution. Their economic power naturally brought them a certain amount of ill will, especially when they abused their position. But they also helped many people to avoid starvation in times of famine or political turmoil and as a result contributed greatly to social stability. Hence, beginning already in the late fifth century, large numbers of Chinese entered Buddhist monasteries, and popular support for the foreign faith burgeoned.[14]

Meanwhile, Buddhism in China developed syncretically, so that it addressed Chinese concerns and reflected the interests of Chinese cultural traditions. From a very early date, the two most popular schools of Buddhism in China were the Chan and Pure Land sects, both of which were deeply influenced by Daoism. Chan and Pure Land exponents had limited interest in the texts and doctrine that engaged the imagination of Indian Buddhists. Instead of textual study and formal reasoning, they emphasized the importance of disciplined meditation, unswerving faith, spontaneous intuition, and instantaneous enlightenment—all interests that Daoists had long cultivated. Once again, then, Daoism served as a cultural bridge between China and India—in this case a bridge that helped to bring Chinese converts to the Indian faith.

Chinese Buddhism benefitted from a process of syncretism at the level of popular as well as elite culture. To be sure, a series of imperially sponsored temples made official Buddhist doctrines and observances known throughout China, and they encouraged all classes of people to support the local Buddhist establishment. In practice, though, village clergy generally had little or no education in Buddhism and continued to serve their clients in a most traditional way. They conducted weddings and funerals, predicted the future, cured illnesses, performed magic tricks, and related exemplary tales of moral significance. Meanwhile, Buddhist shrines often went up at sites already associated with local tutelary deities. Gradually, the identities of indigenous deities became confused with boddhisatvas, while images of the Buddha acquired an increasingly Chinese cast. Festivals and rituals likewise blended Indian and Chinese elements. The Feast of All Souls, for example— one of the most prominent rituals of popular Buddhism—acknowledged the strong Chinese interest in family by making a place in its Chinese manifestations for the observance of family and ancestor cults. The syncretic movement progressed so far, in fact, that from the eleventh to the nineteenth century, one cult of some popularity combined the observances of Confucius, Laozi, and the Buddha.[15]

Buddhism thus accommodated Chinese interests and traditions at the levels of both elite and popular culture, but by no means did it completely lose its own basic character. The main reason for the maintenance of its identity was the vast quantity of cross-cultural traffic linking India and China. Between the third and the ninth century, thousands of Indian missionaries traveled to central Asia and China, where they received patronage and support at courts friendly to Buddhism. Meanwhile, thousands of Chinese pilgrims traveled to India, where they learned Sanskrit, collected and copied religious texts, and visited sites holy to Buddhists. The activities of Indian missionaries are not well known, since they left few accounts of their lives and works. It is clear, though, that their teaching and translations provided a doctrinal foundation without which a recognizably Buddhist tradition could not have developed in China.

The work of Chinese pilgrims who visited India is much better known, thanks to numerous accounts written by the travelers themselves or by colleagues who knew of their journeys. Their long, difficult, and dangerous expeditions merit some mention here. (See map 3 for the routes they traveled.) The monk Faxian traveled in India and Ceylon during the period from 399 to 414; he learned Sanskrit, copied numerous texts, visited holy sites, venerated relics, and became acquainted with the legends and lore of Buddhism; he suffered the loss of one traveling companion while crossing a mountain range during a snowstorm, and on his return trip to China he survived a shipwreck in southeast Asian waters. In 518 the monks Song Yun and Huisheng embarked on a four-year trip to India; they returned with 170 texts of the Mahayana school of Buddhism, as well as a great deal of information on the life of the Buddha. Inspired directly by Faxian's example, the monk Xuan-zang traveled throughout India between the years 629 and 645; he visited holy sites, studied with famous sages, and learned the lore of his faith; he returned to China with 124 new Mahayana texts as well as relics, statues, and Buddhist paraphernalia, all in a baggage train loaded onto twenty-two horses. The monk Yijing spent nearly twenty-five years in India and southeast Asia during the period from 671 to 695; he studied Sanskrit and Buddhist doctrine, and he closely observed Buddhist customs and rituals; he collected more than 400 Buddhist texts; he composed biographical sketches of fifty-six other pilgrims to India; after returning to China he translated some 56 works in 230 volumes.[16]

Yijing's reflections perhaps best express the emotional difficulties that all the missionaries and pilgrims of his age must have expressed: "I passed through thousands of different stages during my long solitary journey. The threads of sorrow disturbed my thought hundred-fold. Why did the shadow of my body walk alone on the borders of Five Indies?" But his lines bespeak also the will and determination that drove the long-distance travelers of premodern times: "An excellent general can resist an aggressive army, but the resolution of a gentleman will never change. If I am sad for a short span of life and be sorry for that, how can I fill up the long Asankhya age?"[17] In the absence of such mettle—founded upon convictions strong enough to survive suffering and personal sacrifice—it would have been impossible for Buddhism to become securely established in China. Except for the communication between India and China sustained over a long term, it seems inevitable that Buddhism would have been largely or wholly absorbed into traditional Chinese cultural alternatives.

Even with the aid of missionaries, pilgrims, and patrons in high places, Buddhism encountered considerable resistance in China. Spokesmen for the Confucian and Daoist traditions naturally attacked Buddhism from an early date. Already by the fourth century, gentry Buddhists in south China had to defend their faith from a variety of charges: that the Buddhist establishment diminished the authority of the state; that monasteries contributed nothing to economic prosperity; that Buddhism was a barbarian faith inferior to Chinese cultural traditions; and that monastic asceticism violated the natural social order and disrupted the family.[18] Criticism of this sort followed Chinese Buddhists through the centuries. One of the most famous attacks came from the Confucian scholar Han Yu, who in the year 819 protested the Tang emperor's veneration of a finger bone said to have come from the Buddha. In an eloquent memorial he denounced Buddhism as a barbarian creed relatively recently imported into China. An intelligent man like the emperor should not engage in silly rites like veneration of relics, said Han Yu, lest he confuse and mislead the unlettered masses. He continued by emphasizing the unattractiveness of the alien:

> Now the Buddha was of barbarian origin. His language differed from Chinese speech; his clothes were of a different cut; his mouth did not pronounce the prescribed words of the Former Kings, his body was not clad in the garments prescribed by the Former Kings. He did not recognize the relationship between the prince and subject, nor the sentiments of father and son.

If the Buddha himself should miraculously appear in China, the emperor should treat him courteously, Han Yu said, and grant him the honors of one formal audience, one banquet, and one gift of fine clothes — then have him promptly escorted to the border. His moldered bone, however, deserved no honor at all.[19]

Buddhism in China overcame this sort of resistance, and even flourished in its face, so long as it enjoyed imperial support. During the ninth century, though, the Tang emperors faced serious political and economic difficulties that encouraged them to persecute Buddhists and adherents of other foreign religions in China. Domestic rebellions and invasions by Turkish nomads strained the Tang treasury and provoked a reaction against foreign cultural traditions. Buddhism was especially vulnerable in this situation because temples and monasteries had accumulated vast tracts of land that did not return tax revenues. Beginning around 841, the Japanese monk Ennin — then traveling in China as a pilgrim in search of Buddhist texts and instruction — noticed that Buddhists were falling out of imperial favor. Between 842 and 845 the Tang emperor issued a series of edicts that placed Buddhist monks under increasingly strict controls. In 845 the emperor ordered the suppression of some 4,600 monasteries, the closing of 40,000 temples and shrines, and the return to lay status of more than 260,000 monks and nuns. The persecutions affected Zoroastrians, Nestorian Christians, and Manichaeans, too, but Buddhists absorbed the brunt of the attack.[20] By no means did the persecutions rid China of Buddhism — which has survived there even into the twentieth century — but they damaged its cultural and economic foundations severely enough that it has never been able to recover the status and prosperity that it enjoyed during the Sui and early Tang dynasties.

Meanwhile, however, the experience of Buddhism in China illustrates two points of interest for the analysis of cross-cultural encounters and exchanges. In the first place, the long-range spread of Buddhism originally took place by means of a process clearly recognizable as conversion through voluntary association. Especially in northern China, traders found its universal ethics an attractive alternative to traditional value systems arising from the foundation of intense loyalty to family and clan. At the same time, ruling elites discovered political uses in Buddhism: it not only provided a source of legitimization for a dynasty or ruling house but also helped to bring about the cultural unification of subject peoples. As northern Buddhists established links with the representatives of gentry Buddhism in the south, the appeal of Buddhism extended throughout China. The official Buddhist establishment of the Sui and early Tang dynasties then consolidated its presence in east Asia and almost guaranteed its survival there over a long term.

In the second place, at the level of both elite and popular cultures, Buddhism blended with indigenous cultural traditions rather than displacing them. Indeed, this point largely accounts for the success of Buddhism in bringing about social conversion on a large scale in China. Sophisticated exponents of Buddhism presented its doctrine in terms familiar to Chinese scholars and philosophers, and they emphasized those elements of Buddhism that most closely resembled Confucian and Daoist teachings. Meanwhile, in the villages and countryside, Buddhism found a place alongside the popular cults of Confucian, Daoist, and other religions. Indeed, in some cases it eventually blended with them so thoroughly that there remained little to distinguish Buddhist priests or temples from their Daoist counterparts.

This does not mean that Buddhism became so submerged in foreign cultural seas that it left no trace of its presence. To the contrary, Buddhism clearly made its mark on Chinese language and culture, introducing new words, deities, rituals, festivals, and concepts, such as karma and the notion of an afterlife, that long continued to have a place in Chinese culture. Equally important was its role in shaping Neo-Confucian thought, which became in essence the official philosophy and ideology of China during the Ming and Qing dynasties.[21] Thus, largely because of its assimilation and accommodation to indigenous traditions, Buddhism left a deep imprint on Chinese thought and culture over the long term.

Chinese Trade and Expansion
in Southeast Asia and Central Asia

The exotic products of the south attracted Chinese attention from the earliest days.[22] Qin Shi Huangdi, first emperor of China, reportedly sent five armies — half a million troops — to guarantee access to such items as rhinoceros horns, elephant tusks, kingfisher feathers, tortoise shells, and pearls. During the Han dynasty, Chinese iron went south in exchange for exotic products that brought prestige to imperial and princely courts. Political instability disrupted Chinese trade with southern regions for several centuries following the collapse of the Han empire. The revival of imperial unity under the Sui and Tang dynasties not only lent new impetus to the southern trade but also served as a foundation for a considerable expansion of Chinese presence in southern regions. In a remarkable outburst of administrative energy, the emperor Sui Yangdi (605–616) organized the construction of the Grand Canal — really a series of canals linking Hangzhou, Changan, and Zhuo (near modern Beijing) — and brought the valley of the Chang Jiang within effective reach of imperial bureaucrats and tax collectors. A powerful demographic surge followed, and south China fell increasingly within the orbit of Chinese civilization. The aggressive emperors of the early Tang dynasty extended Chinese authority even further south, well into Vietnam. These movements brought Chinese into increasingly frequent and intense encounters with the native peoples of the south — Cham, Mon, Khmer, Lao, and others — as well as with Persian and Arab merchants who sailed into the South China Sea.[23]

Chinese for the most part did not look forward to southern journeys. The poet Zhang Ji bade farewell to a Vietnam-bound traveler with these lines:

> Away, away — far-ranging traveler!
> Amid miasmas waste your blighted body!
> Blue hills and roads without limits;
> White heads — of men who do not return.
>
> Countries by the Sea — they mount elephants in battle,
> Countries of the Man — they use silver in market.
> The family unit split — in several places —
> And who may be seen in spring, South of the Sun?[24]

Given this attitude toward the southern regions, it is no surprise that many Chinese who traveled to Vietnam did so involuntarily: soldiers, administrators, and exiles accounted for a great deal of the Chinese population in Vietnam.

Rarely did Tang Chinese find good things to say about Vietnam. For the most part, they despised the land, the food, the animals, the climate, the malaria, and the lack of culture they encountered in the south. They also despised the native peoples of the region.

Chinese referred to them in general terms as "barbarians," but often used more specific language with reptilian and simian connotations when speaking of indigenous peoples.

One notable exception to this general truth was Liu Zongyuan, who in the early ninth century was sent into exile in Vietnam. Liu considered himself unjustly persecuted and longed for China, like his compatriots in the south, and he often scorned the native peoples of Vietnam. In a work recommending the repression of Huang rebels, who came out of the hills to attack Chinese settlements during the eighth and ninth centuries, Liu likened the indigenous raiders to vermin and pests:

> Though not as mean as foxes and rats,
>   Not deserving a display of our might,
> Yet even tiny things like wasps and tarantulas,
>   Can bring destruction on living creatures.

Yet Liu came to appreciate the different world of nature that he found, and he largely made his peace with the south. More important for present purposes, he sought to extend the benefits of Chinese civilization to the peoples of the south. Thus he encouraged the establishment of Buddhism in Vietnam in hopes that it would help to wean indigenous peoples from their irrational cults and improve their morals. He built Buddhist shrines and temples, provided for the maintenance of students, and organized Buddhist services. Eventually, so he said, the formerly superstitious natives "began to reject their phantoms and to desist from killing, and to press on with devotion towards humanity and love."[25]

Liu's compatriots in Vietnam shared his faith in the superiority of northern culture, and they thought it inevitable that indigenous peoples would recognize the value of Chinese ways and organize their lives accordingly. For the most part, their expectations went unfulfilled. If Liu truly succeeded in promoting Buddhist values, his was a very unusual experience. Other Chinese also built schools, offered instruction, introduced technological improvements, and attacked superstition — with disappointing results. They often enough reported that native youths showed interest in their messages, but only to the extent that Chinese culture brought them status and power. Upon disappearance of the immediate material and political rewards that accompanied Chinese culture, the native peoples of Vietnam quickly reverted to their traditional beliefs and values.

Though not immediately obvious to contemporaries — especially Chinese contemporaries — a long-term process of cultural adjustment could not fail to take place in Vietnam, given the immense Chinese presence there. Vietnam did not become completely sinicized by any means; throughout the Tang dynasty the native peoples of Vietnam offered spirited political and military resistance to the Chinese expansion, even as they maintained their beliefs in traditional spirits and deities and continued to participate in family-oriented cults. But Buddhism — arriving both from the west, along with Indian and Indonesian merchants, and from the north, in the cultural baggage of Chinese immigrants — eventually established a secure foothold in Vietnam. Meanwhile, ethnic Chinese born in Vietnam developed an appreciation for southern nature, life, and customs that their immigrant parents had rarely ceased to scorn. Over the long term, then, Chinese adjusted to life in the southern regions, and the sheer weight of numbers ensured that Chinese beliefs and values would influence the cultural experience of Vietnam.[26]

Within China proper, the most notable cultural result of Tang expansion into southeast Asia was perhaps the cultivation of a taste for the exotic. Trade in exotic and luxury items had long had large political significance, since they served as symbols of status and power for the ruling elites who controlled their use and distribution.[27] But during the eighth and ninth centuries, the Chinese taste for the exotic became much more popular and widespread than ever before. The wealth and power of the Tang state were so great that they stimulated trade throughout much of Eurasia. Merchants arrived in China from all quarters and formed diaspora communities in the major entrepôts. Eighth-century Guangzhou had a population of some 200,000, many of them traders from southeast Asia, Indonesia, Ceylon, India, Persia, and Arabia. When the rebel Huang Chao seized and sacked the city in the year 879, he reportedly killed 120,000 foreigners during a brief reign of terror. The unusual or rare products that foreigners brought — aromatics, animals, foreign finished goods, slaves — whetted the Chinese appetite and helped to sustain trading relations with distant parts of Eurasia.

Most of this trade passed through the South China Sea, but a sizeable portion also came by caravan over land routes. Because of their interest in western trade, the Tang emperors reestablished a Chinese presence in central as well as southeast Asia. During the seventh century, Tang armies imposed Chinese authority in Mongolia, Turkestan, Tibet, and Transoxiana. Most extensive of all the Chinese dynasties from a territorial point of view, the Tang empire abutted almost directly on the recently established Abbasid empire in Persia. Like their expansion in southeast Asia, their presence in western lands brought Chinese into intense commercial and political relationships with peoples of different cultures and civilizations. Like their counterparts in southeast Asia, the products and peoples of central Asia stimulated the Tang sense of the exotic. Tang officials tried diligently to minimize the influence of foreigners in China: they closely supervised trade, segregated foreigners into specially designated quarters, and restricted relations between foreign men and Chinese women. But foreign products, fashions, and customs nonetheless enjoyed widespread popularity in China. Many aristocrats affected Turkish ways. Most notably, perhaps, an imperial prince, son of the great emperor Tang Taizong, spoke Turkish in preference to Chinese and lived in a Turkish camp that he built within his palace. So pervasive was the foreign influence in the Tang capitals (Changan and Luoyang) that a tradition-minded poet, Yuan Zhen, versified his complaints:

> Ever since the Western horsemen began raising smut and dust,
> Fur and fleece, rank and rancid, have filled Hsien and Lo
>   [that is, the Tang capitals].
> Women make themselves Western matrons by the study of
>   Western makeup;
> Entertainers present Western tunes, in their devotion to
>   Western music.[28]

Chinese cultural traditions, however, did not exercise nearly so much influence in central Asia as they did in Vietnam. One reason they did not is that the Chinese did not sustain their presence in central Asia. The effective spread of Confucian values depended on permanent establishment of Chinese bureaucratic and educational institutions, supported when necessary by political and military power. The Tang presence in central Asia simply did not last long enough for Chinese culture to work much influence there. In any case, though, the peoples of central Asia had become attracted to different cultural traditions. Many of them had already converted to Buddhism, Manichaeism, or Nestorian Christianity. In no case did the survival of these cultural alternatives depend entirely on the wielding of foreign political and military power over long distances. In all cases, though, their spread benefitted from a process of conversion through voluntary association, since the Indian and Middle Eastern religions offered a worldview and ethic that coincided with the interests of peoples who had commercial and other relationships across cultural boundary lines. Little mystery, then, that Chinese cultural traditions did not take root in central Asia.

Indeed, during the period 600 to 1000, Chinese culture made its influence felt in central Asia more under the guise of Buddhism than in the form of indigenous Chinese traditions such as Confucianism or Daoism. Until about the eighth century, the dominant school of Buddhism in central Asia was the Sarvastivada (one of the schools sometimes referred to by the unflattering term "Hinayana"). But Chinese Buddhists inclined from a very early date to the school of the Mahayana. Chinese pilgrims and Chinese Buddhist theologians became so active, however, that between the eighth and eleventh centuries they virtually converted central Asians to Mahayana Buddhism.[29] Scholars have not yet explored these developments to the point that they can explain why central Asian Buddhists originally preferred the Sarvastivada school and Chinese the Mahayana. In both cases, though, it is clear that early converts did not simply accept a doctrine that outsiders presented to them. Instead they selected and emphasized those elements that they found meaningful or attractive. As Buddhism waned in its original Indian homeland, beginning about the tenth century, the weight of Chinese numbers ensured that the Mahayana school would gain ever greater exposure in central Asia and would attract converts because of its popular, lay-oriented message.

The Early Spread of Islam

The sudden, explosive appearance of Islam ranks as one of the most dramatic cultural developments in all of world history. The faith of the prophet spread first to his family and close friends, then to his clan and a larger circle of acquaintances. During his own lifetime, Muhammad (570–632) welded the fledgling Muslim community into a tightly organized and highly disciplined society that brought most of southern and western Arabia under its control. Within a generation of the prophet's death, the early caliphs extended Islamic power to all of the Arabian peninsula and expanded north as far as Armenia, east to Afghanistan, and west through Egypt and north Africa as far as Tripoli. Between 661 and 750, the Umayyad caliphs pushed the boundaries of the Islamic community beyond the Indus River in the east, while in the west they brought the Maghrib and most of Iberia under Muslim control. In a bit more than a century's time, then, Islam had transformed itself from the faith of a merchant into an imperial state ruling a vast swath of territory stretching from the Atlas Mountains of northwest Africa to the Hindu Kush.

Historians have identified several conditions that help to account for the remarkable spread of early Islam.[30] The Byzantine and Sassanian empires had both decayed and could not offer effective resistance to Arab warriors. On the other hand, Muslim forces fought with an intense zeal. Their faith overrode the problems that had weakened Arab society during previous centuries—suspicion, jealousy, and taste for revenge that fueled endless feuds between the various tribes and clans—and united them in common religious and ethnic cause. Meanwhile, early Islam benefitted also from improvements in camel transport.[31] Between about 500 and 200 B.C.E., the camel saddle came into use in Arabia, and during the next several centuries, Arabs developed its commercial and military uses. The camel saddle made efficient use of the animals' energy, while also enabling warriors to wield swords and spears from their mounts. As a result, early Islamic armies could traverse arid regions in numbers and strength previously unattainable. The early Islamic enterprise benefitted further from the revival of long-distance trade begun in the late sixth century.[32] The Sui and Tang dynasties stimulated the development of markets in east and southeast Asia; Turkish tribes, especially the Uighurs, reestablished trade routes through central Asia; the Umayyad caliphs brought north Africa and the Middle East into an ever-larger network of long-distance commercial relationships; finally, the Abbasid dynasty traded with peoples from the Baltic Sea in the north to the Indian Ocean in the south to the South China Sea in the east.

Thus a series of internal and external developments help to account for the rapid spread and consolidation of Islamic society during the early centuries after Muhammad's proclamation of the Muslim faith. But how is it possible to account for the emergence in widely spread and diverse regions of an Islamic civilization — a political, social, economic, and cultural order that rests on specifically Islamic beliefs and values? Once again, a combination of considerations — some internal, others extrinsic to Islam itself — helps to explain the establishment of Islamic faith and values in different cultural regions.

In its earliest days, Islam was a militant, conquering religion. Muhammad imposed political and military order on the community of his followers in Medina. Both Muhammad and the early caliphs led holy wars in order to bring the Arab tribes under the control of Medina. The caliphs also led campaigns to enforce continued loyalty and obedience when several of the tribes attempted to secede from the Islamic community or otherwise hinder the Islamic enterprise after Muhammad's death. These wars brought about a sort of political conversion to Islam on the part of Arab tribal chieftains. A similar process of militarily induced conversion took place when Umayyad armies conquered the Maghrib, where they faced stiff resistance from Berber nomads and used Islam as a weapon in their campaign to impose their rule.

Generally speaking, though, outside Arabia, early Muslims did not coerce individuals to accept their faith. The Qur'an strongly encouraged missionary work and the winning of converts to Islam, but it often forbade compulsion in express terms: "There is no compulsion in matter of faith" (2:256). Muslim missionaries had the obligation of announcing their message, but had explicit instructions not to argue strenuously or violently on its behalf. Those who rejected the message became responsible for their own fates: "If they turn away (you are not responsible); we have not appointed you a warden over them. Your duty is to deliver the message" (42:48).[33]

Many early converts no doubt turned to Islam out of genuine intellectual or spiritual conviction. The spread of the faith proceeded in especially efficient fashion, though, because unlike Buddhism and Christianity, Islam enjoyed almost from its birth the status of a state-sponsored religion. Already during the Umayyad dynasty, as it expanded throughout north Africa and the Middle East, Islam benefitted from advantages such as those that favored Buddhism during the reign of Asoka and Christianity after the conversion of Constantine. As a result, a wide range of political, legal, social, and economic incentives helped to attract converts even in the earliest days of Islam.[34] Muslim rulers for the most part allowed subject peoples to retain their traditional religions. But Muslim subjects had greater access to positions of power and authority, while non-Muslims lived under restrictions, often in specially designated neighborhoods, which prevented their integration into the new Islamic society. Thus, when early Islam transformed whole societies and brought about the building of a distinctive Islamic civilization, it did so with the considerable aid of a process of conversion encouraged by political, social, and economic pressures. Again, this does not mean that early Muslims coerced individuals to adopt their faith but, rather, that state sponsorship resulted in a policy that rewarded conversion to Islam and penalized those who preferred not to receive the new faith.

The most prominent element of this policy, and the one most carefully studied by scholars, was the *jizya*, a poll tax levied on non-Muslim subjects by Islamic rulers.[35] Upon acceptance of Islam, converts won exemption from the tax. The levy was by no means so heavy or crippling that it ruined non-Muslims; large numbers of Christians, Jews, Zoroastrians, Buddhists, Hindus, and others elected to pay the tax and retain their inherited religions. Nonetheless, for those not firmly committed to their inherited faith, or for those not well served by their religious establishments, the prospect of avoiding the poll tax must have provided a powerful incentive for conversion to Islam. Indeed, within a century of the Hegira, converts had claimed so many exemptions that the Umayyad state experienced serious financial difficulties. Some Umayyad governors even tried to reimpose the poll tax on recent converts to Islam. Eventually, the principle of exemption from the poll tax for Muslims prevailed—even in the cases of recent converts—and Islamic states found alternative sources of finance.

Meanwhile, though, the Umayyad experience with the poll tax illustrates clearly the influence of material incentives in the attraction of converts to early Islam. So effective were the material and social incentives that whole societies converted to Islam within relatively short periods of time. Between the years 750 and 900, for example, about 80 percent of the population of Persia adopted the recently arrived faith, and many converts seem to have responded to social and economic inducements. One scholar has recently argued that the earliest converts came largely from the ranks of the especially privileged and the especially oppressed—that is, those who sought to maintain their positions under new circumstances, and those who hoped to take advantage of new opportunities to improve their conditions.[36]

Taxation of land and property worked less directly, but perhaps even more effectively to encourage conversion in the wake of the early Islamic conquests. In Egypt, for example, Umayyad administrators taxed property at differential rates favoring Arab Muslim immigrants and Egyptian converts to Islam. Heavy rates of taxation undermined the social and economic status of the Christian elites and the Coptic church. Thus, while not directly coercing individuals to convert, Umayyad tax policy progressively deprived the Coptic tradition of the financial resources it required to maintain its position in Egyptian society. The Coptic church did not entirely disappear; indeed, it survives in Egypt to the present day. But over the centuries its influence has progressively and continuously waned, at least partly because of state sponsorship of Islam. With reduced and diminishing resources, the Coptic church could neither attract effective cultural leaders nor provide adequate services for Egyptian Christians. Meanwhile, individuals converted to Islam in an effort to maintain or improve their economic and social positions.[37] The establishment of Islamic civilization in Egypt thus represents a classic case of conversion to the standards of a foreign cultural tradition induced by political, social, and economic pressures.

In the early days of Islam, social and material inducements might have attracted converts who were less than totally committed to Islamic doctrines and values. But over the long term the conversion of whole societies, by whatever means, underwrote the consolidation of a widely spread civilization solidly based on Islamic teachings. Political and educational institutions reflected Islamic interests. Merchants responded especially warmly to the universalist ethic of Islam and forged cultural as well as commercial links between the various regions of the Islamic world. In later centuries, saints and Sufis—mystics who elaborated an intensely emotional and spiritual tradition of popular religion in Islam—would enrich yet further the meaning of Islamic civilization by encouraging the development of popular piety and a sense of devotion to Islamic values. Sufis played an especially prominent role in the process by which entire societies joined the larger Islamic civilization: their mysticism and doctrinal flexibility enabled them to serve as agents of syncretism, finding places in the framework of Islam for the inclusion of values and deities traditionally recognized in lands never known to Muhammad. Over the centuries, too, pilgrims from distant lands would visit the holy sites at Mecca and become acquainted with Islamic traditions at first hand. Thus, whatever was their original inspiration—political, legal, social, economic, or spiritual—early conversions to Islam served as the foundation for the construction of a very impressive civilization built around specifically Islamic beliefs and values.

Islamic civilization of course did not develop without facing considerable resistance from the previously established cultural traditions that it confronted. In the Maghrib, for example, Berber nomads cherished their independence and vigorously resisted the incursion of Arab armies. Tradition holds that the Berbers apostatized twelve times before submitting to Islam. Even then the Berbers' acceptance of Islam represented a rather conditional conversion: the Berbers retained many traditional customs that stood at odds with Islamic teachings, and they produced a large number of anti-Muslim prophets during the centuries following their conversion. The militant Almohads enforced the imposition of an orthodox Islam on Berber society during the twelfth and thirteenth centuries, but Berbers did not embrace Islam warmly until Sufi mystics set in motion a process of syncretism that complemented the conquests and the militarily induced conversion of earlier centuries.[38]

As a nomadic people living in a tribal society, the Berbers posed an especially difficult challenge to early Islamic expansionists who sought to extend the boundaries of their political and cultural influence. But settled peoples also resisted the effort to establish Islamic society in their midst. The experiences of Persia and Spain illustrate this point, but they also offer the additional advantage of revealing the extreme responses taken by some early resisters to Islamic expansion.

Islam made its appearance in Persia almost as soon as the faith became established. In the year 652—thirty years after the Hegira—the last Sassanian emperor died, and by then Muslim armies already controlled most of Persia. Beginning about the middle of the eighth century, Persian Zoroastrians converted to Islam in large numbers. Some of them no doubt responded to the various incentives to conversion: access to positions of power, exemption from the poll tax, freedom from slavery, and the like. One Arab commander at Bukhara even offered cash payments as rewards for converts. Other converts no doubt found Islam an attractive faith and not excessively alien. They were already familiar with many Islamic doctrines—heaven, hell, the end of the world, judgment of individual souls—and they found the transition from Zoroastrian to Islamic ethics a relatively easy one to make. Meanwhile, the establishment of the Abbasid dynasty in the year 750 advanced the process by which Persia became an Islamic society. The Abbasids restored some of the luster that the Sassanians had brought to Persia and in many ways made conversion to Islam an attractive proposition by eliminating its bias toward the interests of Arabs. Meanwhile, the emergence of the Shia sect also served to attract the interest of Persians, since it introduced elements of traditional Persian culture into Islam.

For two groups of people, however—the Parsis and the Manichaeans—Islam remained an unacceptable cultural alternative. Their resistance to Islam took the form of flight to distant regions where they could practice their faiths and avoid the pressures and inconveniences that non-Muslims incurred in Abbasid Persia. The Parsis left Iran for India about the early tenth century and settled in Gujarat. They adopted Indian dress and language but retained their Zoroastrian faith and cults, maintaining their sacred fires and performing traditional sacrifices. Indeed, while thoroughly assimilated into Indian society, Parsi communities observe their Zoroastrian traditions and retain their cultural identity even in the present day.[39]

The Manichaean odyssey was even more extensive than that of the Parsis.[40] Even before the emergence of Islam, Manichaeans had spread their faith into Transoxiana. The Islamic conquest of Persia encouraged Manichaeans to emigrate in much larger numbers than before. In Transoxiana, their faith became popular among Sogdian merchants, who carried it along the restored silk roads throughout central Asia and even into China, where it became prominent in the diaspora communities of foreign merchants. During its early days in China, Manichaeism won few if any Chinese converts, but it attracted a great deal of interest from the Uighur Turks. In the year 757, when the Uighurs liberated Luoyang from the rebellious army of An Lushan, they found some Sogdian Manichaeans among the grateful survivors. After a long discussion with Manichaean priests, the Uighur khakhan and his army converted to their faith; thus for the first and only time of its career, Manichaeism became an official, state-sponsored religion.

The attraction of the Uighur elite to Manichaeism represents a clear case of conversion through voluntary association. Uighurs had long known of Manichaeism because of their dealings with the ubiquitous Sogdians. They certainly recognized that Sogdians could help them to flourish in the larger commercial and diplomatic world. Indeed, during the eighth and ninth centuries, Sogdian civilization worked a profound influence on Uighur culture and society. Sogdians served as ministers, diplomats, advisers, and secretaries to the Uighurs. They provided the Uighurs with a written language based on their own script. Many Uighurs, though by no means all, formally adopted the Sogdians' Manichaean faith. Finally, the Uighurs—originally nomads—even built a permanent city. Located on the Orkhon River, Karabalghasun was probably the first genuine city ever to arise on the steppes. It featured an enormous castle and twelve iron gates. It bustled with markets and trades, including those of metalworkers, potters, blacksmiths, sculptors, masons, and weavers, among others. An agricultural belt surrounded the city itself, which became a prominent station on the trade routes—thanks largely to the volume of silk that the Uighurs obtained from China. Thus Sogdian influence did much more than bring Manichaeism to the Uighurs: it also worked to extend the tentacles of settled civilization into steppelands previously dominated almost exclusively by nomadic warriors.[41]

But the influence of Sogdian merchants and their Manichaean faith did not stop with the Uighurs; more surprising and unexpected by far was their building of a following in China.[42] The explanation for the Manichaeans' success and survival in China has to do largely with their intellectual flexibility. Manichaeans always maintained a strong and characteristic doctrinal framework featuring dualism, the cosmic struggle between the forces of light and those of darkness, and asceticism as the prime moral virtue. But from the earliest days of the faith, they also had freely adopted Christian, Zoroastrian, and other vocabularies for their own purposes. Little wonder, then, that when they communicated or propagated their faith in central Asia and China, Manichaeans made use of other cultural traditions in representing their views. When the Chinese pilgrim Xuanzang visited Bactria in the mid-seventh century, he heard of the Manichaean community there — but they made so much use of Buddhist terms and concepts that he thought they were Buddhist heretics.

A fair number of Manichaean texts survive from the libraries and scriptoria of Dunhuang, and they show that Manichaeans readily used Buddhist terms and concepts when representing their faith in central Asian and Chinese languages. Mani himself came to be known in eastern regions as the "Buddha of Light." In China, Mani was associated further with Laozi, the legendary founder of Daoism. Their willingness to accommodate Chinese traditions and assimilate to Chinese ways enabled Manichaeans to maintain their culture and community in east Asia for some eight hundred years. It is clear that they eventually began to attract converts among native Chinese, since popular Buddhist stories warned of evil fortune that befell Manichaean converts. After the Tang dynasty's persecutions of foreign religions in the mid-ninth century, Chinese Manichaeans lost contact with foreign priests, who were expelled or in some cases even executed for their faith.

Nevertheless, a sizeable community of Chinese Manichaeans survived from the ninth to the sixteenth century in Quanzhou (Marco Polo's Zaiton) in the bustling commercial district of Fujian in southern China. The community sought to avoid persecution by developing a reputation for respectability and strict observance of the law — also by adhering scrupulously to Chinese ways and assimilating to the Daoists. The Manichaeans of Quanzhou worshipped in Daoist temples and even had some of their scriptures included in the officially recognized Daoist canon. Over the long term, though, official persecution and continued assimilation brought an end to the distinctively Manichaean community in China. Buddhists took over some of the Manichaean shrines in Quanzhou, and the faithful themselves eventually underwent conversion by assimilation to Buddhism or Daoism.

The Manichaeans' doctrinal flexibility thus enabled them to extend the appeal of their faith across cultural boundary lines and to attract converts from foreign cultural traditions. Doctrinal flexibility facilitated syncretism, since Manichaeans readily made accommodations for the beliefs and values, and even for the specific deities and vocabularies of other religious and cultural traditions. In China, however, their small numbers could not sustain a permanent and distinctive community, at least not in the face of persecution. By the end of the sixteenth century, after especially vigorous efforts of the Ming dynasty to eradicate their community, the Manichaeans of Quanzhou disappeared from history, absorbed into the larger society and culture of China.

While Parsis and committed Manichaeans chose flight as their manner of resisting the establishment of Islamic society, some Christians in Spain opted for a more direct, confrontational approach. In and of itself, the military conquest of Spain by Islamic forces did not provoke an extreme reaction. Indeed, to many Iberians, Muslim conquerors brought liberation from the much-despised Visigothic regime. Some cities voluntarily submitted to the invaders, exchanging their allegiance for local autonomy and protection. There was little forced conversion of individuals, if any, and the conquerors allowed Christians to continue their observances. Indeed, during the early decades following the conquest, it looked as though the tiny Muslim population might become absorbed by the huge Christian majority. Yet by about the year 1000, most peasants outside the kingdom of Asturias in northwestern Spain had converted to Islam. A Christian community survived in Islamic Spain until the twelfth century. Known as the Mozarabes — Christians subject to the caliphs of Córdoba — its members resisted absorption into Islam and occasionally rose in rebellion against their Muslim lords. Only after the invasions of the Berber Almoravids (1086) and Almohads (1146) did the Mozarabes disappear as an influential force in Spanish society.

During the ninth century, though, a group of fanatical Mozarabes resisted Muslim rule in such extreme fashion — by provoking their own martyrdoms — as to unsettle both Christian and Muslim communities.[43] The troubles began in the year 850, when a crowd in the marketplace at Córdoba goaded the Christian monk Perfectus into a public denunciation of Muhammad, which led to his execution. Shortly thereafter, a series of devout Christians from Córdoba and the surrounding regions deliberately and publicly antagonized Muslim authorities by denouncing Islam and insulting its prophet. Within a decade, at least forty-eight Christians had voluntarily brought about their own martyrdoms in this manner.

The deliberate search for martyrs' crowns did not permanently disrupt the society of Islamic Spain, but its analysis helps to refract the tensions caused by cross-cultural encounters. Some of the martyrs were descendants of the Roman and Visigothic ruling classes; they no doubt loathed Muslims for political and social as well as theological reasons. Others came from families that included both Christians and Muslims; in some cases, evidence makes it clear that personal and family tensions deeply influenced the martyrs' decisions and behavior. Whatever motives prompted the martyrs' actions, Muslim authorities worried that excessively harsh punishment would provoke reaction or even rebellion by the Christian majority population. Moderate Christians, on the other hand, feared that the behavior of their fanatical brethren would bring persecution on their entire community. Church officials and Christians prominent in the business community of Córdoba seem to have worked diligently to discourage the search for martyrdom and to defuse the situation. The martyrs' movement found sympathy, however, in the work of the priest Eulogius, later bishop of Córdoba, who recorded their stories and defended their zeal, though he did not encourage or instigate additional martyrs. The layman Paulus Alvarus went further: he condemned Christians who acknowledged or cooperated with Muslim rule, and he called for all Christians to demonstrate their faith publicly. In their writings and in conversations with Christians—though presumably not openly or in public—Eulogius and Alvarus viciously attacked Muhammad as an immoral monster and Islam as an impious creed.

Thus a complex set of political, social, personal, and religious motives inspired zealous Christians to resist the newly established Islamic order, even to the point of courting martyrdom. Their extreme behavior posed a challenge to both the dominant Muslim minority and the subject Christian majority. The principal long-term result of the cultural clash was the inauguration of a tradition of bitter anti-Muslim polemic on the part of western Christians, a polemic that fueled conflicts between Christians and Muslims for a millennium and more. Cross-cultural encounters often led to the expansion of cultural traditions and the conversion of peoples to new systems of beliefs and values. But they also generated tremendous social tensions—and no doubt did so in many venues other than ninth-century Córdoba.

The Experiences of Christian Missions to the East and West

Constantine and his successors ensured for Christianity an opportunity to establish itself in the Roman empire. But the Christian emperors could not guarantee that their faith would penetrate, and still less that it would dominate the culture of the western world. The collapse of the Roman empire and its displacement by Germanic successor states could conceivably have resulted in the disappearance of Christianity as an important cultural force. At the least, it looked as though the Arian Christianity favored by Germanic peoples might very well prevail over the Catholic faith embraced by the emperors and bishops of Rome.

As in the case of other religious and cultural traditions that attracted large followings in foreign lands, Christianity succeeded largely because of syncretism—its willingness to baptize pagan traditions and its capacity to make a place for them within a basically Christian framework. But the survival of Roman Catholic Christianity and its eventual domination of western culture depended also on two other especially important developments: the emergence of a strong source of authority and agent of organization in the papacy, and the alliance of the popes with Germanic rulers of the northern lands who could provide political and military support for the Roman church. The importance of these developments is clear not only from the success of Catholic missions in Europe but also from the ultimate failure of Nestorian missions in Asia. A dual process of syncretism and conversion induced by pressure established Christianity as the dominant cultural tradition in Europe. In Asia, however, Christian syncretism did not enjoy the benefits of strong organizational leadership or state sponsorship.

Christians there were unable to maintain distinctive communities, and eventually they themselves underwent conversion by assimilation to indigenous cultural traditions. The following pages will briefly examine the expansion of Catholic Christianity in western and northern Europe, then analyze the contrasting experience of Nestorian Christianity in central Asia and China.

In most parts of the world, merchants figured prominently as bearers of culture. In early medieval Europe, however, missionaries came mostly from the monasteries.[44] Among the most effective of them were Celtic monks of the fifth and sixth centuries who preached their faith and established new communities throughout Ireland, Wales, Cornwall, and Brittany. Some of them ventured into northern England and Scotland; others traveled south to Gaul, Switzerland, and Italy. All of the Celtic missionaries worked independently of the church and bishop of Rome. They differed from the Romanists in their more pronounced asceticism, looser institutional discipline, and method of calculating the date of Easter, among other points. Their popularity and sincerity, however, enabled them to establish Celtic Christianity as a powerful cultural force in lands beyond the reach of the Roman church.

Beginning in the sixth century, however, the Roman church took the cultural initiative in Europe. Pope Gregory I (590–604) — sometimes called Gregory the Great — brought energy and determination to his office, which he fashioned into a powerful tool of cultural leadership. Gregory provided guidance on Roman Catholic observances and institutional discipline. He established relationships with Franks, Lombards, Visigoths, and other Germanic peoples who threatened the Roman church. So far as the expansion of Christianity goes, his most important project was the evangelization of Britain. In the year 596 he dispatched a group of forty missionaries under the leadership of St. Augustine of Canterbury (not to be confused with the more famous theologian, St. Augustine of Hippo). They soon won a prominent patron with the conversion of King Ethelbert of Kent, who helped them to establish churches, monasteries, and episcopal sees in southern England. The tight organization and strict discipline observed by this outpost of Roman Christianity — along with the sponsorship of King Ethelbert and his successors — enabled it to grow at the expense of the Celtic church. By the mid-seventh century it had become plain that in order to avoid fruitless competition, the English church needed to decide in favor of either Roman or Celtic observances. At the synod of Whitby (664) English clerics opted for the Roman alternative, and the Celtic church entered a period of decline that led ultimately to its complete disappearance. The revived papacy of Gregory I thus developed as a powerful source of authority and cultural influence, one capable of organizing missionary efforts and attracting religious allegiance over very long distances.

Quite apart from the reinvigoration of the Roman church's leadership, alliances with Germanic rulers also promoted the spread of Christianity in Europe. The Roman church did not necessarily benefit immediately from all Germanic conversions. Beginning about the late fourth century, for example, the Visigoths had turned increasingly to Arian Christianity—rank heresy from a Roman point of view. In fact, from a modern, analytical point of view, their conversion to Christianity of any variety reflected the Visigoths' progressive assimilation into the society and culture of the late Roman empire.[45] This subtlety provided little comfort, however, for representatives of the Roman church eager to preserve the purity of its doctrine.

More important and far more useful for the Roman church were the Franks. Some of them had lived within the Roman empire since the third century and very likely had converted to Christianity at an early date. Not until the conversion of Clovis, however, did Frankish policy favor specifically Christian interests. A combination of personal and political motives seems to have brought about Clovis's conversion.[46] His wife, Clotilda, was Roman Catholic and constantly urged Clovis to accept her faith. The turning point, however, came only after Clovis had defeated the Alamanni in the year 496, a victory that he attributed to intervention by the Christians' God. He delayed his baptism—perhaps until as late as 508, twelve years after his victory over the Alamanni—but eventually joined a large number of his fellow Franks in officially converting to Roman Catholic Christianity.

The entry of the Frankish ruling elite into the Roman Catholic community set the stage for the process of conversion induced by political pressure in northern Europe. Royally sponsored missionaries and monks spread the Christian message to rural communities throughout the Frankish realm. They scorned pagan customs and beliefs and strenuously argued the superiority of the Christian God over pagan deities and fertility spirits. They also attacked pagan morality, which they sought to replace with their own more stringent code. They even destroyed temples and shrines, replacing them with churches and monasteries.[47]

The significance of the Frankish conversion to Christianity became most clear during the reign of Charlemagne (768–814), whose many services not only enabled the Roman church to survive but also helped it to establish a presence in previously pagan lands. On several occasions Charlemagne protected the papacy from threats posed by Lombards and other Germanic peoples, and he sponsored educational programs designed to prepare priests for their work. Perhaps most important of his services for present purposes was his long, intermittent campaign of more than thirty years to impose order in Saxony. Both Charlemagne and his adversaries clearly recognized religion as an important element of their conflict. Thus Widukind, an especially fiery and effective Saxon leader, sought to overthrow Frankish authority, destroy Christian churches, expel missionaries, and restore pagan ways. Besides establishing garrisons and leading armies against rebel forces, Charlemagne used his faith as an ideological weapon against the pagan Saxons. In a moment of temporary superiority in 785, he forced Widukind to accept baptism along with other prominent Saxons, and he imposed on their land a famous and especially harsh ordinance providing the death penalty for those who forcibly entered a church, violated the Lenten fast, killed a bishop or priest, cremated the dead in pagan fashion, refused baptism, plotted against Christians, or disobeyed the Frankish king. Charlemagne's efforts of course did not result in immediate and enthusiastic conversion of the Saxons to Christianity. Nonetheless clearly, however, they enabled the Roman church to establish a secure presence that over the long term brought about the Christianization of Saxony.[48]

Charlemagne's difficulties with the Saxons serve as an effective reminder that Christianity met with stiff resistance as missionaries promoted their faith across cultural frontiers. In the Saxon case, of course, resistance to Christianity reflected political as well as cultural conflict. But even in the Frankish heartland, culture-based resistance to Christianity continued for a very long time indeed. In the middle of the seventh century, for example, St. Eligius, bishop of Noyon, preached zealously against pagan drunkenness and dancing in his diocese. According to his biographer, he received a straightforward and unambiguous response: "Roman that you are, although you are always bothering us, you will never uproot our customs, but we will go on with our rites as we have always done, and we will go on doing so always and forever. There will never exist the man who will be able to stop us holding our time-honoured and most dear games." Only after many decades of preaching by monks and missionaries did the Frankish realm gradually become a Christian land.[49]

Throughout Europe, the process of social conversion to Christianity proceeded the more effectively when missionaries agreed to honor established cultural traditions and to absorb them into a syncretic but fundamentally Christian synthesis. To some extent this policy of accommodation continued the practice of the earliest Christians, who endowed pagan festivals and heroes with Christian significance, turning them into holy days or saints, in order to bridge the gap between established pagan culture and the new Christian alternative. In like fashion, later missionaries baptized pagan beliefs and customs concerning fertility and health; they built churches and shrines on sites traditionally recognized as having special power or cultural significance; and they associated Christian saints with the virtues and powers ascribed to local heroes. In a famous letter, Pope Gregory the Great instructed St. Augustine, his missionary in England, that

> the idol temples of that race should by no means be destroyed, but only the idols in them. Take holy water and sprinkle it in these shrines, build altars and place relics in them. For if the shrines are well built, it is to the service of the true God. When this people see that their shrines are not destroyed they will be able to banish error from their hearts and be more ready to come to the places they are familiar with, but now recognizing and worshipping the true God.[50]

The syncretic approach thus helped to establish lines of continuity between pagan and Christian traditions, thereby easing the process of conversion to foreign cultural standards. When bolstered by the leadership of the revived papacy and the sponsorship of newly converted kings, syncretism helped Roman Catholic Christians to spread their faith to all corners of Europe. Their religious cousins, the Nestorian Christians, did not enjoy the advantages of organizational energy and political sponsorship, at least not over the long term. Nestorians spread their faith to Mesopotamia, Persia, central Asia, and even to China. Nestorian communities in Mesopotamia and Persia survived for more than a millennium, although the expansion of Islam deprived them of their vitality and severely reduced their numbers after the seventh century. In central Asia and China, however, Nestorians had an even more difficult experience. In some ways they lost their distinctively Christian identity: they did not remain in communication with other Christian communities, and they dropped a large amount of specifically Christian doctrine. Their beliefs and values inclined over time toward those of Buddhists, Daoists, and Muslims, and indeed most Nestorians eventually became absorbed into one or another of those cultural alternatives. The Nestorian experience thus differed markedly from the Roman Catholic, and a comparative analysis of the two throws particularly interesting light on the dynamics of cross-cultural encounters.

Nestorian doctrine arose out of Christological debates of the late fourth and early fifth centuries. In combatting the teachings of Arians and other early Christian heretics, the patriarch of Constantinople, Nestorius, advanced the idea that two distinct natures, divine and human, coexisted in Jesus' person. Because of his arrogance and difficult personality, Nestorius had many enemies, and they gleefully attacked his teachings. Some of them argued that Nestorius overemphasized Christ's human nature; others held that his distinction between human and divine natures implied a belief in two Christs. In the year 430 Pope Celestine excommunicated Nestorius, and in 431 a church council at Ephesus deposed him and banished him to his monastery. Yet Nestorius's ideas survived and for two centuries even flourished in the east. By the late fifth century, Nestorians had become solidly entrenched in Mesopotamia and Persia, where their hostility to Byzantine and Roman churches worked to their advantage, endearing them to Christian communities already established in those lands. The Sassanian kings persecuted Nestorians and Manichaeans in their efforts to favor officially approved Zoroastrianism. The arrival of Islam presented even greater difficulties for Nestorians in the Middle

East. Islamic rulers allowed Nestorians to keep their faith, and the Abbasid caliphs permitted a Nestorian patriarch to reside at Baghdad and to govern his church, under close supervision of the caliphate. But taxation undercut the economic foundations of Nestorian church and society, and most Nestorians eventually converted to Islam.[51]

Already, however, the Nestorian church had begun to spread its influence even further to the east. Nestorian merchants traded actively not only throughout Mesopotamia and Persia but also in India, Ceylon, central Asia, and China. Because the Mesopotamian and Persian churches had already gone into eclipse during the early days of Islam, Nestorians in central Asia and China had at best sporadic contact with their patriarch and other cultural authorities. They attracted limited political support, so that their tradition led a precarious existence in Asia. They exhibited the same inclination toward syncretism that marked Roman Catholic missions in Europe. Absent large populations and political support, however, the Nestorians' syncretism in Asia did not attract many converts from local cultural traditions. Instead, it served as a bridge for the Nestorians themselves to undergo conversion by assimilation to Asian traditions. Several writings of high interest survive, mostly from the libraries and scriptoria of Dunhuang, to represent the experiences of Nestorian communities in central Asia and China.[52]

Nestorians had entered China by the early seventh century at the very latest. The first identifiable Nestorian there was the missionary Alopen, who visited Changan and was received by the Emperor Tang Taizong in the year 635. Alopen brought with him Christian scriptures and other writings, which he had translated into Chinese. The emperor himself read and approved the works, as indicated in a remarkable decree of the year 638:

> The Way had not, at all times and places, the selfsame name; the Sage had not, at all times and places, the selfsame human body. Heaven caused a suitable religion to be instituted for every region and clime so that each one of the races of mankind might be saved. Bishop Alopen of the Kingdom of Persia, bringing with him the sutras and images, has come from afar and presented them at our capital. Having carefully examined the scope of his teaching, we find it to be mysteriously spiritual, and of silent operation. Having observed its principal and most essential

points, we reached the conclusion that they cover all that is most important in life. Their language is free from perplexing expressions; their principles are so simple that they "remain as the fish would remain even after the net of the language were forgotten." This teaching is helpful to all creatures and beneficial to all men. So let it have free course throughout the empire.

As a result, in spite of Buddhist and Daoist opposition, Nestorians established a monastery for twenty-one monks in Changan.[53]

During the early years of their community's life in China, Nestorians taught a recognizably Christian doctrine. This is clear from several doctrinal statements, attributed to Alopen, from the mid-seventh century, which outline the basic story and ethical teachings of Christianity. The "Jesus-Messia Sutra," for example, briefly relates Jesus' birth, life, teachings, and death. The "Discourse on Monotheism" and "Discourse on the Oneness of the Ruler of the Universe" both emphasize the Christian God as sole creator of all things. The "Lord of the Universe's Discourse on Alms-Giving" paraphrases Jesus' Sermon on the Mount. The fundamentally Christian character of the Nestorians' faith emerges clearly also in the inscription of a famous Nestorian monument, erected in the year 781 at Changan. The inscription began by recognizing the existence of one triune God, the creator of the world and of pure humankind, unstained by sin. Satan then corrupted God's human creatures and introduced evil into the world. One person of the divine trinity thereafter arrived on earth as both mortal man and messiah. He set an example of perfection, destroyed the power of Satan, opened the road to human salvation, then returned to his heavenly abode. His ministers preach equality, practice asceticism, and promote holiness.[54]

Unlike Buddhists and Manichaeans, however, the Nestorians never negotiated the leap from the diaspora community to the host society. To some extent, their failure to attract large numbers of Asian converts was due to the difficult language and alien concepts that they presented. Buddhists had employed Daoist and Confucian vocabularies when they entered China, and Manichaeans skillfully appropriated Buddhist and Daoist terminology. The Nestorians also relied heavily on Buddhist and Daoist vocabularies in their documents, but some of their doctrines were so specific to Christianity that they could not convey them very well with borrowed terminology. Nestorians called their treatises "sutras," in the Buddhist manner, and they used terms like "buddhas" or "devas" as synonyms for saints or angels. But the early Nestorians made little effort to accommodate Asian tastes in certain other respects. Whereas Manichaeans had referred to Mani as the "Buddha of Light," using a term that resonated nicely in both Sanskrit and Chinese, Nestorians devised an awkward and unpolished transliteration when they represented the name of Jesus in Chinese as "Yishu" — which could be interpreted to mean "a rat on the move."[55] And Nestorians persistently emphasized concepts like the corporeality of Christ and the physical resurrection of individual bodies, which Asians found alien and unattractive.[56]

Quite apart from the difficulty of attracting Asian interest in their doctrines, the Nestorians also faced hostility and persecution from established political authorities. As a part of its attack on foreign religions in the ninth century, the Tang dynasty targeted Nestorians for suppression, alongside Buddhists, Manichaeans, and Zoroastrians. An imperial edict of the year 845 ordered some three thousand Zoroastrians and Nestorians out of their monasteries, returning them to lay society with the stipulation that "they shall not mingle and interfere with the manners and customs of the Middle Kingdom."[57] The policy worked its effects gradually but nonetheless effectively. This is clear from the work of al-Nadim, a Persian encyclopedist of the late tenth century, who reported the findings of a Nestorian monk who had traveled from Baghdad to China with instructions to oversee the church there. The monk returned with the news that "the Christians who used to be in the land of China have disappeared and perished for various reasons, so that only one man remained in the entire country."[58]

Only vestiges of Nestorian Christianity survived the Tang persecutions. It is true that the church reappeared: the next chapter will show that Nestorians successfully propagated their faith in China a second time during the thirteenth and fourteenth centuries. Between the tenth and thirteenth centuries, though, Nestorians presumably either departed from China or became absorbed by Buddhist and Daoist communities. In a way, the Nestorians' willingness to accommodate their message to a Chinese audience — by employing Buddhist and Daoist concepts to represent Christian doctrine — eased the process by which they themselves adopted different beliefs and values. A document of the early eighth century illustrates in striking fashion how accommodation could lead Christians to esteem and even to adopt the values of other cultural traditions.

The document in question is the "Sutra on Mysterious Rest and Joy," attributed to Bishop Cyriacus, a Persian missionary and head of the Nestorian church at Changan during the early eighth century. The treatise portrays Jesus teaching Simon Peter and other disciples, but the doctrines advanced there are specifically and almost exclusively Daoist. To attain rest and joy, according to the Jesus of this sutra, an individual must avoid striving and desire but cultivate the virtues of nonassertion and nonaction. These qualities enable an individual to become pure and serene, a condition that leads in turn to illumination and understanding. Much of the treatise explains four chief ethical values: nondesire, or the elimination of personal ambition; nonaction, the refusal to strive for wealth and worldly success; nonvirtue, the avoidance of self-promotion; and nondemonstration, the shunning of an artificial in favor of a natural observance of these virtues. The treatise in fact does not advance a single recognizably Christian doctrine but offers instead moral and ethical guidance of the sort that Daoist sages had taught for a millennium. The Jesus of the treatise even likened himself explicitly to Laozi, the legendary founder of Daoism, by mentioning ten streaks on his face—marks traditionally associated with the ancient sage.[59] In the light of the "Sutra on Mysterious Rest and Joy," it is not difficult to understand how Nestorians in China could make a relatively easy transit from Christianity to Daoism through a process of conversion by assimilation.

Culture, Religion, and the Spread of Civilization

A double dynamic—long-distance trade and imperial expansion— drove the process of cross-cultural encounter during the period 600 to 1000. Merchandise crossed central Asian steppes and the waters of the southern seas in quantities vastly larger than earlier times had seen. As a result, cultural traditions also gained wider exposure than earlier conditions had permitted. The spread of Hinduism and Buddhism best exemplify the capacity of religions and values to travel the roads of traders. Meanwhile, the restoration of imperial unity to China and the establishment of an Islamic empire inevitably brought about encounters between peoples of different cultural traditions. Western Eurasia experienced similar developments, though on a smaller scale, as Franks and other Germanic peoples attempted to fill the political vacuum created by the collapse of the Roman empire. The various empire builders of this period occasionally used culture as a political tool and insisted that subjugated peoples adopt the beliefs and values of their conquerors. More commonly, though, a combination of political, social, and economic incentives led to gradual acceptance by subject peoples of cultural traditions, without need for conquerors to order conversion by main force.

In light of the traditional characterization of this period from 600 to 1000 as a dark age, one point bears special emphasis: the seventh to tenth centuries without doubt witnessed more political and imperial expansion, more commercial and cultural exchange than any previous period of human history. Expansion and exchange in turn brought about the spread of literacy and technology, of faiths and values, and indeed of civilization itself.[60] Cross-cultural encounters of necessity played a prominent role in promoting these developments. By no means did all efforts at cultural expansion succeed; many of them lacked the political, social, or economic support necessary for long-term survival, and others faced such stiff resistance from indigenous traditions that they could not survive the crossing of cultural boundaries. By no means, either, did efforts at cultural expansion result in the replication of a given tradition in a new region; when crossing cultural boundaries, beliefs and values necessarily adapted and made accommodations to the political, social, and economic, as well as cultural traditions of different peoples. Thus, when it occurred on a large scale, cross-cultural conversion followed a process of syncretism rather than wholesale cultural transformation, or the refashioning of one people according to the cultural standards of another. Nevertheless, cross-cultural encounters of the period 600 to 1000 left rather deep impressions whose outlines remained visible for a long term, continuing in many cases even to the present day.

4

The Age of the
Nomadic Empires

By the time of [Kubilai Khan] the land within the Four Seas
had become the territory of one family, civilization had spread
everywhere, and no more barriers existed. For people in search
of fame and wealth in north and south, a journey of a thousand
li was like a trip next door, while a journey of ten thousand *li*
constituted just a neighborly jaunt. Hence, among people of the
Western Regions who served at court, or who studied in our
south-land, many forgot the region of their birth, and took delight in living among our rivers and lakes. As they settled down
in China for a long time, some became advanced in years, their
families grew, and being far from home, they had no desire to
be buried in their fatherland. Brotherhood among peoples has
certainly reached a new plane.

    Wang Li, quoted, Chen Yüan, *Western and Central Asians*
under the Mongols

The centuries from about 1000 to 1350 C.E. did not witness the
establishment of new trade routes such as those pioneered during
the era of the ancient silk roads. Nor did merchants of that period
revive routes that had fallen into disuse, as the Turks and others
had reestablished links across central Asia after the collapse of
classical Chinese and Roman empires. The period from the early
eleventh to the mid-fourteenth century nonetheless stands out as a
distinctive age in the history of cross-cultural encounters, one that
warrants analysis in its own right. Even without the creation of
new roads or revival of old ones, this period beheld a remarkable
intensification of dealings across cultural boundary lines. Indeed,
during the twelfth and thirteenth centuries, the various regions of

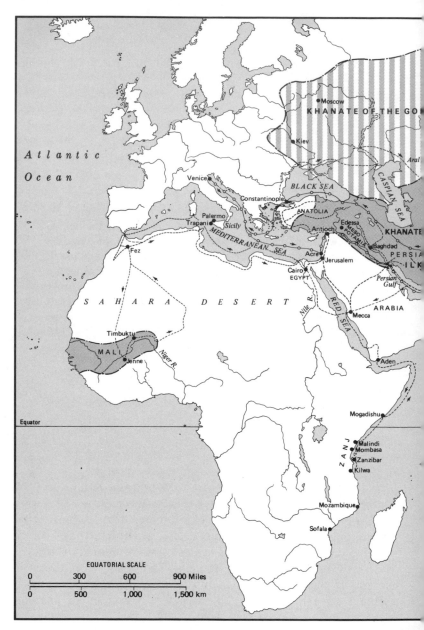

MAP 4. The Mongol Age.

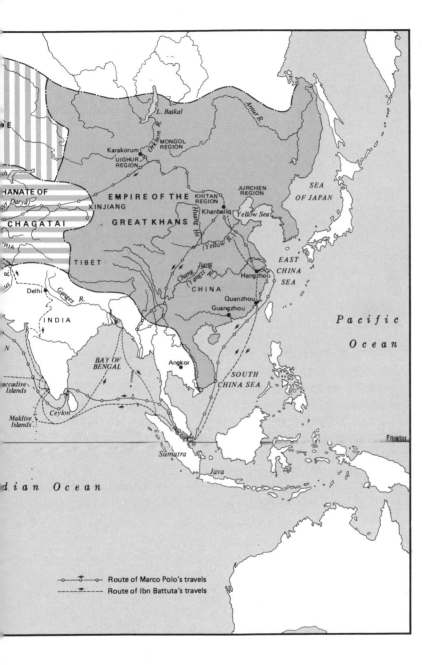

EMPIRE OF THE
GREAT KHANS

XINJIANG

TIBET

CHINA

INDIA

Delhi

Karakorum

UIGHUR
REGION

MONGOL
REGION

L. Baikal

Orkhon R.

Amur R.

KHITAN
REGION

JURCHEN
REGION

Khanbaliq

Huang He

Yellow R.

Yellow Sea

SEA
OF JAPAN

Chang Jiang
(Yangzi R.)

Hangzhou

Quanzhou

Guangzhou

EAST
CHINA
SEA

Pacific

Ocean

HANATE OF

CHAGATAI

Darya

Ganges R.

BAY OF
BENGAL

Angkor

SOUTH
CHINA SEA

accadive
Islands

Maldive
Islands

Ceylon

Sumatra

Java

Equator

dian Ocean

○——○ Route of Marco Polo's travels
------- Route of Ibn Battuta's travels

the Eastern Hemisphere became more tightly integrated than at
any period of history before modern times.[1] Integration in turn
brought about a quickening in the process of cross-cultural encounter, with results that in some cases influenced historical and cultural development over an extraordinarily long term.

One of the most fascinating side effects of this integration was
the fact that it enabled individuals to undertake long-distance travels on a scale never before possible. Many long-distance travelers
will make individual appearances during the course of this chapter.
Two of them warrant special mention, however, because their accounts of their experiences are quite important for purposes of
understanding cross-cultural encounters in this era. The first was
Marco Polo, who left his native Venice in 1271 in order to accom-
pany his father and uncle on a commercial expedition to China.
The party traveled through Mesopotamia, Persia, and Turkestan,
reaching the court of Kubilai Khan in 1275. They remained in
China until 1292, when they sailed from Quanzhou and returned
to Venice, arriving in 1295 by way of Sumatra, Ceylon, India,
Arabia, and Asia Minor. The second of these travelers was the
Moroccan Ibn Battuta, who in 1325 departed his home in Tangier
in order to make his pilgrimage to Mecca. Instead of returning
immediately, however, he proceeded on to Mesopotamia, Persia,
India, the Maldive Islands, Ceylon, and China. In 1346 he left
China and returned to Morocco by way of India, the Persian Gulf,
Syria, and Egypt, arriving at Fez in 1349. The following year he
made a quick trip to the kingdom of Granada but still had not
ended his travels; in 1351 he crossed the Sahara and began a visit of
more than two years to the kingdom of Mali. One scholar recently
calculated that Ibn Battuta visited the equivalent of forty-four
modern countries and logged some seventy-three thousand miles
during the course of his travels. Ibn Battuta himself made the point
quite nicely when he told of meeting "the pious shaikh Abdallah
al-Misri, the traveler, and a man of saintly life. He journeyed
through the earth, but he never went into China nor the island of
Ceylon, nor the Maghrib, nor al-Andalus [that is, the kingdom of
Granada], nor the Negrolands [that is, Mali], so that I have out-
done him by visiting these regions."[2] (See the routes traveled by
Marco Polo and Ibn Battuta on map 4.)

Three particular developments stood behind the pronounced integration of the Eastern Hemisphere's various regions. First was the establishment of transregional empires by nomadic peoples. During the eleventh century, for example, the Saljuq Turks built an empire extending from Anatolia through the Middle East and Persia into central Asia. During the thirteenth century, the Mongols established the largest empire in all human history, stretching from Manchuria, Korea, and China in the east to Russia and the Danube in the west. By pacifying vast territories and ensuring the safety of roads, these empires — especially that of the Mongols — encouraged rapid growth in the volume of long-distance travel undertaken for purposes of trade, diplomacy, and missionary work.

Meanwhile, as the empires of nomads encouraged travel over land, Eurasian mariners increasingly exploited the opportunities offered by the sea lanes of the Indian Ocean. The second agent promoting large-scale integration, then, was the rapid development of sea-based trade over long distances. Beginning about the early eleventh century, Chinese merchants sailed regularly to India and perhaps even visited east African ports. About the middle of the thirteenth century, a port official from Fujian was well informed enough about the larger world to compile a book describing the peoples, customs, and products of an astonishing number of foreign lands, including southeast Asia, Indonesia, Ceylon, India, Arabia, east Africa, Anatolia, Egypt, and even Sicily.[3] Even more prominent, however, were Muslim traders, whose ubiquity in the Indian Ocean helps to account for the spread of Islam to east Africa and southeast Asia.

Finally, the remarkable growth of European economic and political power also encouraged integration by involving Europe more directly in the larger hemispheric economy. This development was not so spectacular as the establishment of the Mongol empire, perhaps not even so impressive as the emergence of the intricate trading patterns of the Indian Ocean. Yet it helped to drive and sustain long-distance trade throughout Eurasia, and it served to bring Europeans more directly than ever before into the larger political and economic life of Eurasia. Thus it played a significant role in fostering Eurasian integration and cross-cultural encounters during the period examined in this chapter. Over the longer term, this economic and political development also underlay the vast expansion of European influence during early modern times.

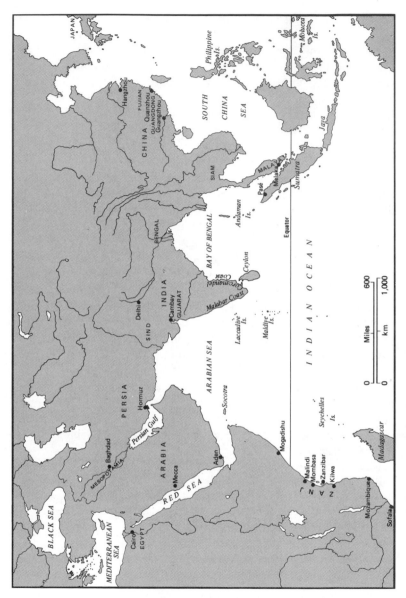

MAP 5. The trading world of the Indian Ocean.

A New Round of Islamic Expansion

The quickening tempo of cross-cultural encounters and exchanges benefitted Islam more than any other cultural tradition. Two developments in particular promoted the expansion of Islam during the period from 1000 to 1350. The first was a series of conquests by Turkish peoples, which helped to consolidate Islam most notably in India and Anatolia. The second was the emergence of elaborate commercial networks, which enabled Islamic traders to introduce their faith through a process of voluntary conversion into India, southeast Asia, east Africa, and west Africa. This section will examine the ways that conquerors and traders helped to spread Islamic faith and civilization.

The presence of Islam in Transoxiana had attracted several Turkish tribes to the faith by the late tenth century, and the new converts soon began to play a prominent role in Islamic history. As Turkish peoples spread south and west from their central Asian homelands, they took their new faith to lands where it had not established a secure presence. Among these lands were India and Anatolia. Turkish Muslims encountered Indian Hindus and Buddhists under conditions quite different from those governing their clash with Anatolian Christians. A comparative look at the Turkish encounters in India and Anatolia can shed useful light on processes of conversion induced by political, social, and economic pressures. In India, a small group of warriors imposed a veneer of Turkish rule on the vast subcontinent. Their political dominance and fiscal policies naturally encouraged some Indians to convert to Islam, but they did not promote their faith in an especially active fashion. As a result, Islam attracted large numbers of Indians only after Sufi mystics popularized their faith and syncretized it with native cultural traditions. In Anatolia, by contrast, Turkish peoples used their new faith as an ideological weapon in their campaign of conquest. They ruled Anatolia—a relatively compact land compared to India, and one that was culturally well integrated for centuries— much more tightly than did their cousins in India. They also aggressively promoted Islam and penalized those who chose not to convert. As a result, they brought about a much more thorough conversion to a foreign cultural tradition.

Islam had made an appearance in India as early as the seventh century, when missionaries and traders began to visit the southern coasts and to win local converts. An Umayyad force conquered the Sind region in the early eighth century. As a result of these developments, small Muslim communities established themselves in India from the earliest days of Islam. Hindus tolerated these early Indian Muslims, and Hindu rulers often employed them as administrators. But during its first three centuries in India, the Islamic faith attracted few native converts, and it exercised little political influence in the subcontinent.

This situation changed dramatically beginning in the early eleventh century. Between 1001 and 1026, Mahmud of Ghazni carved out an enormous state in the Punjab. Later generations of Turkish conquerors established the sultanate of Delhi and extended their political claims to Bengal and the Deccan. As a result of these conquests, Islam gained the support of an aggressive and dynamic state in India. Turkish conquerors attacked the established cultural as well as political order in India. They destroyed temples, monasteries, and shrines. They confiscated the wealth that they found in holy places, and they broke the statuary and religious icons that offended pious Muslim sensitivities.[4]

Yet compared to its experience in other lands — most notably Egypt, Persia, and the Middle East — Islam attracted few native converts in India. One reason for this was a lack of incentives. Conversion of course brought exemption from the *jizya*, the poll tax levied by Muslim rulers on their non-Muslim subjects, but in India the *jizya* was imposed sporadically at best, so that it did not represent a serious burden for Hindus, Buddhists, or others to bear. Conversion also brought escape from the strictures of the caste system, but this opportunity appealed only to the most oppressed members of Indian society. Indeed, most Indian converts generally maintained their traditional caste and social relationships even after their acceptance of Islam. Meanwhile, political incentives that might have attracted Indian elites to Islam were almost entirely lacking. Turkish conquerors completely dominated politics and society within their states until the fourteenth century, and they made little room even for Indian Muslims. Only during the dynasties of the Khaljis (1290–1320) and the Tughluqs (1320–1414) did native Indians begin to find places as governors and administrators.

Quite apart from a lack of incentives for conversion, the Turkish conquerors of India regarded their new subjects with suspicion and hostility. Already upon first encounter they developed an unattractive impression of the Indian people and their civilization. The work of the central Asian astronomer al-Biruni makes this point clear. Mahmud of Ghazni captured him in his native Khwarizm in 1017 and sent him to Ghazni and later to Delhi. On the basis of about ten years' life and experience there, al-Biruni composed a long work on Indian beliefs, customs, and sciences. He by no means idolized the Turkish conquerors — he pointedly criticized Mahmud's cruelty and ferocity — and he found some achievements to respect in Hindu mathematics, science, and philosophy. But he recoiled at "the innate perversity of the Hindu nature." The Hindus, he said, "believe that there is no country but theirs, no nation like theirs, no kings like theirs, no religion like theirs, no science like theirs. They are haughty, foolishly vain, self-conceited, and stolid." Even more scandalous to al-Biruni were Hindu religious beliefs, sexual habits, and social customs. Taken together, they demonstrated to his satisfaction the "essential foulness" of Indian culture as against the manifest superiority of Islamic institutions.[5]

In the light of these conditions — lack of incentives for conversion and a hostile conqueror's mentality — it is perhaps not surprising that Indians converted to Islam only gradually and in small numbers. Probably the most successful proponents of Islam were Sufi missionaries, who worked among the masses and attracted converts by their reputations for humanity and spiritual power. Their methods represented a process of religious syncretism rather than the arbitrary imposition of an alien doctrine. They related traditional Hindu and Buddhist stories — traditionally the primary sources of moral and religious instruction in India — but adapted them to Islamic purposes by substituting Muslim saints for the original actors. They built new shrines on the sites of Hindu temples and Buddhist monasteries, thus appropriating the existing sacred character of the sites for a new faith. They even accepted secret converts — Indians who privately acknowledged Islam but who practised Hinduism and observed traditional caste obligations in public.

Religious and cultural syncretism also took more systematic and organized form in India, most notably in the form of the *bhakti* movement, which emerged in southern India during the twelfth century as a cult of love and devotion. In its early decades it represented a purely Hindu development that drew most of its inspiration from the *Bhagavad Gita*. As it moved north, especially during the period from the thirteenth to the seventeenth century, the *bhakti* cult progressively encountered the spreading faith of Islam. *Bhakti* proponents — traditionally referred to as "saints" — came under the influence of certain Islamic values, especially monotheism and the spiritual equality of individuals. The saints thus elaborated an egalitarian doctrine that transcended the caste system and encouraged individuals to seek personal union with the divine. Like Sufis, then, they offered a spiritual alternative that appealed strongly to members of the oppressed castes. To that extent, it had the potential to limit the spread of Islam by competing for the allegiance of the same audience that the Sufis addressed.

Over the longer term, though, the *bhakti* movement served to blend two spiritual traditions. This point came most clear in the late fifteenth and early sixteenth centuries in the work of Kabir and Nanak, who popularized the *bhakti* movement in the urban society of northern India. Kabir (1440–1518) rejected the exclusive authority of either Muslim or Hindu deities, whom he indeed identified with one another:

> O servant, where dost thou seek Me?
> Lo! I am beside thee.
> I am neither in temple nor in mosque:
> I am neither in Kaaba nor in Kailash [home of Siva]. . . .
>
> Hari is in the East: Allah is in the West. Look within your
>   heart, for there you will find both Karim [Allah] and Ram
>   [incarnation of Visnu];
> All the men and women of the world are His living forms.[6]

Nanak (1469–1539) avoided specific Hindu and Muslim connotations altogether but seemed instead to envision a new and more universal deity than either of the existing traditions that influenced his thought. His disciples later founded the independent community of the Sikhs, who ultimately rejected both Hinduism and Islam. In the shorter term, though, the work of both Kabir and Nanak clearly illustrated the mutual influence of Hindu and Islamic traditions on each other. They illustrated moreover the potential of syncretism not only to facilitate cross-cultural communication but also to blend various cultural traditions so thoroughly as to generate altogether new cultural configurations.

Even when adorned by Hindu and Buddhist cultural elements, Islam held little appeal for many Indians. Some paid as little attention to Islam as Turkish rule permitted. Others actively resisted the Islamic faith and Muslim rule. Resistance became especially effective during the fourteenth century, as the sultanate of Delhi entered a long period of decline. During the eight years that he spent in India (approximately 1333 to 1341), the Moroccan traveler Ibn Battuta learned from several harrowing encounters with rebels and bandits that the sultan's writ did not run far beyond Delhi. It was one thing to enforce Islamic law in Delhi and at the sultan's court; as *qadi* of Sultan Muhammad Ibn Tughluq, Ibn Battuta himself once sentenced a military officer to eighty lashes and imprisonment because he had drunk wine in the past.[7] It was quite another matter, though, to introduce and enforce Islamic law throughout the vast Indian subcontinent.

In several notable cases, resistance took a serious political and military turn. The most notorious case involved Khusrau Khan, an Indian of low caste who converted to Islam, then rose to high position as homosexual lover of the Khalji sultan. In 1320 Khusrau turned suddenly, murdered the sultan and his family, seized power for himself, desecrated mosques, reinstituted Hinduism, and ordered the expulsion of Muslims from Delhi. His rule lasted only four months and so had no permanent effect, except to bring the Khalji dynasty to an end. But it demonstrated both the vulnerability of Muslim rule in India and the explosive potential of resistance associated with Hinduism.

More significant than Khusrau's rebellion was the establishment of the Hindu kingdom of Vijayanagar in southern India. Ironically, Turkish expansion in the south precipitated the series of events that resulted in the consolidation of the Hindu kingdom. While attempting to extend the authority of Delhi to the south in the early fourteenth century, the sultan's army captured two Hindu princes, Harihara and Bukka, and transferred them to Delhi. There they converted to Islam and entered the sultan's service. Later they returned to the south as the sultan's governors. Ultimately, though, they could not resist the temptation to establish themselves as independent rulers. In 1336 Harihara had himself proclaimed king in his own right. The brothers then abandoned Islam and returned to their native Hinduism. They did not mount an anti-Islamic crusade by any means, but the founding of an officially Hindu kingdom helped to limit the expansion of Islam as a political force in India.

During the same centuries that Mahmud of Ghazni and his successors promoted the spread of Islam in India, their Saljuq Turkish cousins took Anatolia by storm and brought about a far more thorough cultural transformation than had taken place in India. On the eve of the Turkish invasions, Anatolia perhaps seemed more united and defensible than India, thanks to the long-established authority there of the Byzantine empire. In fact, though, a great deal of internal dissension plagued the Byzantine order. Saljuq raiders easily found openings to exploit, and each success contributed to the disruption of existing society. Turks first appeared in Anatolia in 1016. By 1071 they had shattered the Byzantine army at the battle of Manzikert. From that point on, Byzantine authority progressively collapsed, as ambitious Byzantines, Turks, Armenians, Normans, and others vied to establish states that would fill the void. During the late thirteenth and fourteenth centuries, new rounds of invasions—most notably by Ottomans, as well as by other Turkish peoples—sealed the fate of both Byzantine authority and Christian culture in Anatolia. In effect, all Anatolia fell into the sort of confusion that in India afflicted only the Sind and the Punjab.

The more serious disruption of Anatolian society helps to account for the more thorough cultural transformation that took place there.[8] Famine, disease, and military casualties reduced the Christian population. Many survivors fled before Turkish invaders; others fell captive and went into slavery. The conquerors tolerated Christians, if they observed their faith quietly, but they imposed discriminatory restrictions upon them: Christians had to wear distinctive dress, and they could not ride saddled horses or carry swords. They also of course paid the obligatory *jizya* in addition to other tax levies. Clergy as well as laity experienced this fate. As in India, the Turkish invaders targeted religious as well as political sites for destruction. Thus spoke the Muslim hero in the Turkish epic: "I am Malik Danishmend Ghazi . . . the destroyer of churches and towers."[9] The invaders sometimes forbade clergy to visit their churches, and they often appropriated income from religious properties for their own uses. By the fifteenth century, the Christian clergy had lost its confidence and much of its discipline, and the ecclesiastical structure of Anatolia had fallen into ruin.

Thus it was far more difficult to remain a Christian in Anatolia than to remain a Hindu in India following Turkish invasions of the eleventh century. At the same time, there were more incentives to convert to Islam in Anatolia than in India. As a result, already by the late thirteenth century, a great many Christians had become integrated into Muslim society in Anatolia, and by the late fifteenth century few Christians remained there. Economic and social inducements were particularly effective in attracting Anatolian converts. Whereas in the Punjab Turks showed scant interest in opening the ranks of ruling class society to Indians, even to Muslim Indians, the conquerors of Anatolia displayed considerable generosity to Christians who adopted Islam. Many Christians received gifts, grants, and other rewards for casting their lots with the conquerors. Some of them rose high in the Turkish service, a point well illustrated by the case of the Gabras family. Long an important and powerful clan in eastern Anatolia, the Gabras figured prominently in the defense of Trebizond against the Turks in the eleventh century, and one member of the family suffered martyrdom for his efforts. By the twelfth century, however, the name Gabras occurred frequently in the ranks of Saljuq servants. Several members of the family held high military positions; one served as an envoy in negotiations with Byzantines; and another even won an emirate for his services.[10]

By no means did all converts volunteer their services to the Turks so readily as did the Gabras family. But even involuntary recruits generally found it possible to make satisfying lives for themselves in Turkish Muslim society. One of the more distinctive Turkish institutions was the *devshirme*, a levy of Christian children who were removed from their homes to be educated and socialized as Muslims. Though officially slaves — that is, servants of the sultan — these recruits had tremendous opportunities opened to them, and they made significant contributions to political, military, cultural, and religious affairs in Turkish Anatolia. During the early days of Turkish rule, Christian families naturally tried to avoid losing children to the *devshirme*. Gradually, however, it became clear that children so recruited had many more opportunities opened to them than they would otherwise find. Hence, by the fifteenth century, it was not unknown for Christian families to volunteer their offspring for the *devshirme*.

Quite apart from material incentives, Turks in Anatolia sought to provide psychological and spiritual rewards for conversion to Islam. Religious and educational foundations prepared potential converts and helped them to enter the Muslim cultural world; social welfare foundations provided food, clothing, shelter, and even money for new converts in straitened circumstances. Meanwhile, several orders of Sufi dervishes took it as a special part of their mission to convert Christians to Islam. Their efforts succeeded partly because of their humanity and kindness: they provided charity for Christians who lacked the necessities of life but could no longer rely upon the increasingly moribund Orthodox church for support. Their work benefitted also, though, from the ritual and doctrinal flexibility traditionally associated with Sufis. Some of them attracted converts through music, dance, and emotion-charged rituals that sought to bring individuals into personal union with Allah. Others discovered that a syncretic approach helped to ease the spiritual journey from Christianity to Islam: they emphasized the importance of a general attitude of religious awe and reverence, for example, rather than acknowledgment of a specific doctrine, or they emphasized the common elements of Christianity and Islam so as to suggest that the two were only different versions of the same faith.

The Sufis' various methods brought huge numbers of Christians into the Islamic fold. Yet in Anatolia, as everywhere, a new cultural arrival exercised less than universal appeal, and in various ways the established culture negotiated its survival. A small minority of Byzantine Christians held to their inherited faith even after adopting Turkish language and customs. In the late fifteenth century, these holdouts accounted for approximately 8 percent of the Anatolian population. More dramatic but less common was overt resistance to Turkish rule and Muslim religion. Voluntary martyrdom did not become a popular movement in Anatolia, as it had in ninth-century Córdoba, but determined individuals provoked the ire of Muslim rulers and faithful for centuries after the arrival of Turks in Anatolia. These individuals gave offense sometimes gratuitously, sometimes inadvertently, but in numerous recorded cases they suffered martyrdom for their efforts. Though obviously self-destructive, these martyrdoms passed into the lore of the remaining Christian communities, where they served to reinforce a legacy of resistance. As a result, in spite of the hugely successful cultural transformation that took place in Turkish Anatolia, at least small Christian communities survive there even in the twentieth century.

Thus in India and especially in Anatolia, Turkish conquests promoted the expansion of Islam through processes of conversion largely induced by political, social, and economic pressures. Meanwhile, thousands of anonymous Islamic traders quietly spread their faith through processes of voluntary conversion in port cities and coastal regions throughout the basin of the Indian Ocean. Information that could help to illuminate the ways and means by which merchants spread Islam is both rare and fragmentary. Enough survives, however, to permit at least a general understanding of the process, which resembled the spread of Hindu and Buddhist culture in southeast Asia. Traders established small diaspora communities in ports and regions where they did business, and they cultivated their Islamic faith primarily for their own purposes. Some of the local inhabitants who dealt extensively with the merchants adopted their faith, which provided them with a set of values and a code of ethics well suited to their participation in the economic activities of a large and cosmopolitan world. Small Islamic communities gradually expanded: *qadis* arrived to administer justice and adjudicate disputes among Muslims; theologians arrived, serving both as intellectual links to the larger world and as agents promoting a degree of standardization in the transregional culture of Islam; Sufis arrived and sought to penetrate existing cultural boundaries by spreading Islam broadly among native inhabitants. Meanwhile, new converts made pilgrimages to Mecca, where they became acquainted at first hand with Islamic customs and traditions — became initiated, as it were, into the larger world of Islam. Finally, in many cases, ruling elites recognized political or economic advantages in Islam, and as a result they lent official support that enabled the new faith to establish itself securely in their lands.

This process or something like it unfolded many times over in sub-Saharan west Africa and in most regions of the Indian Ocean basin—southern India, southeast Asia, coastal east Africa, and even in some of the islands of the Indian Ocean, such as the Maldives and Laccadives. The cumulative result of the process was to expand vastly the range of Islamic cultural influence.

There were inevitably uneven degrees of commitment to Islamic doctrine and values in the many lands where the new faith found a following, a point well illustrated by Ibn Battuta's experience. After his departure from India, Ibn Battuta visited the Maldive Islands, where Sultana Khadija soon appointed him *qadi*. Here, perhaps more than any other land he visited during his many travels, Ibn Battuta sought to introduce Islamic values and to enforce Islamic law with genuine zeal. During his sojourn of about twenty months in the Maldives, Ibn Battuta established lashing as punishment for men who missed Friday prayers, and he often ordered lashings for men who took sexual advantage of their former spouses whom they had divorced. In one case, abiding strictly by Islamic law, he ordered severance of a thief's right hand, a punishment so severe and unexpected that several witnesses fainted at its execution. Loss of a hand perhaps discouraged thievery, but multiple lashings suggest that Ibn Battuta experienced less success in his efforts to develop respect for Islamic values in the Maldives. In one connection Ibn Battuta frankly admitted his failure to introduce Islamic morality. When he arrived in the islands, he said, he found that women

> wear only a waist wrapper which covers them from their waist to the lowest part, but the remainder of their body remains uncovered. Thus they walk about in the bazaars and elsewhere. When I was appointed *qadi* there, I strove to put an end to this practice and commanded the women to wear clothes; but I could not get it done. I would not let a woman enter my court to make a plaint unless her body were covered; beyond this, however, I was unable to do anything.[11]

Nevertheless, the establishment of the faith on an institutional foundation—often officially supported and patronized by ruling elites—ensured that over the long term, Islam would survive across a vast swath of the Eastern Hemisphere.

The spread of Islam by merchants took place so quietly that the earliest mention of the process often appeared long after it began.

The first clear indication of Islam's arrival in southeast Asia, for example, appeared only in the late thirteenth century in Marco Polo's discussion of the kingdom of Perlak in northern Sumatra:

> This kingdom, you must know, is so much frequented by the Saracen merchants that they have converted the natives to the Law of Mahomet—I mean the towns-people only, for the hill-people live for all the world like beasts, and eat human flesh, as well as all other kinds of flesh, clean or unclean.[12]

The report itself indicates clearly that the conversion process unfolded over a considerable period of time. It has the effect also of lending credence to the notion that a process of conversion through voluntary association took place in Perlak: converts to Islam came from the ranks of city dwellers—those who worked closely with Muslim merchants and who thus participated in the affairs of a large, cosmopolitan world—while the newly arrived faith held no attraction for inhabitants of the surrounding hills and hinterland, who consequently held fast to their traditional ways.

Similar developments took place elsewhere in the commercial communities of southeast Asia. One recent interpretation suggests, for example, that economic relations with foreign traders encouraged Javanese to convert gradually to Islam. Ruling elites controlled trade in their realms and thus became acquainted with Islam at an early date. Most likely, though, ruling elites inclined toward Islam, and eventually converted, because of the political advantages that it offered them. In traditional southeast Asia, leadership was closely associated not only with personal prowess but also with divine sanction and energy. Islam appealed to elites, then, as an additional source of divine power that could legitimize their rule. The elites do not seem to have pushed their subjects to convert to Islam in any very zealous manner. Indeed, they most likely maintained their own associations with Hindu and Buddhist cultures, additional sources of divine sanction for their rule, even after adopting Islam. Meanwhile, on the popular level, Islam spread in a personalized and mystical rather than systematic and doctrinal form. Only in the fifteenth century did the spread of Islam in southeast Asia pass into written records to the extent that historians can document it today. From such evidence as survives, however, it seems most likely that a process of conversion through voluntary association explains the early presence of Islam in south-east Asia.[13]

In the case of sub-Saharan Africa, both east and west Africa, the evidence shows much more clearly that traders played the most important roles in the early spread and establishment of Islam. In east Africa merchants took part in the seaborne commercial networks that linked the Indian Ocean basin. The Swahili—in Arabic, the term means "coasters," that is, those who traveled up and down the coasts—traded between the fishing and farming villages in the Zanj region, the east African coast between Mogadishu and Sofala.[14] Besides trade goods—pottery, glass, ironware, and textiles exchanged for such local products as gold, ivory, slaves, aromatics, and animal skins—they brought Arabic language, Islamic religion, and sophisticated political institutions to the east African towns they visited. Trade itself encouraged rapid development in the coast's major towns—Mogadishu, Malindi, Mombasa, Kilwa, Mozambique, and Sofala—which not only grew in size but also organized trade networks in the hinterland. Trade also brought considerable prosperity to these towns. Their elites wore silk and placed imported chinaware on their tables, and stone buildings went up in place of the wooden and coral structures that had previously adorned the towns.

A high volume of trade also encouraged far-reaching cultural developments. In some cases Swahili traders forged alliances with indigenous aristocracies that promoted the interests of the foreign merchants; in other cases the traders founded their own ruling dynasties and imposed them on the coastal towns. In all cases, though, the major trading sites of east Africa saw the development after about 1100 of an alliance between Islam and kingship. Islam provided a kind of cultural unity for all the Swahili trading and ruling classes. Indeed, their adoption of Islam represents an especially clear case of conversion through voluntary association. Indigenous culture emphasized the importance of local genealogies, magical abilities, and mastery over the spiritual world, interests of too parochial a nature for those who lived and worked in a cosmopolitan world of trade and travel. Islam, however, supplied a system of values and ethics recognized throughout the Indian Ocean basin, and one moreover that enhanced the legitimacy of local ruling houses. Thus rulers, merchants, and others engaged in long-distance trade gravitated naturally toward Islam, which linked them culturally with their counterparts in all areas of the Indian Ocean. By the thirteenth century, stone mosques dominated the larger trading towns. Local rulers patronized the Islamic establishment: they supported construction projects, introduced Islamic jurisprudence, and publicly observed their ritual and charitable obligations. In return they gained both the endorsement of the local Islamic establishment and a larger legitimacy implicitly conferred by the Islamic world as a whole.

Ruling elites did not forcibly impose Islam on their subjects. Indigenous beliefs and values—interest in genealogy, magic, spirits, and the local microcosmic world—remained prominent among the popular classes of the Swahili towns. Indeed, the elites themselves recognized the continuing significance of indigenous culture and sought its imprimatur as an additional sanction for their rule. In a way, then, the local elites served as links joining microcosmic worlds governed by traditional cultural norms to a diverse and cosmopolitan society that stretched throughout the Indian Ocean basin and beyond.

Thus, Islam by no means displaced or uprooted indigenous cultures in east Africa. During its early days there, it simply offered a cultural alternative that appealed primarily to traders and rulers. Yet it seems all but inevitable that, over the longer term, Islam would become established as the principal cultural alternative in east Africa. As trade in the Indian Ocean increased, it encouraged further political, social, and economic development of the Zanj region. Sophisticated development in turn created an environment favoring the expansion of Islamic culture. The increasing complexity of the Indian Ocean basin thus promoted the spread of Islam along with trade and political hierarchy.

Though not a part of the Indian Ocean trading network, continental west Africa had an experience very similar to that of the eastern coastal cities. From about the eighth century, traders crossed the torrid stretches of the Sahara by camel caravan in search of west African gold and slaves. In west Africa, trade and Islam became so closely identified that they were virtually synonymous—to the point that some merchants adopted Islam while engaged in commerce but gave up the faith and their identities as Muslims when they ceased trading. By the eleventh century, west

African rulers had begun to adopt the traders' Islamic faith as their own. At midcentury, the king of Takrur on the lower Senegal River went so far as to impose Islamic law on his subjects and to proselytize vigorously in neighboring lands. Most local rulers, however, adopted a less aggressive policy. They employed literate Muslims as secretaries and interpreters, and they accepted Islam for themselves, without forcing it upon their subjects. Their interest in controlling trade, the primary source of their income, helps to account for their adoption of Islam. They no doubt found that a common faith facilitated dealings between themselves and merchants from afar. Conversion to Islam also brought political advantages for west African rulers: they gained ready access to a group of talented and educated entrepreneurs who could provide useful services as bureaucrats and royal servants; they established close relationships with an itinerant class of people who could provide useful information about developments in other lands; and they won recognition from established Muslim rulers in north Africa.[15]

West African rulers no doubt hoped to benefit politically, diplomatically, and economically when they adopted Islam, but the prospect of material advantage did not necessarily mean that royal converts did not feel genuine devotion for their new faith. Mansa Musa, the king of Mali, was perhaps the best example of a royal convert who developed a strong and sincere interest in Islam. In 1324 he made a memorable pilgrimage to Mecca. Though accompanied by thousands of subjects, slaves, soldiers, and attendants, he undertook the journey in a spirit of penitence and devotion. He made lavish gifts of gold throughout the course of his travels. Indeed, he distributed so much in Cairo that the value of gold dropped by as much as 25 percent while his entourage was there. The pilgrimage seems to have strengthened his commitment to Islam: he invited several descendants of Muhammad to Mali, he built mosques in his own land, and he sponsored students studying in the Islamic schools at Fez.

Their interest in stability, though, discouraged royal converts to Islam from undertaking campaigns to transform all west African society, except in the rare cases of especially zealous converts like the aforementioned king of Takrur. Like their Swahili counterparts, west African rulers adopted Islam as a cultural bridge to the larger world, but they continued to recognize traditional beliefs and honor established values in the interests of effective governance in their own societies. Muslim merchants generally occupied a separate quarter of west African towns, and they dealt with the local inhabitants only on matters of commerce or official business. Outside the larger towns, Islam left little if any mark on west African society before the nineteenth century. Even within the towns and the royal courts, pagan traditions survived, while Islamic law became established in limited and selective fashion. Once again, Ibn Battuta illustrates the point. On his last major journey, undertaken between 1351 and 1354, he visited the kingdom of Mali and other sub-Saharan lands. As a pious Muslim, he was scandalized by the relationships between the sexes that he found there. Men spoke in easy and familiar fashion with women other than their wives, and even in the sultan's court he witnessed scores of female slaves and servants whose public nudity violated Ibn Battuta's sense of propriety.[16]

Once again, then, in west Africa as in east, kings who converted to Islam served as links tying a parochial society into a larger world order. But in west Africa, it was not so certain as on the east coast that trade would continue and increase. The Indian Ocean offered calm waters and regular wind patterns to legions of mariners, some of whom were bound to find their ways to east Africa. Though it did not constitute an absolute barrier, the Sahara made travel between north and west Africa a much more difficult affair than sailing the Indian Ocean. Trade across the desert never disappeared completely, but political instability on either side of the desert could severely diminish its volume, with startling cultural results. Thus, as the kingdom of Mali declined in the fifteenth century, conditions in Timbuktu, Jenne, and other trading centers became uncertain enough that the Muslim merchants departed. The kingdom as a whole returned gradually to paganism, and those Muslims who remained lost interest in spreading their faith. The case of west Africa illustrates better perhaps than any other the significance of trade for the spread of Islam to new regions.

The Waning of Indian Cultural Influence

One result of the expansion of Islam between the eleventh and fourteenth centuries was gradual but consistent decline in the influence of Indian cultural traditions, both at home and in foreign lands. During the first millennium C.E., Hinduism and especially Buddhism had spread broadly and influenced beliefs and values throughout Asia. The appearance of Turkish conquerors and the spread of Islam, however, placed Indian traditions under tremendous political and cultural pressure. Islam attracted Indian converts rather slowly, to be sure, but Indian traditions lost the cultural initiative in the face of the more dynamic new faith and its aggressive proponents.

The waning of Indian cultural influence did not result exclusively from foreign developments such as the Turkish expansion and the spread of Islam. To the contrary, indigenous developments worked toward the same end. Most significant of these was the decline of Buddhism in India — or to put it more properly, the absorption of Buddhism into the Hindu tradition from which it had originally emerged. In any case, after the eleventh century, India progressively ceased to be a source of intellectual and cultural leadership for Buddhism. Indian missionaries no longer spread the Buddhist message in foreign lands, and pilgrims no longer found it worthwhile to visit India, for lack of opportunities to learn Buddhist doctrine or to observe rituals at sites of genuine religious authority. Buddhism no longer served to carry Indian cultural influence to foreign lands. Meanwhile, since Hindus had never developed much interest in proselytization, Islam became the principal missionary religion reaching out from the Indian subcontinent.

Whether caused by internal or external developments, the waning of Indian cultural influence in foreign lands manifested itself in two ways. In some places, most notably in China, Buddhism suffered an absolute decline in popularity and influence. In other lands, including China as well as southeast Asia, Indian traditions increasingly entered into cultural compromises with indigenous traditions. This continuing process of syncretism guaranteed the survival of Indian traditions in foreign lands. But in the lack of continuing contact with Indian sources of authority and inspiration, it also led to a progressive decline of the specifically Indian character of originally Indian traditions. Buddhism especially came to reflect the interests and values of other peoples much more than those of its original Indian creators.

Already during the Tang dynasty, as noted in the previous chapter, Buddhism began to encounter serious resistance in China, including opposition sponsored by the imperial court. During the Song dynasty, Chinese Buddhism experienced even more difficulties than during the Tang.[17] The revival of the Confucian civil service examination system attracted intellectually talented Chinese who might otherwise have cast their lots with Buddhism. Meanwhile, the quality of the Buddhist clergy and community declined noticeably, due to Song financial difficulties. Perpetually short of funds, the dynasty sold monastic licenses to individuals who had not undergone thorough education or preparation for their positions. Since the flow of Indian missionaries to China and Chinese pilgrims to India had diminished, and ultimately ceased altogether, there was no external source of correction or inspiration for more conscientious observance of Buddhism in China.

Buddhism certainly did not disappear from China during the Song dynasty, but it increasingly took on the characteristics of Chinese cultural traditions — sometimes at the expense of traditional Buddhist values. The Pure Land and Chan schools continued to be the most popular Buddhist sects in China. Both of them deemphasized texts and doctrine in favor of meditation, faith, intuition, and instantaneous enlightenment. Thus both of them recalled the interests, values, and methods of Daoism at least as much as those of Indian Buddhism. Popular cults of the Song dynasty illustrate in even more dramatic fashion the displacement of Indian Buddhist by traditional Chinese values. Among the most popular of these was the cult of Maitreya, which featured a fat, jovial, worldly monk as the future Buddha. The original Indian Maitreya had represented the future Buddha as a rather serious and austere figure dedicated to high moral standards and salvation. The Maitreya of the Song dynasty, however, clearly enjoyed life: he ate and drank well, and his generous girth bespoke prosperity and leisure; when not laughing he wore a perpetual smile on his face, and groups of children surrounded him wherever he went. The Song Maitreya thus reflected Chinese interests in food and family, retaining little substantive association with Indian Buddhism.

Indian culture had sunk deeper roots in southeast Asia than in China, and so Indian influence did not decline so sharply in the southern lands. Indian legal and political culture had accompanied Hinduism and Buddhism on their travels to southeast Asia. Ac-

cordingly, when Indian religions blended with indigenous traditions, or even went into decline, other Indian traditions continued
to influence southeast Asian culture in an important way. Both in
the islands and on the mainland, for example, southeast Asian
rulers recognized the continuing authority of Indian political traditions. Thus an eleventh-century Javanese king, Erlangga, followed the precepts of the *Arthasastra* and attributed his victories
over his enemies to the sound doctrine of the Indian political treatise. As late as the fourteenth century, the law code of the Maja-
pahit dynasty of Java drew its inspiration primarily from the Laws
of Manu.[18]

Yet in southeast Asia as in China, Indian religions gradually lost
their distinctiveness and merged with indigenous traditions. This
development became clearly noticeable in the thirteenth century,
as Mongol incursions jeopardized political stability in southeast
Asia, while traders established Muslim communities in the region's
commercial centers.[19] The syncretic tendency sometimes led to a
remarkable cultural fusion, as at the kingdom of Singosari, which
ruled much of Java from 1222 to 1293. The Singosari court was
the site of a merger of Hindu, Buddhist, and indigenous traditions.
Court sculptures depicted Hindu and Buddhist personalities, but
they represented indigenous magical and divine powers rather than
Indian values. Meanwhile, the ritual cement for this cultural blend
came from Tantric Buddhism, which supplied Singosari syncretism
with a variety of magical, mystical, alcoholic, and sexual observances.

Thanks to the monumental architectural remains of Angkor, the
Khmer civilization provided an even more spectacular example of
cultural syncretism than did the kingdom of Singosari. As in Java,
the sculpted images at Angkor represented recognizable Hindu and
Buddhist personalities, but behind them stood indigenous interests
and values. Khmer civilization depended for its survival on a sophisticated waterworks — a complex network of reservoirs and canals that enabled the people to capture the waters that arrived with
the monsoons, to store them for months at a time, and to distribute
them to fields during the dry season. The principal function of the
Khmer kings was to ensure fertility and prosperity by serving as an
effective mediator between divine powers and human subjects, a
duty that entailed careful maintenance and regulation of the com-

plex hydraulic system.[20] Indian deities no doubt added to the luster of the Khmer kings, but the society at large placed more value on the indigenous, agricultural religion that sought to guarantee a regular supply of water and sun. If the trappings of exotic doctrines helped the Khmer kings to mediate between divine and human, so much the better. But the water spirit remained the central and pervasive figure of popular religion. As one scholar put it, Angkor the city was

> a system of canals and waterworks which transformed it into a blossoming garden. The labour represented by these works is far more impressive than the building of temples, which were merely chapels crowning a cyclopean undertaking, built at small cost and all the more willingly in that they provided a moral guarantee of success for this deeply religious people.[21]

Nomads and the Cultures of Settled Peoples in Eurasia

Nomads have already played a role of some prominence in this chapter, as Turkish peoples adopted Islam and helped to establish it in India and Anatolia. The vigorous expansion of nomadic peoples and their establishment of large empires between the eleventh and fourteenth centuries ensured that cross-cultural encounters would take place on a systematic basis throughout central Asia and east Asia. The experiences of steppe peoples such as Khitans and Mongols differed considerably, though, from those of Turks in the more southern and western regions. Turkish conquerors attacked the established religious and cultural order in India, and in Anatolia they used their newly acquired Islamic faith even more explicitly as an ideological weapon. The Turks' commitment to Islam provided them with a rationale and justification for a spirited attack on the Hindu and Christian cultural establishments that they encountered. This cultural dimension of their expansion naturally complemented their political and military campaigns. It also helped to secure the establishment of Islamic faith and institutions in new lands.

In central and east Asia, nomadic peoples did not undertake the sort of cultural campaign that Turkish conquerors did in India and

Anatolia. They naturally took their beliefs and values with them on their imperial campaigns, but they did not attempt to displace existing cultural establishments or to impose foreign values on the peoples they conquered. Indeed, more often than not, they eventually adopted the cultures of the settled peoples whom they ruled. Of course nomadic peoples left their marks on the sedentary civilizations that they conquered. But their influence did not carry far beyond the realm of economy and material culture. Generally speaking, then, nomadic peoples in central and east Asia did not spread cultural traditions so much as adopt those that they encountered and found attractive or useful for their purposes.

Nomadic tribes and confederations had long dominated the central Asian steppes. As they organized political life on progressively larger scales, they established powerful states that threatened sedentary civilizations in China and the Middle East. With the collapse of the Tang dynasty, for example, the Khitan people established the Liao dynasty (907–1125) in the steppelands north of China. The Jurchen, a seminomadic people from Manchuria, conquered the Khitans, ousted Song authority from northern China, and established their own Jin dynasty (1115–1234) in northern China itself. Ultimately, the Mongols and their nomadic allies overran both steppe and settled regions and dominated most of Eurasia. The Mongols conquered the Jin state in northern China in 1234. By 1279 they had toppled the Song dynasty and brought all of China under Mongol control. For almost a century thereafter, the Mongols dominated political and military affairs in east Asia, especially during the period of their Yuan dynasty (1279–1368) in China. Meanwhile, during the early thirteenth century, Mongols established a presence in eastern Europe and the Middle East. By 1240 the Mongols of the Golden Horde had imposed their authority in Russia, and in 1258 the Mongol general Hülegü sacked Baghdad, put an end to the Abbasid caliphate, and established the ilkhanate of Persia as a kingdom for himself.

All of these conquests set the stage for systematic encounters and cultural dealings between the nomadic and the sedentary peoples of Eurasia. Most complex of these encounters, due to the variety of cultural alternatives available, were those that took place in and around China. During the Liao dynasty, when the Khitan nomads ruled a powerful kingdom north of China, relations between Chinese and nomads closely resembled those that developed during the Han dynasty between Chinese and Xiongnu. A certain amount of cultural transfer and exchange took place, especially in border regions, but for the most part the period saw the coexistence of Khitan culture in the north and Chinese in the south. Cultural exchange intensified during the Jin dynasty, when the seminomadic Jurchen ruled not only their native Manchuria but also north China itself. Perhaps the most notable development of this period was the absorption of the Jurchen into Chinese society and culture. The potential for cultural exchange reached its high point, however, during the period when the Mongols dominated most of Eurasia. The relative safety of roads encouraged traders and missionaries to undertake long-distance travel. Meanwhile, the Mongols themselves moved certain peoples around their empire for military or administrative purposes. As a result, China and Mongolia became rather cosmopolitan lands, especially during the Mongol Yuan dynasty in China. The following section will examine these patterns of cross-cultural encounter between Chinese, nomads, and others, and will offer an explanation of the sometimes surprising results.

The Khitans largely retained their traditional ways in spite of dealings with the Chinese.[22] They looked to the steppes for military leadership; they continued to hunt and herd; and they organized their political life on a traditional tribal basis. In the northern regions of their Liao state, Khitan culture persisted in uninterrupted and undiluted form. The occasional presence of silk represented the extent of Chinese influence there. Intermingling and intermarriage resulted in a great deal more cultural exchange in the southern regions, approaching the borders of Song China, but even there Chinese and Khitan peoples largely went their separate ways. Chinese living in the Liao realm largely spoke their native language but often took Khitan honorific names, dressed in Khitan fashion, married Khitan women, and developed a taste for certain Khitan activities such as riding, hunting, and fishing. Meanwhile, a certain amount of influence passed also from China to the Khitans. Imperial ceremonies at the Liao court derived mostly from Chinese practice. In the early tenth century, a Khitan written language and script was elaborated, partly on the model of Chinese and Uighur scripts. With Chinese language, there came also the influence of

Chinese values, at least in certain quarters of Khitan society. For the most part, the Khitans held to their traditional reverence for the sun, the heavens, and spirits that they recognized, and they continued to observe ceremonies conducted by their shamans. Some Khitans found Buddhism adaptable to their religious traditions, but Confucianism and Daoism were cultivated almost exclusively by Chinese living in Khitan society.

Yet occasionally signs appear that indicate the influence of Chinese values among Khitan elites. The most remarkable of these signs occurs in a document revealing the unmistakably Confucian views of Xiao Yixin, a Khitan royal princess. The document, dated about the mid- to late eleventh century, records a dispute between Xiao and her brothers' wives at the Liao court. The other women held that the elimination of evil spirits was an important means of gaining the favor of one's husband, but Xiao thought differently: "The repression of evil spirits is not as good as proper behavior." When questioned about this opinion, she explained:

> To cultivate yourself with purity, to honor elders with respect, to serve husbands with tenderness, to direct subordinates with generosity, and not to let gentlemen see one frivolous—this is proper behavior. It naturally gains the respect of one's husband. Are you not ashamed to gain favor by repressing evil spirits?

The document plainly communicates the point that Xiao held unusual views: "The listeners were deeply mortified."[23] It looks as though Chinese values attracted a few of the Khitan ruling class but did not win widespread allegiance even in elite society. Indeed, even in elite society, communication between Khitans and Chinese was a haphazard affair. Even after two centuries of encounter, the last emperor of the Liao dynasty did not realize that his Chinese subjects gagged at the thought of drinking kumiss—fermented mare's milk that was a staple in the diet of steppe peoples and that Liao courtiers continued to enjoy.

The experience of the Jurchen differed significantly from that of the Khitans. Two considerations help to account for the difference. In the first place, the Jurchen were not steppe nomads, like the Khitans, but rather a seminomadic people from Manchuria. They depended heavily upon agriculture, and even before their encounter with Chinese, many of them had settled in villages and even walled towns. For most Jurchen, their nomadic heritage survived principally in the form of hunting, herding, and sometimes migration to more attractive regions. Though highly mobile when compared to Chinese, the Jurchen had enough experience with sedentary agricultural life that they were able to adapt reasonably well to Chinese society. In the second place, unlike the Khitans, the Jurchen did not stop at the borders of China. In the twelfth century, their state included not only their native Manchuria but also northern China down to the Huai River. Thus they dealt much more directly with Chinese than had the Khitans, and they had to develop methods of effectively governing Chinese. This entailed considerable accommodation to Chinese cultural standards. The result, over a long term, was the effective absorption of the Jurchen into Chinese society and their conversion by assimilation to Chinese cultural standards.

Almost immediately upon the conquest of northern China, the Jurchen ruling elite sought to legitimize its rule by adopting the symbols and methods of Chinese authority.[24] Imperial ceremonies, political organization, recruitment of scholarly bureaucrats, governance in accordance with Confucian ethics and traditional Chinese law — in all these respects the Jurchen modeled their rule on Chinese examples. Chinese values naturally accompanied the other elements of Chinese culture, and in some cases they thoroughly displaced traditional Jurchen culture. The early Jurchen emperor Wanyan Dan (ruled 1123–1149) reportedly read Chinese literature, wrote Chinese poetry, gave up his Jurchen manners, and regarded his ancestors as rude barbarians. Likewise, Xiyin, a Jurchen shaman with great political influence, collected the Chinese classics and provided his offspring with a Chinese education. On a popular level, too, Chinese influence shaped the Jurchen experience. During the century that the Jin dynasty ruled northern China, the Jurchen people there came to speak Chinese, wear Chinese clothes, marry Chinese spouses, raise their children in Chinese society, and convert to Buddhism or Daoism. A few traditional Jurchen customs survived into the period of the Ming dynasty, but over the long term, the Jurchen people who settled in northern China gradually became absorbed into Chinese society and culture.

The Mongols' relationship with the Chinese recalled that of the Khitans in some respects and that of the Jurchen in others.[25] The

Mongols came to China with a cultural and social background very similar to that of the Khitans, their cousins from the steppes. Their nomadic customs and values did not naturally incline them to appreciate or adopt Chinese ways, but like the Jurchen, the Mongols conquered China and soon enough found it necessary to make some accommodations in order to govern effectively. In time, some of them fell into the orbit of Chinese culture and society, though not so many as in the case of the Jurchen.

When they conquered the Jin dynasty and moved into northern China, in the early thirteenth century, the Mongols exalted the military virtues of the steppes — riding, hunting, fighting, and the forging of alliances between the noble leaders of the various tribes of Mongolian-speaking peoples. They knew little if anything of Buddhism, much less of the Confucian and Daoist traditions. Their religious observances centered on the shaman, who communicated with spirits, offered sacrifices, interceded with the gods on behalf of his companions, and divined the future. The Mongols recognized numerous deities — some of them powerful gods, others lesser spirits but still capable of influencing individual human fortunes — and they suspected the existence of others as well. Their densely populated pantheon perhaps accounts for the toleration they exhibited toward the various institutional faiths that they encountered while building their empire. Though little interested in adopting the cultural traditions of settled peoples, they certainly had no desire to attack established traditions or to impose their own beliefs and values on the peoples whom they conquered.

When they entered China, the Mongols had to develop policies for administering the institutionalized cultural traditions that they found. The earliest such policy derived from the personal interest — almost a whim — of Genghis Khan, conqueror of northern China. During the course of a long campaign in Persia and Afghanistan, Genghis felt the pangs of mortality and decided to call the noted Daoist sage Chang Chun to his camp. He dispatched a flattering letter to the sage acknowledging his need, as a ruler with heavy responsibilities, for sound advice: "To cross a river we make boats and rudders. Likewise we invite sage men, and choose out assistants for keeping the empire in good order." Chang Chun first balked at Genghis's invitation, but eventually agreed to undertake the long journey. In the year 1222, he met several times with Genghis in Afghanistan and Samarkand. Genghis's main concern was to learn the secret of immortality from the wise man. Chang Chun disappointed him in this respect but nonetheless won the conqueror's favor and admiration. Genghis generously rewarded the sage for his advice and ordered his doctrine to be recorded in both Chinese and Mongolian languages. Unfortunately, he also regarded Chang Chun's teachings as mysterious and secret, and he strictly limited access to them. As a result, no details of his advice survive.[26]

Genghis's interest in Daoism set the stage for a bitter controversy between Buddhists and Daoists, a contest that caused considerable difficulties for the Mongol rulers of China. Upon his return to China, Chang Chun received an appointment as supervisor of monks and clergy, including Buddhists, Nestorians, and others as well as Daoists. The arrangement was especially offensive to the Buddhists, since Chang Chun seized many of their properties and converted them to Daoist use. His appointment thus helped to bring Buddhists and Daoists into an extended dispute concerning points of doctrine as well as the disposition of religious properties. The controversy culminated in several formal debates held between 1255 and 1258 in the presence of Genghis Khan's successors, Möngke and Kubilai. By this time the Mongols had begun to feel more attraction to egalitarian Buddhism than to native Chinese cultural traditions — especially the Confucian but to a lesser extent the Daoist as well — that regarded Chinese as superior and nomads as inferior, barbarian peoples. At one of the formal debates, Möngke Khan expressed his own views in picturesque fashion. He recognized the claims of Daoists, Confucians, Nestorians, and Muslims but found none of them so persuasive as those of the Buddhists. Holding up his hand, he then likened Buddhism to the palm and the other religions to the fingers that branched off from the common source.

During the reign of Kubilai Khan (1260–1294), the Mongol ruling class broadened its cultural interests. Kubilai himself observed the traditional Confucian rituals and took pains not to disappoint the educated Chinese elite. He had little appreciation for Daoism, but he occasionally sponsored the building of Daoist temples in exchange for public recognition of his authority. He showed special favor to Buddhists: even before becoming great khan, he had sided with Buddhists in their dispute with the Daoists, and he appreciated their efforts to provide ideological justification for his rule. But Kubilai also protected Muslims, many of whom he employed in his government. He even looked with interest on Christianity, and in conversations with Marco Polo and other westerners, he went so far as to predict mass conversions of his subjects to their faith. Kubilai patently formulated his cultural policy with political considerations in mind: as lord of an enormous, multicultural, polyglot empire, he sought to win the respect of all the various peoples of his realm, or at least to avoid alienating them through neglect or insult of their cultural traditions.[27]

The single tradition that drew most benefit from Mongol rule in Asia was Buddhism, especially Lamaist Buddhism of Tibetan origin. Deeply tinged by Tantric influences, Lamaist Buddhism featured a variety of ritual sexual practices and a strong interest in magic. It is possible that the Mongols responded to the Lamaist tradition because of its superficial resemblance to their own shamanist culture. In any case, they paid little attention to the fine points of Buddhist doctrine. Instead, the Mongol ruling elite found the Lamaist tradition attractive primarily because of its political uses. Tibetan princes endeared themselves to Mongol rulers by adopting them into the family of Buddhist universal emperors, thus providing a sense of legitimacy for their rule. Lamaist clergy associated the Mongol khans with boddhisatvas and even recognized them as incarnations of the Buddha. Their reward was strong and consistent support of the Mongol ruling elite for the Lamaist tradition. The Mongol masses showed little interest in Buddhism or any other foreign cultural tradition until the sixteenth century, when a Lamaist revival swept the steppes and largely displaced the Mongols' traditional shamanism. Meanwhile, however, the attraction of the khans to Lamaism illustrates well the tendency of the Mongols to adopt cultural traditions of the settled peoples whom they conquered and to use them for their own purposes.[28]

Though not personally attracted to it, the Mongols even found some use for the Confucian tradition. The most important personality in this connection was a Khitan noble named Yelü Qucai (1189–1243).[29] Born near Beijing during the Jin dynasty, Yelü received a formal Confucian education and served in the Jurchen bureaucracy. Like most other officials, he suffered greatly during and after the Mongol conquest of northern China. Indeed, for three years he devoted himself to the study of Buddhism, from which he took some comfort. In the year 1218, though, he re-entered public life when Genghis Khan called him into his government. For the next twenty years Yelü served as secretary, adviser, and an increasingly important minister to Genghis and his immediate successor, Ögedei Khan. During that period he helped in several ways to mitigate the difficulties of Mongol rule in China. During the 1230s, for example, he opposed a party of militant Mongols who wanted to annihilate the Jin dynasty and turn northern China into grazing lands. He argued that a traditional Chinese taxation system would enrich the Mongols far more than would the militants' radical plans. His arguments persuaded Ögedei, and tax receipts came in as he had predicted. As a result, his credibility rose, and he received appointments to high offices.

Yelü often used his influence on behalf of the Confucian cultural tradition. He intervened in the cases of numerous Confucian scholars — including a direct descendant of Confucius in the fifty-first generation — in an effort to spare them punishment and persecution by the new Mongol rulers. He helped some to obtain posts as bureaucrats in Mongol service or even as tutors to Mongol princes. He worked also to reinstate the Confucian examination system, which the Mongols had abolished, as a means of recruiting sophisticated government officials educated in the Confucian tradition.

By no means did Yelü Confucianize the Mongols. During his official career he struggled continuously against parties of militant Mongols who sought to rule China according to the principles of steppe politics. Eventually, during the last years of Ögedei's reign, his enemies undermined his position and eased him out of the government. In the absence of any voice urging moderation, the Mongols embarked upon a policy of harsh and sometimes reckless exploitation of their Chinese subjects and resources. Even during the reign of Kubilai Khan — perhaps the high point of Mongol rule in China — serious tensions strained relations between Mongols and Chinese. Marco Polo put the point in plain terms: "The Cathayans detested the Grand Kaan's rule because he set over them governors who were Tartars, or still more frequently Saracens, and these they would not endure, for they were treated by them just like slaves."[30]

As the Mongol rulers of China honored the various cultural

traditions generated by settled civilizations of Asia, and sometimes even adopted them for their own purposes, their cousins in Persia found uses for Islam in their part of the Mongol realm. In 1253, the Mongol prince Hülegü departed the Mongol capital at Kara-korum with the intention of subduing the Abbasid caliphate. By 1258, he had toppled the dynasty, executed the caliph, ravaged Baghdad, and begun to carve out a state for himself as the Mongol ilkhan of Persia. From this base, Hülegü and his successors men-aced much of the Middle East. During the early years of their state, they posed a serious threat especially to the local Islamic establishment, which had vigorously resisted their invasion. The early ilkhans sponsored the reintroduction of Buddhism to Persia, and they allowed Nestorian Christians to practice their faith openly.

In 1295, however, the Ilkhan Ghazan converted to Islam, and most of his fellow Mongols in Persia followed his lead.[31] Ghazan's motive was largely political — he needed the support of the local Muslim community against the Egyptian Mamluks, who sought to organize an anti-Mongol campaign on the foundation of Islam — and he seems to have retained his interest and commitment to shamanism even after his conversion. Whatever his motive, though, Ghazan's conversion had large cultural ramifications. Christians, Jews, and Buddhists all faced intense persecution. A Syriac docu-ment records the fury unleashed against the Nestorian community during the late thirteenth and early fourteenth centuries: when the Nestorians lost the protection of the ilkhans, Muslim crowds de-stroyed their churches, looted their homes, and assaulted individu-als, many of whom were killed or enslaved.[32] Meanwhile, the Mon-gols progressively assimilated into the Islamic culture of Persia. By the fifteenth century, they no longer maintained a distinctive iden-tity in Persia, having long since blended into the Turkish commu-nity there.

Thus in both China and Persia the Mongols found it necessary or useful to adopt the cultural traditions of the settled, civilized peoples whom they ruled. Marco Polo expressed this point in plain and straightforward terms. During the late thirteenth century he had observed the Mongols at close quarters in both China and Persia. After describing the Mongols' traditional customs in his memoirs, he remarked on the changes that recent decades had brought:

All this that I have been telling you is true of the manners and customs of the genuine Tartars. But I must add also that in these days they are greatly degenerated; for those who are settled in Cathay have taken up the practices of the Idolaters of the country, and have abandoned their own institutions; whilst those who have settled in the Levant have adopted the customs of the Saracens.[33]

Quite apart from their own experiences, the Mongols sponsored an enormous amount of long-distance travel and intermingling of other peoples from different cultural traditions. Especially notable was a large amount of travel to China by peoples from points west: central Asia, the Middle East, and even western Europe. Thus Wang Li (1314–1389), a sinicized native of the western region of Jiangxi, offered the remarkable observation quoted at the head of this chapter. Wang Li made his point in the course of reflections on public cemeteries in China. In many of them he found signs that natives of central Asia and western lands had adopted Chinese burial customs. Already before the Mongols' conquests, he noted, peoples from western lands had appeared frequently in China and contributed their services there. By the time of Kubilai Khan, however, China and the rest of Eurasia had become much more tightly integrated than before. Indeed, to quote him again,

the land within the Four Seas had become the territory of one family, civilization had spread everywhere, and no more barriers existed. For people in search of fame and wealth in north and south, a journey of a thousand *li* was like a trip next door, while a journey of ten thousand *li* constituted just a neighborly jaunt. Hence, among people of the Western Regions who served at court, or who studied in our south-land, many forgot the region of their birth, and took delight in living among our rivers and lakes. As they settled down in China for a long time, some became advanced in years, their families grew, and being far from home, they had no desire to be buried in their fatherland. Brotherhood among peoples has certainly reached a new plane.[34]

Wang Li's reflections suggest that a good deal of conversion by assimilation took place during the Mongol era, as western peoples found China to their liking and adopted Chinese ways as a result. By no means did all visitors from western lands find China so appealing. The Mongols, for example, lived in China as long as it formed a part of their Eurasian empire. But with the collapse of their Yuan dynasty, they returned to the steppes, taking with them many of their Khitan, Turkish, Alan, and other nomadic allies. A good deal of evidence survives, however, to show that when small groups of westerners went to China and remained there over a long term, they often found it desirable to observe Chinese ways.[35] Some westerners adopted Daoism or Chan Buddhism, which of course represented a thoroughly sinicized form of the Buddhist faith. In many cases, though, especially those involving educated foreigners who hoped to find bureaucratic posts in China, they gravitated toward the Confucian tradition. Peoples of Nestorian, Islamic, Buddhist, and Manichaean faiths all studied the Confucian classics and honored the tradition. In some cases, even with limited access to formal instruction, they won recognition as *jinshi*, the supreme academic rank of the Confucian educational system. According to a native Chinese scholar, they had great literary and scholarly potential:

> On reading the poems of Ang-fu, I became convinced that scholarship is capable of transforming a man's personality. Ang-fu issued from the aristocratic class of the Hsi Jung [a tribe on the western frontier of China]. Their clothes were made of felt and fur; their drink kumiss; their homes depended on water and pasture; they shot game from the backs of fleet horses; they filled themselves with meat, and were men of courage. These were the customs of his people. But Ang-fu devoted himself to brush and ink. He read widely and took on the life of a scholar. He composed poetry and [popular verses] which were all outstanding, vigorous and beautiful, unmatched by Confucian scholars of several generations past. Remarkable![36]

In a few cases, surviving evidence even sheds a bit of light on the motives of individuals who underwent conversion by assimilation to Chinese ways. Especially articulate on this point was the Öngut Turk Ma Zuchang, a Nestorian Christian whose family had come to China about the late eleventh century. Some of his ancestors had served as bureaucrats for the Liao and Jin dynasties, and he took special pride in his family's adoption of Confucian ways:

> How admirable was our forefather!
> Here for a hundred years.
> The succession of caps and gowns —
> It was he who began it.
> Many are the princes and dukes of this world

Who came under the influence of China.
But because they did not discard their customs,
Their Chinese learning did not continue.

Another set of verses provides more detail about the experiences of his family:

Seven generations ago
My ancestors were raising horses west of the
    River T'ao.
Six generations back they moved to T'ien-shan;
Daily they listened to the beat of the drums.
When the royal house of Chin hunted on the
    river banks
My forefathers were among the first to follow it.
The *Shih* and the *Shu* [Confucian classics]
    enriched us for a hundred years.
We are not like the pelicans which roost on the
    beams and just happen to wet their wings. . . .
Because I have been brought up under the
    family influence,
I have exerted every effort to climb the terrace
    steps of Confucius.
In spreading culture I have assisted in the
    progress of the times.
Their brightness corresponds to resting places
    of the moon [37]

In the case of Ma Zuchang, acceptance of a new cultural tradition seems to correlate reasonably closely to his own career and his family's appointment to government positions. In other cases, though, it is clear that intellectual, moral, and spiritual concerns led individuals to experimentation with different cultural traditions. Ding Henian (1335–1424), for example, came from a family of Muslim merchants who traded across central Asia during the period of Mongol domination there. Though quite wealthy, he closely studed the Confucian classics with a prominent teacher — and with his sister, who by some unknown means acquired an impressive literary education. When asked why he did so, he replied that he wanted to honor his family, which never before had produced distinguished scholarly or literary figures. But the fall of the Mongols' Yuan dynasty (1368) seems to have shaken his intellectual confidence, and he became progressively interested in

Buddhism. Eventually, he even opened a Buddhist school and composed several sets of verses announcing his allegiance to the new faith.

So little information survives concerning Ding that it is difficult to explain satisfactorily his cultural odyssey from Islam to Confucianism and Buddhism. A social concern for the reputation of his family perhaps helps to account for Ding's interest in Confucianism. He certainly did justice to the Chinese tradition: he wrote sophisticated Chinese poetry and prose, strictly observed Confucian ethics and values, and took a *jinshi* degree along with three of his brothers. It seems that he first turned to Buddhism when he sought refuge in a Buddhist monastery in order to escape some enemies. Before too long, however, he became intrigued with Buddhism and committed his last years to its study. He corresponded with at least thirty-one monks and wrote numerous poems expressing his devotion to his new faith. From one set of verses in particular it appears that Ding underwent a thorough conversion to Buddhism:

> The autumn moon is empty and bright;
> The Ch'an heart is pure and clean.
> Both the heart and the moon are without deficiencies,
> They form a great round mirror,
> Shedding their streaming light on the myriad objects,
> They make all the objects fresh and lustrous.
> The reflected shadow is in a thousand rivers,
> And they are completely illuminated.
> If the dust of sentiment be not swept away,
> It might soon obliterate one's true character.
> Therefore, the success or failure of students of the Way
> Depends upon whether or not they do this.
> The body may be looked upon as being hollow and empty.
> Nothing is gained and nothing proved.
> Great is Han-shan weng [a famous Buddhist hermit];
> He has enabled you to have peace of heart.[38]

Whatever the precise personal explanation for the cultural odysseys of Ma Zuchang, Ding Henian, and others like them, one point remains clear: except for the Mongols' pacification of Eurasia and their sponsorship of travel across the landmass, cultural exchange could not have taken place on the scale that it did. The Mongols' political achievement underlay cross-cultural encounters of intensity high enough to bring about widespread cultural experimentation and even cross-cultural conversion.

Even in the Mongol age, however, cross-cultural conversion had its limits. It is not surprising to find that western and central Asians who settled in China often adopted Chinese cultural traditions. It was far more difficult during the century of Mongol dominance in China for western peoples to attract Chinese interest in their own traditions. The experiences of Roman Catholic Christians in the Middle East and China will help to illuminate the difficulties of cross-cultural conversion during this era.

Crusaders and Missionaries

As mariners established dense networks of trade and travel in the basin of the Indian Ocean, and as nomadic peoples brought the steppes and civilized lands of Asia under their domination, important changes in western lands enabled Europeans to enter more deeply than ever before into the circuits of trade and travel that linked Eurasia. An earlier generation of historians thoroughly explored the economic, social, and technological foundations that underlay the dynamism of medieval Europe. As a result, scholars now understand quite well that certain agricultural, commercial, and military developments — many of them sparked by techniques that diffused from the Middle East and Asia — stood behind the crusades, long-distance trade, and other expansive ventures of medieval Europeans.[39] The most important of these ventures for present purposes were the crusades and missionary efforts to spread Roman Catholic Christianity to Asian lands. The following section will analyze the resulting cross-cultural encounters in the light of the other such encounters of the period from 1000 to 1350.

European expansion began in Europe itself.[40] Already by the mid-eleventh century, ambitious feudal nobles began to organize military expeditions against Muslim states in Spain and Sicily. They readily won the support of church authorities, who welcomed both the opportunity to extend the reach of their spiritual authority and the prospect of having Christians for their political neighbors. As a result, Europeans undertook officially sanctioned holy wars designed to conquer Spain and Sicily and to Christianize them at the same time. In both lands they mounted successful campaigns to induce the conquered Muslim populations to convert to Christianity. These campaigns merit attention both as efforts that precipitated intense cross-cultural encounters and as preludes to the massive crusades that Christians dispatched to the Middle East.

In Spain, the Umayyad caliphate of Córdoba collapsed in 1031, and a series of weak successor states tempted Christian ambitions. The resulting *reconquista* brought Iberia gradually but inevitably under Christian domination. Military conquests led to cultural contests, as Christians confronted large numbers of Muslims and Jews who resisted assimilation. In some ways the *reconquista* resembled the Turkish conquest of Anatolia. Castilians, who led the drive to conquer and Christianize Iberia, were not nomads, but neither had they developed an urban society. Compounded of Cantabrian and Basque elements, they were a people of shepherds and peasants, unsophisticated and even rude by comparison with the settled, city-oriented civilization at whose expense they expanded. Like the Turks, who also attacked a sophisticated urban civilization in Anatolia, the Castilians used their faith as an ideological weapon in their campaign. They set as their goal not only the conquest but also the outright Christianization of Iberia.

Recent scholarship has thrown a great deal of useful light on the cultural dimensions of this confrontation.[41] As in all frontier societies, individuals found and explored opportunities on both sides of the cultural boundary. There are numerous recorded cases of individuals' conversions to another religion, followed by the same individuals' reconversions to their inherited faiths. Castilian power, however, ensured that the long-range advantage in Iberia lay with the Christians. Thus, in Valencia, for example, hard on the heels of the conquest there came systematic efforts to convert the Muslim population to Christianity. About thirty Dominicans preached assiduously throughout Valencia during the mid- to late thirteenth century. When addressing intellectuals, they employed high-powered, rational arguments derived from Aristotle, whose thought commanded great respect in Islamic cultural circles. When addressing others, they often spoke to captive audiences surrounded by crowds of Christians, whose boisterous behavior encouraged many hasty conversions to Christianity. In the early days following the conquest, one social incentive in particular encouraged conversion: adoption of Christianity brought liberation for Muslim slaves. Christian lords themselves sometimes hindered conversion in order to protect their supplies of labor, to the point that they eventually won the right to keep recent converts in slavery. Nonetheless, the lure of liberation continued to attract slaves of non-Christian lords. As in other cases of economically or socially induced conversion discussed earlier, the original motivation for conversion hardly mattered in the long run, as Iberian society progressively took on Christian coloration.

Though not so well studied, the experience of Sicily seems to have resembled that of Spain.[42] Following their conquest of the island, the new Norman rulers offered inducements and applied pressures in the search for converts. Thanks no doubt to its relatively compact size and geographical unity, Sicily underwent a much more rapid process of cultural transformation than did Anatolia and Spain. The Muslim pilgrim and traveler Ibn Jubayr told of numerous conversions in Sicily of the late twelfth century: some Muslims turned to Christianity as a result of political pressure; others adopted the new faith after bitter family quarrels. Whatever the individual reasons, the numbers of converts had grown so large in Trapani that the remaining Muslims there feared that their community would soon disappear altogether. Especially devout Muslims went to extreme lengths to protect their faith; in an effort to ensure that his daughter would not convert to Christianity, Ibn Jubayr reported, one man sought to marry her to a fellow Muslim scheduled to depart for the kingdom of Granada.[43]

And yet in both Spain and Sicily, despite the political and military forces favoring conversion to Christianity, a complete cultural and social transformation required a very long time. Arabic language and Islamic institutions survived intense pressures in thirteenth- and fourteenth-century Spain. Muslim *mudejar* society there succumbed to efforts at Christianization only in the fifteenth and sixteenth centuries. Meanwhile, alongside an alarmingly high rate of conversion to Christianity, Ibn Jubayr found abundant signs of Islamic survival and resistance during his sojourn of about three months in Sicily. He encountered Muslims observing their faith openly and in great numbers throughout the island. More strikingly, at the court of King William II himself, he found nominal converts to Christianity who continued to practice Islam in secret. Servants, pages, chamberlains, and even ministers, he said, fasted during Ramadan, gave alms, intervened on behalf of Muslim prisoners, and said their daily prayers. Ibn Jubayr spoke at length with one of the most important pages at the Norman court, who eagerly inquired about the pilgrim's visit to Mecca. "You can boldly display your faith in Islam," the page said:

> But we must conceal our faith, and, fearful of our lives, must adhere to the worship of God and the discharge of our religious duties in secret. We are bound in the possession of an infidel who has placed on our necks the noose of bondage. Our whole purpose therefore is to be blessed by meeting pilgrims such as you, to ask for their prayers and be happy in what precious objects from the holy shrines they can give us to serve us as instruments of faith, and as treasures on our bier (in token of the life to come).

Ibn Jubayr commiserated with his companion, told him stories about his pilgrimage, and left with him some of the mementos he had brought from Mecca.[44]

If conversion and social transformation proceeded slowly in Spain and Sicily, lands conquered by Christian armies, it should come as no surprise that Christianity brought about little long-term cultural change in the Levant and Middle East, even within the states that crusaders established around Jerusalem, Antioch, and Edessa.[45] Chronicles and documents show that Muslim converts served in crusader armies, and the objections of Christian lords show that Muslim slaves frequently sought conversion as an avenue to liberation. As in the case of other religions in other lands, early converts to Christianity in the crusader kingdoms seem to have come from the very high and the very low social classes, so that they represented those looking to maintain their status under new circumstances and those hoping to improve their condition by taking advantage of new opportunities.

It is certainly possible that some conversions came about because of genuine moral or spiritual conviction. The Arab gentleman Usamah Ibn Munqidh recorded the case of a captive Christian boy taken with his mother into the household of Usamah's father. The boy accepted Islam, said his prayers, observed the fasts, learned stonecutting, and eventually took a Muslim wife, by whom he had two sons. When the youngsters reached five or six years of age, the father took his family and all his goods and joined the crusaders, in whose company he and his sons converted to Christianity. Usamah did not say whether social or spiritual considerations stood behind the conversion, but contented himself with a curse: "May Allah, therefore, purify the world from such people!"[46] It is possible that some social incentive or economic problem or family quarrel led to these conversions, but it is also conceivable that residual memory of a childhood faith prompted the return to Christianity. Whatever the explanation in this particular case, it seems unwise to rule out the possibility that spiritually motivated conversions occasionally took place in the crusaders' states. Yet it is clear that in no part of the Levant or Middle East did there occur a large-scale conversion to Christianity.

Indeed, the crusades might well have produced more recruits for Islam than for Christianity. Like other cross-cultural clashes, the crusades offered opportunities for all talented parties who would exchange one cultural allegiance for another. If Muslim warriors bolted and entered crusader armies, Christians did the same. The heroism and gallantry of Saladin seems to have been especially effective in drawing Christian soldiers into Muslim ranks. In one especially notable case, an English Templar, Robert of St. Albans, converted to Islam in 1185, joined Saladin's forces, and later married Saladin's granddaughter. In some cases coercion or military threats encouraged Christians to turn to Islam. During the siege of Acre (1189–1191), for example, many Christians fled the city, sorely afflicted by famine and disease. Some eventually returned; others lived as Christians among Muslims; but at least a few converted to Islam. In any case, by various means and for various reasons, large numbers of Christians who traveled to eastern parts found their ways into the house of Islam. One contemporary estimated the number of Christian renegades in fifteenth-century Cairo at twenty-five thousand![47]

Whatever the motivations that prompted individual Christians to convert to Islam, it seems clear that to some extent, European crusaders underwent a process of conversion by assimilation to the cultural standards of the Levant. A few sources of information survive to throw light on this process. One especially interesting reflection by Fulcher of Chartres bears a close look. Fulcher served as chaplain to Baldwin of Boulogne, first crusader king of Jerusalem, and he composed an important account of the first crusade. Writing about 1126 or 1127, barely thirty years since crusaders had begun to arrive in eastern lands, Fulcher reflected on the remarkable cultural transformations he had witnessed:

> For we who were Occidentals have now become Orientals. He who was a Roman or a Frank has in this land been made into a Galilean or a Palestinean. He who was of Rheims or Chartres has now become a citizen of Tyre or Antioch. We have already forgotten the places of our birth; already these are unknown to many of us or not mentioned any more. Some already possess homes or households by inheritance. Some have taken wives not only of their own people but Syrians or Armenians or even Saracens who have obtained the grace of baptism. . . . People use eloquence and idioms of diverse languages in conversing back and forth. Words of different languages have become common property known to each nationality, and mutual faith unites those who are ignorant of their descent. . . . He who was born a stranger is now as one born here; he who was born an alien has become as a native.[48]

Usamah Ibn Munqidh offered several observations that reinforce Fulcher's points. Writing approximately a half-century later than Fulcher, Usamah noticed sharp differences between crusaders who had recently arrived and those seasoned by long experience in eastern lands: "Everyone who is a fresh immigrant from the Frankish lands is ruder in character than those who have become acclimatized and have held long association with the Moslems." He cited several examples of offensive behavior on the part of overzealous crusaders who had recently arrived. On the other hand, he mentioned the case of an unnamed knight who had come to Syria on one of the crusaders' earliest expeditions and who had become quite comfortable indeed with local Muslims and their ways. He set an excellent table, which he shared with Muslims. He allayed their dietary concerns by pointing out that he employed Egyptian women as cooks, never partook of Frankish food, and never allowed pork into his house. After one such meal, he went to some additional trouble to protect Usamah's servant from a crowd of boisterous Franks, who accused the man of killing a Christian.[49]

Finally there is the testimony of Jacques de Vitry, who lived almost ten years in Syria and Egypt and who served as bishop of Acre from 1216 to 1228. In a letter composed shortly after his arrival at Acre, in late 1216 or early 1217, Jacques offered an extremely pessimistic assessment of the people whom he encountered there. It is perhaps not surprising that he complained about Jacobites, Nestorians, Armenians, and other Christians who employed rites different from those of the Roman church. But he also found great fault with westerners who had adopted foreign ways. Most disappointing were those whom he called the Suriani and the Pullani. By Suriani he meant westerners who had lived among Muslims so long that they had forgotten their native religion and culture. They used leavened bread in the sacrament and allowed priests to marry, in the manner of the Greek church, and they veiled their daughters. By Pullani Jacques meant half-westerners born in the holy land — presumably from liaisons between crusaders and local women — who had never become socialized as Christians at all. They never contracted respectable marriages, he said, and never heard the word of God; instead they lost themselves in lust and devoted their lives to the pursuit of luxury.[50] Small wonder that Jacques returned to Europe in 1225 and resigned his post as bishop of Acre in 1228.

Thus, from radically different points of view, three witnesses — Fulcher, Usamah, and Jacques — testified to a process by which western Christians gradually entered Islamic society. Vastly outnumbered by indigenous Muslims and unable to bring overwhelming military force to bear, as they had in Spain and Sicily, Christians in the holy land had no alternative but to adjust to a new society and culture or return to Europe. Those who adjusted did so by learning the local languages, taking local spouses, observing local diets, and at least tolerating if not adopting local faiths. In short, they underwent a process of conversion by assimilation to the standards of a different cultural tradition.

Whether successful or not, efforts to spread Christianity in Spain, Sicily, and the Middle East all depended heavily on sustained military and political support. In other, more distant lands, Christian missions had no such support. Not surprisingly, they largely failed in their goal to win converts. Their experiences nonetheless repay examination because they throw light on the dynamics of cross-cultural encounters during the period 1000 to 1350. The Roman

Catholic church dispatched numerous missions during the course
of these centuries to Persia, Ethiopia, and India. Better known,
however, were several missions to China during the era of Mongol
domination there. Since contemporary sources illuminate them
much better than the others, the missions to China will receive the
emphasis in the following pages.[51]

The Asian missions of the medieval church did not spring from
a pure and disinterested desire to convert pagans to Christianity.
To the contrary, they represented the cultural dimension of a fundamentally political campaign to establish alliances between eastern powers and the Roman church. In some cases the principal
Roman objective was to convert the Mongols outright, in the hope
that they would spare western Christendom the ravages that they
had inflicted on other lands. In other cases the Roman objective
was to win the political and military support of the Mongols, in
the hope that they would then join western Christians in attacking
Muslim Arabs and Turks in the Middle East. Despite sustained
efforts, the missionaries never attracted many Mongol converts.
They found enough supporters from other peoples, though, to establish at least a limited and temporary presence of the Roman
Catholic church in China.

The initiative for these contacts came originally from Pope Inno-
cent IV, who in the 1240s became nervous about the Mongol invasions of Hungary and Russia. Hence, he dispatched a series of
well-documented diplomatic missions to represent Roman political
interests at the Mongol court. In 1245 the Franciscan John of Pi-
ano Carpini set out with his companion, Friar Benedict the Pole,
on a mission to convert the khan and seek a Mongol alliance.
Güyük Khan refused the overture, however, and demanded that
the pope submit to Mongol supremacy. John returned disappointed, but he gathered a great deal of intelligence about Mongol
customs, which proved to be immensely popular with European
audiences. Dominican envoys led at least four additional diplomatic missions between 1245 and 1251, with similar results: neither
pope nor khan would agree to recognize the other's supremacy,
and the parties could find no grounds for an alliance.

Failure of the diplomatic missions, however, did not bring an
end to communication between Mongols and Christians. Between
the mid-thirteenth and mid-fourteenth centuries, a series of evangelical and ecclesiastical missions represented the faith and values

of the Roman church, rather than its political interests, in Mongolia and China. The Franciscan William of Rubruck undertook the first such mission between the years 1253 and 1255. He had little success, owing largely no doubt to his rather severe and uncompromising attitude, but he left a rich account that throws considerable light on the cosmopolitan character of the Mongol empire. At Karakorum, the Mongols' capital, he encountered not only Alans, Georgians, Armenians, Persians, Turks, and Chinese but also Slavs, Greeks, Germans, Hungarians, at least one Englishman, and French, including the Parisian sculptor Guillaume Boucher, who had fashioned a remarkable silver drinking fountain for the khan.

William's departure inaugurated a long hiatus in official communications between Mongols and Christians. Contact resumed in 1287, when Arghun, the ilkhan of Persia, dispatched the Turkish Nestorian Rabban Sauma as an envoy to Rome.[52] Arghun sought an alliance with Christians that would help him to conquer Jerusalem and crush Islam as a political force in the Middle East. The embassy failed in its diplomatic aim, and the ilkhans themselves soon adopted Islam, thus precluding further consideration of a Christian alliance. As a native of Khanbaliq (modern Beijing), however, Rabban Sauma reignited the interest of the Roman church in Mongolia and China. He traveled extensively in the Byzantine empire, Italy, and France, and he had friendly relations with the pope and cardinals of the Roman church. His visit went well enough, in fact, that the pope decided to try again to establish the Roman church in Asia. Thus in 1290, two years after Rabban Sauma's departure from Europe, the Franciscan John of Montecorvino went to China to guide the Christian community there. In 1307 he was named archbishop of Khanbaliq, where he won wide respect and admiration as he led a small but thriving Roman Catholic community until his death in 1328. A series of Franciscan reinforcements joined him in the early fourteenth century, and they established Christian communities in Quanzhou (Marco Polo's Zaiton), Hangzhou, and Yangzhou. The last known expedition was that of John of Marignolli, who went to Khanbaliq in 1342 as a replacement for John of Montecorvino. He remained at his post for about three years, leaving in 1345, perhaps because of the disorder that afflicted China during the latter days of the Mongols' Yuan dynasty.

The evangelical and ecclesiastical missions of the Roman church succeeded better than its diplomatic initiatives, in that they led to the establishment of Roman Catholic institutions and communities in China. Yet these missions actually won few outright converts to Christianity. Mongols rarely found Christianity attractive, and Chinese hardly ever. Nestorians regarded representatives of the Roman church with suspicion at best, and often with undisguised hostility. The largest part of the Roman Catholic community in China seems to have come from the ranks of European traders and others, like the Alans, who already had committed themselves to Roman Catholic or Greek Orthodox Christianity before going to China. In short, Roman Catholic Christianity primarily served the various diaspora communities that were able to become established in China because of the high incidence of long-distance trade and travel that linked the regions of Eurasia during the Mongol era. Unlike Buddhism, however, Roman Christianity did not successfully negotiate the leap from the diaspora communities to Chinese society. When the diaspora communities disappeared, at the end of the Mongols' Yuan dynasty, Roman Christianity also disappeared from China.

The Mongol khans patronized Roman Catholics at Khanbaliq, just as they supported Nestorians, Buddhists, and others at the capital. This support partly derived from the Mongols' toleration of foreign faiths, but partly also no doubt from their need to maintain order. Official recognition and financial support offered the khans a kind of leverage that discouraged foreign religious communities from acting with excessive independence. Many contemporary reports mention the khans' consistent and generous financial support for the Roman Catholic community in Khanbaliq.[53] Despite the missionaries' hopes, however, the khans never seriously entertained notions of converting to Christianity. As mentioned earlier, the Mongol ruling elites developed considerable sympathy for Lamaist Buddhism. Throughout their rule in China, though, Mongol elites and commoners alike held strongly to their traditional shamanism and resisted complete conversion to the faith of any settled people.

Perhaps even more serious a blow to Roman Catholic missions was their failure to win the cooperation and support of Nestorians in China. As mentioned in the previous chapter, the earliest Nestorians arrived in China from central Asia during the seventh century; but the original Nestorian community there had largely disappeared by the late tenth century, following the persecutions of the Tang dynasty. The Nestorian church itself survived, however, both in its Persian heartland and in central Asia, where many Turkish tribes maintained its traditions. Since these Turkish peoples used writing and possessed a relatively high order of administrative skills, they often served as secretaries, advisers, or ministers for other nomadic peoples in central Asia. Genghis Khan and most of his successors as khan employed Nestorian Turks as secretaries. Thus, as nomadic peoples moved into China during the twelfth and following centuries, Turkish administrators accompanied them and reestablished a Nestorian presence in China. Though religious and doctrinal writings unfortunately do not survive, the later Nestorians left archeological traces of their presence in China, and Roman Catholic witnesses often commented on their large and well-appointed churches.[54]

From their earliest days in China, Roman Catholic missionaries clashed with the Nestorians already established there. William of Rubruck characterized them as ignorant, immoral, corrupt, and drunken, less pure even than pagans and Mongols. He found fault with their polygamy, their observation of Islamic fasts, and their priests' saying offices in Syriac, which they did not understand. He sternly rebuked one Nestorian priest — an intellectual leader of the Nestorian community at Karakorum — for voicing a doctrine that William considered Manichaean: the priest taught that the devil had fashioned earthly slime into a human body, into which God then breathed the breath of life. In another case, William encountered a Nestorian who seemed willing to entertain notions of reincarnation.[55] Given his uncompromising and undiplomatic approach to missionary work, it perhaps comes as no surprise that William clashed with the Nestorians. But even John of Montecorvino, the successful and widely beloved archbishop of Khanbaliq, experienced difficulties with Nestorians. In his second letter to Rome, dated January of 1305, he reported that the Nestorians tried to prevent the preaching of any doctrine except their own and that they had accused him of espionage, lying, and worse. He announced that he had baptized some six thousand persons during his dozen years in Khanbaliq, but estimated that in the absence of the pestiferous Nestorians the number would have reached thirty thousand. One of his admirers went further to say that he would have converted the whole land, except for Nestorian hostility and opposition.[56]

This prediction notwithstanding, it is clear from several sources that Roman Catholic missionaries attracted few outright converts but, rather, gathered around them communities of peoples already disposed for one reason or another to a western form of Christianity. William of Rubruck, for example, reported that he baptized a total of six individuals during his short sojourn in Karakorum. Three of them, however, were the children of a German captive living there.[57] In south China, Roman Catholic churches seem to have served the needs primarily of western merchants and their families. Thus Andrew of Perugia mentioned that a rich Armenian lady had built the Franciscan church in Quanzhou, the most important trading city in southern China during the Mongol era. He acknowledged that even after active preaching, he and his colleagues attracted few converts from the Jewish and Muslim communities at Quanzhou. He claimed to have baptized a great many "idolators," but his own words raise a question about the depth of their conversions: "when they are baptized," he admitted, "they do not adhere strictly to Christian ways."[58] In Yangzhou, another prominent southern trading center, there came to light in 1951 a monument that clearly indicates the significance of the diaspora trading community there. The monument in question is a tombstone — the earliest known physical evidence of Roman Catholic Christianity in China — that records the death in 1342 of Catherine de Viglione, daughter of a Venetian or Genoese merchant named Dominic de Viglione. From the legend on the tombstone it appears that both Dominic and Catherine were well regarded in the Roman Catholic community and that they had been especially generous in supporting the local church.[59]

Most successful of the early Roman Catholics in China was the first archbishop of Khanbaliq, John of Montecorvino, who won a reputation among all the peoples in the Mongol capital for his hard work and kindness. He went to great lengths in search of converts. He translated the New Testament and the psalter into Turkish and built three churches for his flock in Khanbaliq. He purchased forty slave boys, whom he baptized and raised as Christians; he went so far as to teach them Latin and have them sing hymns in that foreign tongue. He even approached Temür Khan with an invitation to convert; the khan declined, but treated Catholics generously nonetheless. By John's own estimate, his efforts resulted in some six thousand baptisms, including that of a powerful Turkish prince, formerly a Nestorian, named George of Tenduc, who converted many of his people and built a Catholic church in his domain. John's colleague, Brother Peregrine, later amplified this report: he said that Prince George had become an enthusiastic Roman Catholic, and he mentioned further that the community around John of Montecorvino included some thirty thousand Christian Alans.[60]

Recent research by an eminent Chinese scholar has cast some additional light on the supposed conversion of Prince George. Chen Yüan points out that George wholeheartedly accepted Chinese culture and placed special value on Confucian ideals. He built temples and schools, collected classics and histories, and understood Confucian thought well enough to carry on learned discussions with scholars. He sponsored the printing of Confucian writings and compiled a library of some ten thousand volumes of Chinese classics.[61] Archeological evidence confirms Chen's assessment. Prince George's capital city featured a Nestorian and a Roman Catholic church, but also a Confucian temple and a large library. From his tomb, it seems that George received a traditional Chinese burial.[62] Clearly, then, George did not accept Roman Catholic Christianity in any exclusive sense. Possibly, he viewed the Roman church as a counterbalance to the entrenched political power of the Nestorians. In any case, George died shortly after his supposed conversion, and Nestorians reestablished their predominance in his state. The Catholic mission thus drew little benefit from the conversion, whatever its nature, of Prince George.

As in the case of Prince George's conversion, so with respect to the large numbers of baptisms attributed to John of Montecorvino, a story stands behind the bare facts. The Roman Catholic community at Khanbaliq seems to have drawn the vast majority of its recruits from the ranks of the Alans, who were already disposed toward western Christianity.[63] The Alans had converted to Orthodox Christianity during the early tenth century, when they lived in the Caucasus region under Byzantine influence. In the early thirteenth century they allied on favorable terms with the Mongols, who employed Alans throughout their empire as armor makers and bodyguards. Perhaps as many as thirty thousand served as imperial guards at Khanbaliq. William of Rubruck had noticed already during the 1250s that the Alans did not get along well with the Nestorians, whose priests insisted on rebaptism before they would agree to administer sacraments to western Christians.[64] The Alans therefore heartily welcomed the arrival of the Catholic missionaries, who represented a more recognizable and congenial faith than that of the Nestorians. The Alans became so attached to John of Montecorvino and the Roman church in Khanbaliq that in 1336, eight years after John's death, they requested that the pope send a replacement. In December of 1338, the Franciscan John of Marignolli led an embassy to Khanbaliq in response to the Alans' plea.[65]

This last mission of the medieval church to China had few results. Marignolli arrived in Khanbaliq in 1342, following a lengthy overland journey, and departed only three years later. About the same time, China and central Asia began to suffer serious depopulation from epidemics of bubonic plague, which soon disrupted society and economy in nearly all of Eurasia. In 1368, the Mongol regime in China collapsed, and a Chinese rebel leader established the Ming dynasty. With the end of their state, the Mongols themselves departed China, along with the Alans and many of their other non-Chinese allies. The Roman Catholic community in China thus suddenly lost its human foundation.

During the course of its first sojourn in China, then, Roman Catholic Christianity never became much more than the faith of a series of diaspora communities. The communities varied greatly in their composition: they included western merchants, westerners captured during the Mongols' campaigns, and Alans who served the Mongols as bodyguards. But members of all these communities came to China from abroad, and all were already disposed toward Roman Catholic Christianity rather than the Nestorian faith or some foreign cultural alternative. Meanwhile, Catholic missionaries did not find a way to articulate their message so as to attract the attention and allegiance of Mongols, Chinese, or other peoples in the Mongols' empire. Possibly they placed so high a value on doctrinal precision, Latin language, and Roman liturgy that Mongols and Chinese found their faith too alien to understand or accept. In any case, whatever the explanation, Roman Catholic Christianity did not sink roots in Asian society during the thirteenth and fourteenth centuries. Thus, when expatriate Christians departed from China during the mid-fourteenth century, the Roman church there quickly and completely vanished. When Jesuit missionaries ventured into China in the sixteenth century, they found not even a single trace of the earlier Roman Catholic missions there.

End of the Mongol Era

The unraveling of the Mongol state in China coincided with a phenomenon of much larger impact: the spread of bubonic plague, known in the west as the black death, throughout Eurasia. It seems likely that the Mongols unwittingly sponsored the spread of the disease. By pacifying vast regions and facilitating overland travel throughout their empire, the Mongols made it possible for humans and their animal stock to transport microorganisms across long distances much more efficiently than ever before.[66] Wherever it traveled, the bubonic bacillus attacked its human victims in sudden, dramatic, and lethal fashion. In China, the Middle East, and Europe, mortality rates escalated alarmingly. Contemporaries reported that half, two-thirds, three-fourths, and in isolated cases even larger proportions of the population succumbed to the plague. Historians will never determine precisely what were the plague's demographic effects, but enough information survives to show that epidemic plague thoroughly disrupted the political, social, economic, and cultural orders of all the peoples it attacked.

Among the other effects it brought — including an acute shortage of labor, steep declines in agricultural and industrial production, and financial crises with large political and social ramifications — the plague also interrupted the cross-cultural encounters that had flourished during the Mongol era. Long-distance trade probably did not disappear completely, but its volume certainly declined precipitously during the late fourteenth century. Indeed, the plague ranks as the most important single agent in bringing down the complex system of interregional trade that developed during the thirteenth and early fourteenth centuries.[67] Diminished trade and travel implied less frequent, less systematic, and less intense encounters between peoples of different civilizations. Besides that, to the extent that they influenced cultural developments, epidemics of the plague encouraged introspection—a search for explanation or solace within one's own system of beliefs or values—rather than concern with alternative cultural traditions. As a result, there is little to say about cross-cultural encounters during the late fourteenth century.

Beginning early in the new century, however, the plague lost its initial ferocity. It did not disappear by any means. To the contrary, it remained endemic in some parts of Eurasia until the twentieth century. But epidemic outbreaks decreased in both number and intensity, while Eurasian societies and economies reconstituted themselves and reestablished interregional linkages. It very quickly became apparent, however, that the resulting round of cross-cultural encounters would unfold according to a dynamic quite different from the one that had operated in previous centuries. The next chapter will examine cross-cultural encounters of the fifteenth century—the age when the world's various peoples and civilizations moved for the first time toward sustained cross-cultural communications and global interdependence.

5

Toward a
New World Order

You cannot find a peril so great that the hope of reward
will not be greater. . . . Go forth, then, and . . . make your
voyage straightaway, inasmuch as with the grace of God you
cannot but gain from this journey honour and profit.

> Prince Henry the Navigator, quoted,
> Gomes Eannes de Azurara, *The Chronicle of the
> Discovery and Conquest of Guinea*

Outbreaks of the black death plagued the entire Eurasian world
for three centuries and more, and in some areas it even became an
endemic disease. By the time it arrived in the mid-fourteenth century, however, African and Eurasian peoples had established such
extensive trade and communication networks that not even virulent
epidemic disease could permanently destroy them. Within half a
century of the plague's initial, dramatic appearances, Africans and
Eurasians began to recover from its effects and to reconstitute the
links that bridged their civilizations.

By the early fifteenth century, the civilizations of China, Islam,
and Europe had all embarked upon expansive ventures. In the case
of China, the venture came to an early end, and it led to no permanent result in the way of cultural interaction. In the cases of Islam
and Europe, however, fifteenth-century expansion was a sustained
affair that produced cultural consequences on a large scale and
over a long term. Indeed, the cultural legacies of Islamic and European expansion survive to the present day.

MAP 6. The Eastern Hemisphere in early modern times.

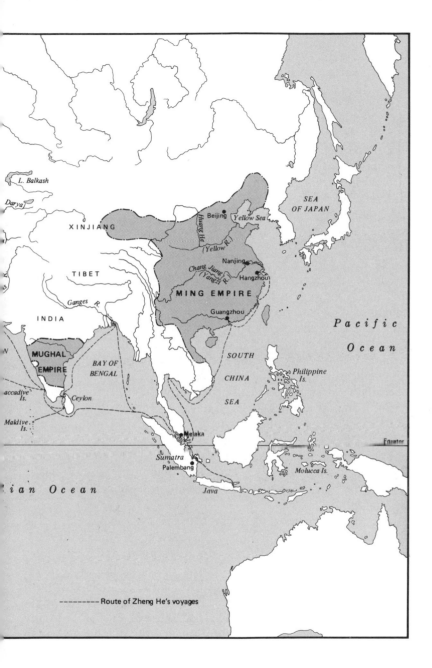

L. Balkash

Darya]

XINJIANG

TIBET

INDIA

Ganges R.

MUGHAL
EMPIRE

BAY OF
BENGAL

accadive
Is.

Ceylon

Maldive
Is.

Huang He

Beijing   *Yellow Sea*

(Yellow R.)

SEA
OF JAPAN

Nanjing

*Chang Jiang
(Yangzi R.)*   Hangzhou

MING EMPIRE

Guangzhou

SOUTH

CHINA

SEA

Pacific

Ocean

*Philippine
Is.*

Melaka

Sumatra
Palembang

Equator

ian Ocean

Java

Molucca Is.

-------- Route of Zheng He's voyages

The Chinese Reconnaissance

In China, the appearance of the bubonic plague coincided with the late stages of the Mongol empire. As the disease ravaged Chinese society, the Mongol lords there quarreled among themselves and faced increasing resistance in the native population. Serious rebellions broke out early in the 1350s, and during the 1360s, China fell into complete disorder. In 1368, the Mongols abandoned China and returned to the steppes. The restoration of order fell to an able, ambitious, authoritarian general who founded the Ming dynasty (1368–1644) and reigned for thirty years as the emperor Hongwu.

The early Ming emperors despised the Mongols and sought to strengthen the hand of China against all the nomads. Among other policies, Hongwu and his successor, Yongle (reigned 1402–1424), sought to eliminate private trade and to bring foreign commerce under the umbrella of the tributary system. To the extent that it succeeded — rather small, by most accounts — this effort perhaps reduced the influence of China in the larger world. But the early Ming emperors sponsored one enterprise in particular that had the potential to extend Chinese influence throughout the Indian Ocean basin. This was a series of seven naval expeditions that called on ports in Indonesia, southeast Asia, Ceylon, India, Arabia, and east Africa. The voyages had little or no permanent result, since court politics brought them to an abrupt conclusion. The voyages nevertheless bear some reflection, since they demonstrated in dramatic fashion the potential for intense cross-cultural exchange in the fifteenth century.[1]

The Ming voyages took place between 1405 and 1433 at the instigation of the emperor Yongle. An old story attributes the expeditions to the emperor's efforts to track down and capture his nephew, whom he had deposed from the Ming throne in 1404. More likely, though, Yongle hoped to gain firm imperial control over foreign trade and to impress foreign peoples with the might and power that the Ming dynasty had restored to China. In any case, under the leadership of the eunuch admiral Zheng He — an accomplished diplomat with a great deal of practical political experience — the voyages certainly advertised Chinese economic and military capacities in effective fashion. The expeditions featured enormous fleets, sometimes numbering more than three hundred ships, including as many as sixty-three mammoth, nine-masted treasure ships capable of accommodating five hundred men apiece. Laden with silk, porcelain, lacquerware, and other finished products, the ships called on nearly every major port on the South China Sea and Indian Ocean. Zheng He used his cargo to open commercial and diplomatic relations in numerous ports, and he returned to China with all manner of exotic foreign goods: spices, aromatics, textiles, gems, drugs, and even animals, such as a famous giraffe transported from Malindi to the Ming imperial zoo by way of Bengal. (Another giraffe later traveled directly from Malindi to China.)

Whenever possible, Zheng He relied upon persuasion and diplomacy in his dealings with foreign peoples. But his entourage included as many as twenty-eight thousand armed troops, and on several occasions he resorted to force in order to achieve his aims. In Sumatra he captured a pirate chief of Palembang and a usurper of the throne of Samudra, both of whom were later executed in China. An uncooperative king of Ceylon also experienced difficulties: after defeating his army in battle, Zheng He captured the king and his family and took them to China, where they later won their release from the emperor Yongle. Zheng He also made displays of military force at La'sa (near Aden in Arabia) and Mogadishu.

Yet on the whole, the Ming expeditions reflected political and commercial interests, not cultural or ideological motivations. Striking testimony to this point comes in the form of a stele erected in 1409 in southern Ceylon. The monument records the visit of the Chinese fleet in three languages — Chinese, Tamil, and Persian — but honors a different faith in each of the three inscriptions. The Chinese text praises the Buddha and the Ceylonese Buddhist community; the Tamil version honors Tenavarai-nayanar, one of the incarnations of Visnu; and the Persian text glorifies Allah and the saints of Islam. The inscriptions record further that Zheng He honored the Buddha, Visnu, and Allah each with lavish gifts, including one thousand pieces of gold, five thousand pieces of silver, one hundred rolls of silk, and large quantities of perfumed oil and ecclesiastical ornaments.

To judge from the Ceylonese monument, the Ming voyagers and their sponsors had no interest in promoting Chinese culture or values in foreign lands. At least in its early stages, the Chinese reconnaissance sought to reestablish orderly commercial and diplomatic relationships with foreign peoples and to foster the recognition of China as the world's central empire surrounded by subordinate vassal states. It is impossible to know whether the Chinese might have developed over time a more explicitly cultural or ideological dimension of their overseas expansion. It seems certain that sustained voyages and cross-cultural dealings would have had some sort of cultural result, but its nature lies purely in the realm of speculation, since a series of problems in the 1420s and 1430s brought the expeditions to an end. Floods, famine, and disease caused serious economic difficulties, which undermined imperial financing of the expensive expeditions. Meanwhile, Confucian scholars at the Ming court mistrusted the coterie of eunuchs who supported and organized the voyages. The Confucians argued that overseas trade was a frivolous and dangerous enterprise, one best suppressed in favor of agricultural and industrial pursuits. They eventually had their way, and resources that had gone into the building of ships were rechanneled into the construction and repair of public works. Before too long, Chinese even forgot how to build the enormous treasure ships that had awed foreign observers from Java to Malindi.

The Continuing Expansion of Islam

While Chinese fleets reconnoitered the Indian Ocean under imperial auspices, the house of Islam continued to expand as a result of both state policies and commercial relationships. In Spain, the *reconquista* gradually but relentlessly pressured the Muslim kingdom of Granada toward its final collapse in 1492. Elsewhere, however, the realm of Islam stretched its boundaries, even in Europe. The Ottoman Turks consolidated the Islamic conquest of Anatolia and used the resulting momentum to expand into Egypt, the Balkans, and eastern Europe as far as Hungary. In India, Islam spread more slowly, but there too Muslim rulers strengthened their positions especially in the Sind, Gujarat, and Bengal. In all these lands,

Islam became established largely by a continuing process of conversion induced by political, social, and economic pressures, as Turkish rulers and conquerors provided official sponsorship and support of their faith.

Several contemporary accounts by travelers to these regions illustrate pressures brought on nonbelievers to convert to Islam if they sojourned for very long in these lands. Johann Schiltberger, for example, who fell captive at the battle of Nicopolis (1396), left an account describing his experiences during almost thirty years in Ottoman service. Schiltberger despised Islam, which he called a "wicked religion," and he himself resisted continuous pressure to abandon his native faith in its favor. Yet it seems that conversions to Islam were by no means uncommon: Schiltberger described an elaborate ritual that he said registered an individual's conversion from Christianity to Islam. The convert publicly recognized Allah as God and Muhammad as his messenger, then received new clothes and participated in a parade of celebration. Poor converts also received large gifts of money as inducements to conversion.[2] Schiltberger's experience shows that it was possible to rebuff the pressures and resist the temptations to convert to Islam. Indeed, after years of planning, he ultimately escaped captivity and returned to his native Bavaria.

Others, however, felt greater pressure to join the cultural majority. The Russian merchant Athanasius Nikitin visited Arabia, Persia, and India in the late fifteenth century. About the time of his fourth Easter away from home, he composed an account of his travels and experiences. Despite intense pressure to convert, he reported that he had diligently observed Christian holy days—but he frankly admitted that he did not know how much longer he could refrain from apostasy. The Italian merchant Niccolò Conti ultimately succumbed to pressures to convert. His case became quite well known because he sought absolution for his apostasy from Pope Eugenius IV, and his story intrigued Poggio Bracciolini, the famous humanist and papal secretary, who wrote an account of it in his widely read work on fortune. Conti had begun his mercantile career in Damascus, where he learned some Arabic; later he traveled to Persia, India, and Sumatra, among other places. On his return trip to Europe, he passed through Egypt, where he faced such intense pressure that he renounced Christianity and accepted Islam. In seeking absolution, he explained that he took this step out of fear and concern for his wife and two children, who had accompanied him on all his travels. Niccolò eventually returned safely to Italy, but his wife and children perished at Cairo in an outbreak of the plague.[3]

Despite the different attitudes and experiences of the authors, all of these accounts throw some light on the process of conversion induced by political, social, and economic pressures. All make it clear that in Islamic lands there was abundant opportunity and considerable incentive for Christians to renounce their faith and convert to Islam. It was possible to retain another faith—but also difficult, especially over a long term, in the absence of regular services and communication with cultural authorities. It certainly required more than usual discipline and determination to resist the various pressures and inducements to accept Islam. Meanwhile, formal acceptance of Islam, for whatever reason, was an event common enough that established rituals and ceremonies marked its occurrence.

Surviving western accounts reflect the experiences of those who resisted Islam to a far greater degree than those who converted. The autobiography of Anselmo Turmeda stands as a rather lonely witness to the fact that Christians sometimes voluntarily converted to Islam. Turmeda was a Franciscan from Mallorca who studied theology at Lérida and Bologna. According to his account, his conversion came after a discussion of New Testament passages concerning the paraclete, who Jesus promised would come in the future and comfort his flock (John 14:16–17, 14:26, 15:26, 16:7–14). Christians identified this comforter as the Holy Spirit, but Islamic theologians had held since the eighth century that the paraclete was none other than Muhammad. Modern scholars have suggested that Turmeda might well have had other reasons for turning to Islam: disillusionment with the decadence of the late medieval church, desire to escape punishment for political activities, or evasion of the Inquisition, since it is possible that he came from a Jewish family. In any case, he made his way to Tunis about 1386, publicly renounced Christianity, and converted to Islam. The sultan showered him with gold dinars and provided him with a new set of clothes, a post as customs official, and a wife, by whom he had a son. About 1420 he composed a work that offered a brief autobiography with an account of his conversion, a history of the sultans at Tunis, and a lengthy attack on Christianity.[4]

How many other medieval Europeans abandoned Christianity and turned to Islam? Their numbers and experiences are lost to history, although it is certainly safe to say that Turmeda was not the only Christian who found opportunities to pursue in the house of Islam. In any case, Turmeda's experience demonstrates that conversion to Islam was a practical alternative for Christians at odds with their inherited society and culture.

The western regions of the Islamic world thus played host to cross-cultural encounters of some intensity, but equally dramatic developments took place as Islam established an enduring presence in southeast Asia. Gujarati merchants had already introduced their faith into the trading centers of Sumatra at least by the thirteenth century, but only in the fifteenth century did Islam gain expansive momentum in southeast Asia. As in other lands where merchants introduced foreign cultural and religious traditions, a process of conversion through voluntary association promoted the expansion of Islam in southeast Asia. The rapid spread of the faith had much to do with the rise of Melaka as the principal entrepôt of southeast Asia. Since a variety of source materials survive to illuminate the development of Melaka, its experience bears investigation.

The origins of Melaka trace to the late fourteenth century and the actions of Paramesvara, a prince of the Hindu trading state at Palembang.[5] During the 1390s, Paramesvara mounted a rebellion at Palembang but had to flee his homeland when the uprising failed. He went to a point near modern Singapore on the Malay peninsula, where he killed the local ruler, a vassal of the king of Siam, and usurped his position. Later he moved up the coast with a band of seaborne retainers and established his presence at Melaka. The early rulers sent out fleets that forced trading vessels to call at Melaka and pay duties there; meanwhile, they either conquered neighboring states or established alliances with them, so that they controlled an increasingly large portion of trade passing through southeast Asian waters. As a result of these policies, Melaka had become a bustling port already by 1403, and it grew rapidly for the next century and more. When the Portuguese conquered the city in 1511, its population approached fifty thousand, and the Portuguese merchant Tomé Pires reported that eighty-four languages could be heard in Melakan streets.

The rapid development of Melaka strongly favored the expansion of Islam in southeast Asia. The rulers of Melaka had tense relations with the Buddhist kingdom of Siam, prompting them to seek external support for their rule. Paramesvara and his two successors each journeyed to the Ming court in order to establish and maintain a Chinese alliance. Meanwhile, they also made common cause with the region's increasingly prominent Muslim traders, who themselves had difficult dealings with Buddhist Siam. As the Muslim community grew in Melaka, *qadis*, *mullahs*, Sufis, and other cultural authorities joined the merchants there. By the middle of the fifteenth century, Melaka had become a center of Islamic studies and a source of missionaries who worked to spread Islam throughout southeast Asia.

The concentrated presence of Muslims brought political repercussions also in the Melakan ruling class. During his reign, Paramesvara maintained his court on the outskirts of Melaka. He had few dealings with foreigners, but entrusted administration of Melaka to his son. When he assumed the throne in his own right, the son moved his court to the city center of Melaka, converted to Islam, and took a new name, Megat Iskandar Shah. It looks as though Iskandar Shah underwent a classic case of voluntary conversion — one that associated his rule with the traditions and values of the larger world of Islam but that did not necessarily indicate rejection of his inherited culture. Instead, Iskandar Shah and later Muslim rulers of Melaka continued to observe the Hindu and Buddhist traditions that they had brought with them from Palembang. They retained Hindu and Buddhist ceremonials at court, and they relied on the political traditions of Srivijaya to legitimize their rule. Indeed, they never completely abandoned the idea of returning to rule in their ancestral homeland.

The term *conversion through voluntary association* suggests a calculated and somewhat cerebral process, but the experience of Melaka shows that it could lead to considerable internal tension and even violence in communities where it took effect. Before the conversion of Iskandar Shah, elites at Melaka fell into one of two classes: the Malay ruling nobility and the wealthy Muslim merchants. After his conversion, the ruling house itself divided into two camps: those favoring retention of Hindu and Buddhist traditions and those accepting Islam as a cultural foundation for commercial and political alliances. The resulting tensions came to a head in 1445, when the regent for the third ruler of Melaka attempted to stage a reaction in favor of the Hindu and Buddhist traditions. His efforts not only failed but provoked a coup organized by the Islamic faction at court. The coup ended with the victory of Muzaffir Shah, who consolidated his hold on Melaka, established Islam as the state religion, and based his rule on Islamic principles. He then proceeded to extend Melakan influence throughout the region, seize control of the Strait of Singapore, conquer and convert rulers in both the Malay peninsula and Sumatra. As a result of these achievements, Muzaffir Shah's fame spread widely — he became well known as far away as China, India, and Arabia — and he became the first of Melaka's rulers recognized throughout the Islamic world as sultan.

As in other lands, the voluntary conversion of elites facilitated the establishment of Islam at all levels of Melakan and southeast Asian society. The elites themselves served as links between the established local society and the larger world of the Indian Ocean basin, but they also served as conduits through which Islam could enter the local society. Following the conversion of elites, Muslim *qadis* and teachers became increasingly influential as cultural authorities in southeast Asian courts and cities. Meanwhile, Indian Sufis, organized in trade guilds, spread their faith on a more popular level: thanks to their doctrinal flexibility, the Sufis built bridges between the established and the new cultural traditions by absorbing Malay pantheism and animism into Islamic mysticism.

This observation points up the survival of indigenous cultural traditions and the significance of syncretism: as elsewhere, conversion to Islam in southeast Asia resulted not in the extinction of an established cultural tradition and its replacement by another but, rather, in a syncretic blend of cultural alternatives. Shadow plays continued to represent episodes from the Hindu epics, and incantations to Siva and Visnu survived alongside prayers to Allah. Indeed, in some cases ritual Hindu incantations were baptized by the simple addition of the Islamic confession of faith as a conclusion.[6] Not until the eighteenth century did cultural and political authorities undertake zealously to root out pre-Islamic cultural elements and to enforce a more orthodox Islamic faith in southeast Asia.

Meanwhile, though, the house of Islam clearly displayed its potential for further expansion during the fifteenth century. Whether by means of conquest and conversion induced by pressure, as in Anatolia and eastern Europe, or through trade and voluntary conversion, as in southeast Asia, the Islamic community continued to grow rapidly. By century's end, as mosques began to dominate urban landscapes in Java, Sumatra, and the Malay peninsula, the faith had made its first appearance in the Moluccan Islands and even in the southern Philippines. Indeed, on the basis of cultural developments in the preceding five centuries, an impartial observer in the year 1500 might well have predicted that Islam would soon become the world's dominant faith, its principal source of beliefs, values, culture, and human consciousness.

The Emergence of the West

Like most of the other regions of Eurasia, western Europe suffered deeply from the black death but began to exhibit signs of recovery as early as the fifteenth century. In the European case, recovery took the form of a resumption of earlier efforts at expansion. One such effort was the *reconquista* of Spain, already examined in the previous chapter. The *reconquista* had stalled in the later fourteenth century, and the complications of Iberian politics prevented its resumption for the first half of the fifteenth century. The fall of Constantinople in 1453 reignited in Spain a zeal for the crusade. Only in the 1480s, however, after the union of the Castilian and Aragonese crowns during the reign of Ferdinand and Isabella, did the *reconquista* again become a serious and sustained affair. By 1492 — thanks partly to internal divisions and weakness in the Muslim kingdom of Granada — it resulted in reestablishment of Christian rule throughout Iberia. In its wake there occurred yet another round of encounter between conquered Muslims and victorious Christians. As in earlier stages of the *reconquista*, the principal pattern that developed from this encounter was that of conversion induced by political, social, and economic pressures. In their zealous promotion of their faith, victorious Spaniards went so far as to order the expulsion, in 1492 and 1502, respectively, of Jews and Muslims who refused conversion to Christianity. Historians have long recognized the *reconquista* as an experience of large significance for the development of the Spanish empire in the Americas. It was in fact the historical crucible from which there emerged the formative attitudes, the policies toward different peoples, and even the specific institutions that Spaniards took to the Americas.[7] The *reconquista* thus ranks as one of the most crucial links between the pre-modern world and the earliest stage of modern world history.

Another indication that Europeans had begun to recover from the epidemics of the fourteenth century was the resumption of efforts at geographical expansion and colonization.[8] Historians once considered the lure of trade in spices as the principal incentive that prompted Europeans to mount expensive voyages of exploration. More recently, though, it has become clear that two additional commodities, sugar and gold, stood behind European expansion during the fifteenth century. Europeans had acquired a taste for sugar during the crusades, and large profits awaited those who could cultivate it and convey it to western and northern markets. Thus, from the early thirteenth century on, Europeans had conquered Mediterranean islands, where they organized sugar plantations. Eventually, the search for land capable of sugar cultivation drew Europeans out of the Mediterranean altogether and into the Atlantic Ocean. During the later fourteenth and fifteenth centuries, Genoese, Spanish, and Portuguese mariners colonized the nearby island groups of the so-called Mediterranean Atlantic—the Azores, Madeiras, and Canaries—where they established sugar plantations to supply the European market.

Meanwhile, as sugar drew Europeans into the Atlantic, the lure of gold tempted them to explore Africa. Since antiquity Africa had enjoyed a reputation among Europeans as a rich source of gold, and since the eleventh century, trade with north African cities had confirmed African wealth in gold, ivory, and slaves. During the fourteenth and fifteenth centuries, accounts of Mansa Musa's pilgrimage to Mecca and his lavish expenditures in Cairo reverberated in Europe and whetted the western appetite for the precious metal. The Catalan atlas, a famous world map drawn about 1375, depicted Mansa Musa as the king of Africa wielding a scepter in one hand and bearing an enormous gold nugget in the other. Little wonder, then, that Portuguese and Spanish mariners carefully explored the western coasts of Africa and sought to move trade to the coasts, where they could deal directly with African suppliers, rather than obtain higher-priced gold transported by caravans and exchanged in the markets of north Africa.

As it happened, these early European ventures into the Atlantic and west Africa resulted in cross-cultural encounters even more difficult and unpleasant than those generated by the *reconquista*. As Portuguese mariners explored the western coast of Africa, rounded Cape Bojador, and approached the Cape of Good Hope, they not only found gold markets but also raided native villages in wanton fashion and forced their captives into slavery. Gomes Eannes de Azurara, who composed the earliest account of Portuguese ventures beyond Cape Bojador, spoke often of these raids and occasionally of the capture of Africans in groups of fifty or more. On the basis of his own observations, he calculated that between 1434 and 1448, his compatriots had transferred some 927 slaves from Africa to Portugal. (Many other slaves, whom he did not number, remained in Africa, but nonetheless worked in Portuguese service in their forts and trading settlements.) The slave trade developed with amazing rapidity: according to the Venetian mariner Cadamosto, by the mid-fifteenth century the Portuguese shipped one thousand slaves per year from their fort at Arguim in Guinea.

Azurara clearly recognized the brutality of the early slave trade. He witnessed the first lot of slaves delivered at Lagos and reflected on their fate as their captors used brute force to divide families, allot parents and children to different owners, and dispatch them to varied destinations:

> But what heart could be so hard as not to be pierced with piteous feeling to see that company? For some kept their heads low and their faces bathed in tears, looking one upon another; others stood groaning very dolorously, looking up to the height of heaven, fixing their eyes upon it, crying out loudly, as if asking help of the Father of Nature; others struck their faces with the palms of their hands, throwing themselves at full length upon the ground; others made their lamentations in the manner of a dirge, after the custom of their country.

Azurara took comfort in the conversion of these slaves to Christianity: almost all of them converted as soon as they learned the Portuguese language, he said, and their children and grandchildren remained firmly in the faith. Azurara maintained that slaves who went to Portugal received especially favorable treatment: they wore no chains and quickly adapted to Portuguese ways; they did not flee, he said, but forgot their homeland and made new lives for themselves in an improved physical and spiritual environment.[9] While sources do not illuminate these experiences from the slaves' point of view, it seems clear from Azurara's testimony that a process of conversion by assimilation and compulsion accounts for the slaves' adoption of the Christian religion and European culture.

If Africans endured captivity and slavery as a result of their encounter with Europeans, the indigenous peoples of the Canary Islands suffered an even harsher fate: the extinction of their culture and their disappearance as a recognizable people. The Guanches of Tenerife and the closely related societies on other islands were a neolithic people, akin to the Berbers, who had gone to the Canaries from north Africa, but had lost contact with the continent at least by the early centuries C.E. Despite their limited technology, and despite the loss of numerous individuals who fell captive to slave raiders, they resisted several Portuguese and Spanish attempts at conquest during the fifteenth century. Beginning in 1478, however, the revived Spanish monarchy of Ferdinand and Isabella mounted a sustained campaign that resulted in the subjugation of all the Canary Islands by 1496. As in the case of African conquests, contemporaries expressed their reservations about the morality of Spanish actions in the Canaries. Thus Alonso de Espinosa, earliest and most reliable of the Spanish chroniclers of the Canaries' conquest, regarded it as

> an acknowledged fact, both as regards divine and human right, that the wars waged by the Spaniards against the natives of these islands, as well as against the Indians in the western regions, were unjust and without any reason to support them. For the natives had not taken the lands of Christians, nor had they gone beyond their own frontier to molest or invade their neighbours. If it is said that the Spaniards brought the Gospel, this should have been

done by admonition and preaching—not by drum and banner; by persuasion, not by force.[10]

To some extent the Spaniards' victory came about because of their horses, which awed and intimidated the islanders, and their weaponry, which featured firearms, cannons, crossbows, and steel swords as opposed to the stones and boulders that dominated the Canary arsenal. Yet even with their superior military technology, the Spaniards could hardly have won their victory—certainly not without much higher losses and much more time—without the aid of infectious and contagious diseases that they brought to the Canaries. During the decades surrounding the conquest, indigenous society reeled as hitherto unknown diseases decimated the indigenous population. The islanders probably numbered about eighty thousand in 1400. When exotic diseases arrived and broke out in epidemic form, their population thinned to the point that they simply did not command the human resources to offer effective resistance to the waves of Spanish invaders.[11]

Those islanders who survived both the diseases and the invasions of the Spaniards witnessed the gradual disappearance of their people and culture. Many of them fell captive and passed into slavery; others intermarried with the conquerors and passed into a new cultural environment. As in the case of African captives, then, a combination of assimilation and compulsion account for the islanders' conversion to Christianity and adoption of European culture.

One peculiar experience in particular sheds a bit of light on the process of the Guanches' conversion to Christianity and the workings of assimilation and compulsion in their case. The experience has to do with an image of the virgin that appeared in Tenerife about 1400.[12] By that time European mariners had long been aware of the Canaries' existence and location, although they had not yet embarked upon a campaign of conquest. The image of the virgin no doubt arrived at Tenerife during some unrecorded ship's call there. The Guanches quickly developed a healthy respect for the image because of its reputation for working miracles. Thus for many years they preserved the image and lived in its awe, without understanding its significance. Then came Anton, a Guanche taken captive by Spaniards early in the fifteenth century. Anton went as a slave to Spain, where he learned Spanish and converted to Christianity. So sincere was his faith, according to Alonso de Espinosa, who chronicled his experiences, that his master allowed him to return to the Canaries to evangelize the Guanches. Thus as a missionary he visited the village of Candelaria, where the image of the virgin resided. The inhabitants showed him the image and asked if he could explain its significance. Anton of course immediately recognized it, fell into prayer, and instructed the others in his faith, explaining to them that the virgin was the mother of Guayaxerax and Achaman, the Guanches' gods of the sky and sun.

Assimilation and compulsion certainly account for Anton's own adoption of European and Christian ways. In later decades the same forces came to bear on all the Guanches and their fellow islanders who survived the diseases and wars of the later fifteenth century. The ultimate result was the absolute deculturation of the Guanches: remnants of Guanche culture that survive to the present include nine sentences, about two hundred words, and little else. Anton the convert could not have prevented the obliteration of Guanche culture, and he perhaps had little desire or inclination to preserve it in any case. Anton served neither as a preserver nor as a destroyer but, rather, as a mediator of culture: one whose ministrations perhaps helped his people to travel a bit more easily the difficult road from their inherited ways and values to an alien cultural tradition.

Toward a New World Order:
The Late Fifteenth Century and Beyond

European ventures in west Africa and the Canary Islands demonstrated in especially dramatic fashion the potential of two elements, sophisticated technology and epidemic disease, to alter the dynamics of cross-cultural encounters. Neither element was absolutely new. To the contrary, in fact, both had influenced cross-cultural dealings from early times. The Roman empire and the various Chinese dynasties, for example, all stood to some extent on the foundation of superior technologies that neighboring peoples did not possess. Meanwhile, epidemic disease devastated the commercial and cultural networks that developed during the era of the ancient silk roads and the age of the Mongol empire.

In earlier centuries, however, technology had not strengthened the hand of a single people in quite the same way that it favored Europeans during early modern times. Several times during the history of Eurasia, centers of civilization had garnered a technological advantage over their neighbors and used it to improve the terms of their military, political, and economic relationships with others. Yet even in early times, useful technology had a tendency to diffuse quite readily, so that no single people was able to gain a permanent, or even a long-term monopoly on advanced techniques.[13] Thus, in spite of countless laws, decrees, and proclamations, Chinese authorities never stemmed the flow of metallurgical techniques or of finished bronze and iron products to neighboring nomadic peoples. Besides that, the combined practical effects of pre-modern technology were not so large that clever peoples could not devise successful countermeasures. Military technology might well enable Chinese forces to prevail over nomads in pitched battle, but pitched battles rarely occurred, since nomadic peoples had horses, mobility, advanced tactical skills, and vast expanses of steppe territory that enabled them to withdraw and evade superior forces.

If technology did not permanently or decisively influence the distribution of power in pre-modern times, disease played hardly any favorites at all. In the earliest days of civilization, diseases such as measles and smallpox became endemic in large societies, where they did not completely disrupt life. It is possible that these diseases devastated small neolithic communities previously unexposed to their pathogens.[14] After the widespread establishment of civilization, though, and especially after the organization of long-distance trade and communication networks, endemic diseases of large communities spread to most parts of the Eastern Hemisphere. As a result they did not favor one people over another but struck instead with approximately equal effect in all the regions they invaded. Meanwhile, when epidemic disease erupted, it ravaged all peoples unfortunate enough to become exposed. The epidemics that traveled the ancient silk roads, for example, decimated the populations of both the Han and the Roman empires—and probably those of the intervening Kushan and Parthian societies as well. Likewise, the bubonic plague of the fourteenth century disrupted society throughout Eurasia, sparing only those regions such as Scandinavia and southern India where the plague-bearing black rat preferred not to dwell.

Beginning in the fifteenth century, and continuing to some extent to the present day, new configurations of technology and new patterns of disease favored Europeans in their dealings with nonwestern peoples. The technology in question was not absolutely new, nor was it always European in origin. Much of it traced ultimately to Tang and Song inventions: gunpowder, the compass, the sternpost rudder, and other elements of nautical technology all came ultimately from China. Other items also came from eastern parts, most notably the lateen sail, which originated in the Indian Ocean and came to the Mediterranean through the agency of Arab merchants and mariners. Thus Europeans borrowed much of their naval and military technology, but they refined, accumulated, and combined it to the point that they at least matched and most often exceeded the technological development of other peoples. When Europeans ventured into the Atlantic Ocean in the fifteenth century, they not only possessed highly maneuverable vessels and the instruments necessary to chart their courses (at least approximately) and return safely but also drew upon an arsenal of powerful weapons that dismembered and profoundly disoriented peoples who had not before encountered such destructive machinery. Sophisticated naval and military technologies by no means provided Europeans with the means to dominate all the peoples they encountered—certainly not before the development of the steamboat and advanced weapons in the nineteenth century—but they underwrote western hegemony in the world over a very long term.

In certain areas, disease favored Europeans even more than technology. When Europeans first ventured into lands previously unexposed to the pathogens of the Eastern Hemisphere—lands such as the Canary Islands, the American continents, and later still the islands of the Pacific Ocean—they introduced diseases that ran their virulent and lethal courses unchecked by inherited or acquired immunities. In extreme cases, entire societies perished: the Arawaks or Tainos of the Caribbean and the aboriginal people of Tasmania followed the Guanches into extinction. In less extreme cases, indigenous peoples managed to survive, but only at the cost of the total disruption of their societies. Since the imported diseases attacked unexposed populations indiscriminately, they carried off not only the sickly or weak but also the political and cultural authorities who led their societies and held them together. Societies ravaged by epidemic disease obviously became extremely fragile and vulnerable to any sustained effort at invasion or expansion by an unafflicted foreign people.

Thus either separately or in combination, sophisticated technology and epidemic disease considerably altered the dynamics of cross-cultural encounters in early modern times. As far as cultural change is concerned, the principal results of technology and disease were to magnify vastly Europeans' potential to inaugurate processes of conversion induced by political, social, and economic pressures, and to increase equally vastly the incidence of deculturation. In some parts of the world, cross-cultural encounters proceeded on the basis of dynamics in operation since the days of the ancient silk roads or even before: trade diasporas introduced new cultural alternatives to a region and offered opportunities for conversion through voluntary association, while campaigns of military or colonial expansion encouraged aggressive peoples to impose their cultural preferences forcibly upon others. In all these cases, cross-cultural encounters produced some sort of syncretic result. In other regions, however—principally the Caribbean, the Americas, and the Pacific islands—technology and disease destroyed societies and seriously threatened their established cultural traditions. It is the task of another volume, however, to analyze the dynamics of cross-cultural encounters in modern times, to examine the processes and results of those encounters, to explore and to question the thoroughness and permanence of the process of deculturation, and to gauge the extent to which long-embattled cultural traditions still survive and have the potential to undergo revival.

NOTES

Chapter 1

1. The works of two scholars demonstrate particularly well the value of this sort of analysis. William H. McNeill has examined cross-cultural exchanges of technology and diseases in pre-modern as well as modern times; see especially *The Rise of the West* (Chicago, 1963), and *Plagues and Peoples* (Garden City, 1976). Philip D. Curtin has outlined patterns of cross-cultural trade in pre-modern as well as modern times; see his *Cross-Cultural Trade in World History* (New York, 1984). This book draws a great deal of inspiration from the works and the insights of both McNeill and Curtin.

2. For an anthropologist's general reflections on cross-cultural encounters and their results, see Melville J. Herskovits, *Acculturation* (Gloucester, 1958).

3. Arthur Darby Nock, *Conversion: The Old and the New in Religion from Alexander the Great to Augustine of Hippo* (Oxford, 1933), especially pp. 1–16. See also T. W. Arnold, *The Preaching of Islam*, 2d ed. (London, 1913).

4. For a careful study of Turmeda's life and work, along with the Arabic text and a Spanish translation of his autobiography, see Miguel de Epalza, *La Tuhfa. Autobiografía y polémica islámica de Abdallha al-Taryuman (fray Anselmo Turmeda)* (Rome, 1971).

5. For a rich analysis of long-term cultural change within a single civilization — without reference, however, to the cross-cultural encounters that this book examines — see two works of Norbert Elias: *The History of Manners*, trans. E. Jephcott (New York, 1978); and *Power and Civility*, trans. E. Jephcott (New York, 1982).

6. On trade diaspora communities, see Curtin, *Cross-Cultural Trade in World History*.

7. Two scholars have recently published works that present especially interesting reflections on these themes. See Mary W. Helms, *Ulysses' Sail:*

An Ethnographic Odyssey of Power, Knowledge, and Geographical Distance (Princeton, 1988); and two articles by Robin Horton: "African Conversion," *Africa* 41 (1971): 85–108; and "On the Rationality of Conversion," *Africa* 45 (1975): 219–35, 373–99. See also some critical literature dealing with Horton's work: Humphrey J. Fisher, "Conversion Reconsidered: Some Historical Aspects of Religious Conversion in Black Africa," *Africa* 43 (1973): 27–40; and J. D. Y. Peel, "Conversion and Tradition in Two African Societies: Ijebu and Buganda," *Past and Present* 77 (1977): 108–41.

8. For a brilliant analysis of Islamic syncretism, see Clifford Geertz, *Islam Observed: Religious Development in Morocco and Indonesia* (Chicago, 1968).

9. For an anthropologist's reflections on the survival of cultural traditions in the face of challenges, see Fredrik Barth, ed., *Ethnic Groups and Boundaries* (Boston, 1969).

10. Irving Rouse, *Migrations in Prehistory: Inferring Population Movement from Cultural Remains* (New Haven, 1986).

11. For the developments mentioned in this paragraph, see William H. McNeill, "The Eccentricity of Wheels, or Eurasian Transportation in Historical Perspective," *American Historical Review* 92 (1987): 1111–26; Richard Bulliet, *The Camel and the Wheel* (Cambridge, Mass., 1975); and Shereen Ratnagar, *Encounters: The Westerly Trade of the Harappa Civilization* (Delhi, 1981).

12. For a recent elaboration of these views, see Thor Heyerdahl, *Early Man and the Ocean* (London, 1978).

13. Joseph Needham, *Science and Civilisation in China*, 6 vols. to date (Cambridge, 1954–), 4:540–53.

14. On the Phoenicians, see especially Donald Harden, *The Phoenicians* (New York, 1962); and Sabatino Moscati, *The World of the Phoenicians*, trans. A. Hamilton (New York, 1965).

15. Owen Lattimore, *Inner Asian Frontiers of China*, 2d ed. (New York, 1951), especially pp. 255–334. See also two essays on the concept of barbarism in other contexts: Romila Thapar, "The Image of the Barbarian in Early India," *Comparative Studies in Society and History* 13 (1971): 408–36; and W. R. Jones, "The Image of the Barbarian in Medieval Europe," *Comparative Studies in Society and History* 13 (1971): 376–407.

16. Karl Jaspers, *The Origin and Goal of History*, trans. M. Bullock (New Haven, 1953), especially pp. 1–21.

17. Miguel León-Portilla, "El processo de acculturación de los chichimecas de Xólotl," *Estudios de cultura nahuatl* 7 (1968): 59–86.

Chapter 2

1. On trade in the ancient world, see Philip D. Curtin, *Cross-Cultural Trade in World History* (New York, 1984), pp. 60–108; C. G. F. Simkin, *The Traditional Trade of Asia* (London, 1968), pp. 1–49; Manfred G. Raschke, "New Studies in Roman Commerce with the East," in *Aufstieg und Niedergang der römischen Welt*, ed. H. Temporini and W. Haase, 2 vols. (Berlin, 1978), 2:9:2, pp. 604–1361; Lionel Casson, ed., *The "Periplus Maris Erythraei"* (Princeton, 1989); and Wang Gungwu, *The Nanhai Trade: A Study of the Early History of Chinese Trade in the South China Sea* (Kuala Lumpur, 1958).

2. Hisayuki Miyakawa, "The Confucianization of South China," in *The Confucian Persuasion*, ed. Arthur F. Wright (Stanford, 1960), pp. 21–46.

3. Along with the classic work of Owen Lattimore, *Inner Asian Frontiers of China*, 2d ed. (New York, 1951), see also two recent books that analyze relations between Chinese and steppe nomads over the long term: Thomas J. Barfield, *The Perilous Frontier: Nomadic Empires and China* (Cambridge, Mass., 1989); and Sechin Jagchid and Van Jay Symons, *Peace, War, and Trade along the Great Wall* (Bloomington, 1989).

4. On the Xiongnu and their relations with the Han dynasty, see two publications by Ying-shih Yü: *Trade and Expansion in Han China* (Berkeley, 1967); and "Han Foreign Relations," in *The Cambridge History of China*, ed. Denis Twitchett and Michael Loewe, 15 vols. (Cambridge, 1987), 1:377–462.

5. For a very interesting record of one such debate, see Huan Kuan, *Discourses on Salt and Iron*, trans. E. M. Gale (Leiden, 1931).

6. Yü, *Trade and Expansion*, pp. 188–219; and H. G. Creel, "The Role of the Horse in Chinese History," *American Historical Review* 70 (1965): 647–72.

7. Sima Qian, *Records of the Grand Historian of China*, trans. B. Watson, 2 vols. (New York, 1961), 2:188–89; Yü, "Han Foreign Relations," p. 385.

8. Sima, *Records*, 2:170–72. For Zhonghang Yue's proper name, rendered incorrectly in Watson's translation of Sima Qian, see Yü, *Trade and Expansion*, p. 11 n. 5.

9. Sima, *Records*, 2:192.

10. Raschke, "New Studies in Roman Commerce," especially pp. 606–22.

11. The principal source of information on Zhang Qian's travels is Sima, *Records*, 2:264–89.

12. The bloody sweat probably came from small lesions caused by para-

sites. On the horses of Ferghana see Creel, "The Role of the Horse in Chinese History."

13. S. A. M. Adshead, *China in World History* (London, 1988), p. 24.

14. See James Heitzman, *The Origin and Spread of Buddhist Monastic Institutions in South Asia, 500 B.C.–300 A.D.* (Philadelphia, 1980); also his article, "Early Buddhism, Trade and Empire," in *Studies in the Archaeology and Palaeoanthropology of South Asia*, ed. Kenneth A. R. Kennedy and Gregory L. Possehl (New Delhi, 1984), pp. 121–37.

15. The best study of Asoka is that of Romila Thapar, *Asoka and the Decline of the Mauryas* (Oxford, 1961). Also recommendable is B. G. Gokhale, *Asoka Maurya* (New York, 1966). Both works include translations of Asoka's rock and pillar edicts.

16. Thapar, *Asoka*, pp. 255–56.

17. The best guide to the ancient encounter of Greeks and Indians is Jean W. Sedlar, *India and the Greek World* (Totowa, 1980). For a convenient collection of ancient western writings on India, see R. C. Majumdar, ed., *The Classical Accounts of India* (Calcutta, 1981).

18. G. Koshelenko, "The Beginnings of Buddhism in Margiana," *Acta antiqua* 14 (1966): 175–83; and R. E. Emmerick, "Buddhism among Iranian Peoples," *Cambridge History of Iran*, 6 vols. (Cambridge, 1983), 3: 2:949–64.

19. Richard Garbe, *India and Christendom*, trans. L. G. Robinson (La Salle, Ill., 1959). See also Sedlar, *India and the Greek World*, pp. 107–89.

20. Jan Nattier, "Buddhism in Central Asia: The State of the Field," unpublished conference paper, delivered before the American Academy of Religion, November 1988.

21. The best study is that of Arthur F. Wright, "Fo-t'u-teng: A Biography," *Harvard Journal of Asiatic Studies* 11 (1948): 321–71.

22. On early Buddhism in China, see especially E. Zürcher, *The Buddhist Conquest of China*, 2 vols. (Leiden, 1959–72); also Liu Xinru, *Ancient India and Ancient China: Trade and Religious Exchanges, A.D. 1–600* (Delhi, 1988); Kenneth K. S. Ch'en, *Buddhism in China: A Historical Survey* (Princeton, 1964); Arthur F. Wright, *Buddhism in Chinese History* (Stanford, 1959); and Tsukamoto Zenryu, *A History of Early Chinese Buddhism*, trans. L. Hurvitz, 2 vols. (Tokyo, 1985).

23. Literature on the early history of southeast Asia bristles with historiographical controversies. The best general guides include George Coedès, *The Indianized States of Southeast Asia*, trans. S. B. Cowing (Honolulu, 1968); and D. G. E. Hall, *A History of South-East Asia*, 4th ed. (New York, 1981). On the cultural issues raised here, see especially O. W. Wolters, *History, Culture, and Region in Southeast Asian Perspectives* (Singapore, 1982); Kernial Singh Sandhu, *Early Malaysia* (Singapore, 1973); and

Kernial Singh Sandhu and Paul Wheatley, "The Historical Context," in *Melaka: The Transformation of a Malay Capital, c. 1400–1980*, ed. Sandhu and Wheatley, 2 vols. (Kuala Lumpur, 1983), 1:3–60. For the Gujarati story, see Sandhu, *Early Malaysia*, p. 8.

24. Sandhu, *Early Malaysia*, pp. 21–49; and Sandhu and Wheatley, "The Historical Context."

25. Sedlar, *India and the Greek World*, pp. 66–67.

26. For a convenient collection of texts on the spread of cults and syncretism, see Frederick C. Grant, ed., *Hellenistic Religions: The Age of Syncretism* (Indianapolis, 1953).

27. On Zoroastrianism, see R. C. Zaehner, *The Dawn and Twilight of Zoroastrianism* (London, 1961); and Mary Boyce, *Zoroastrians: Their Religious Beliefs and Practices* (London, 1979).

28. For an erudite and judicious study, see Samuel N. C. Lieu, *Manichaeism in the Later Roman Empire and Medieval China: A Historical Survey* (Manchester, 1985). This remarkable work surveys the career of Manichaeism from the days of Mani himself until the disappearance of the last Manichaean community in south China during the sixteenth century. Along the way it corrects a great number of long-standing misconceptions about Mani and Manichaeism. The quotation occurs on p. 61. See also Geo Widengren, *Mani and Manichaeism*, trans. C. Kessler (New York, 1965); and Sedlar, *India and the Greek World*, pp. 208–51.

29. Raschke, "New Studies in Roman Commerce with the East," pp. 605–79; Casson, *Periplus*.

30. For the classic argument that Mithra's cult represented influence of Persian culture in the Roman empire, see Franz Cumont, *The Mysteries of Mithra*, trans. T. J. McCormack (New York, 1956). There is by no means scholarly consensus on the origins and significance of the cult, but most scholars today doubt the presence of genuine Persian influence in the Roman cult of Mithra. For two alternative views, see Michael P. Speidel, *Mithras-Orion: Greek Hero and Roman Army God* (Leiden, 1980); and David Ulansey, *The Origins of the Mithraic Mysteries* (New York, 1989). On the cults of Orpheus, Isis, Baal, and others, see Grant, *Hellenistic Religions*.

31. Ramsay MacMullen, *Christianizing the Roman Empire (A.D. 100–400)* (New Haven, 1984), esp. pp. 17–42.

32. For a summary of his career, ibid., pp. 34, 59–61. On the miracles of St. Martin of Tours, see Aline Rousselle, "From Sanctuary to Miracle-Worker: Healing in Fourth-Century Gaul," in *Ritual, Religion, and the Sacred*, ed. R. Forster and O. Ranum (Baltimore, 1982), pp. 95–127.

33. Johannes Geffcken, *The Last Days of Greco-Roman Paganism*, trans. S. MacCormack (Amsterdam, 1978), esp. pp. 1–113, 281–304.

34. Ibid., pp. 223–80; MacMullen, *Christianizing the Roman Empire*, pp. 52–67, 102–19; and Pierre Chuvin, *A Chronicle of the Last Pagans*, trans. B. A. Archer (Cambridge, Mass., 1990). On the changes that state sponsorship brought for Christian doctrine, see the remarkable study of Elaine Pagels, *Adam, Eve, and the Serpent* (New York, 1988).

35. William H. McNeill, *Plagues and Peoples* (Garden City, 1976), pp. 106–47.

Chapter 3

Translations of verses from the Qur'an in this work come from *Al-Qur'an: A Contemporary Translation*, trans. A. Ali (Princeton, 1988).

1. Long-distance trade in this period is a fascinating topic that has generated a substantial body of literature. Among the more interesting works, see Philip D. Curtin, *Cross-Cultural Trade in World History* (New York, 1984), pp. 90–108; C. G. F. Simkin, *The Traditional Trade of Asia* (London, 1968), pp. 49–124; Richard W. Bulliet, *The Camel and the Wheel* (Cambridge, Mass., 1975); William H. McNeill, "The Eccentricity of Wheels, or Eurasian Transportation in Historical Perspective," *American Historical Review* 92 (1987): 1111–26; Wang Gungwu, *The Nanhai Trade: A Study of the Early History of Chinese Trade in the South China Sea* (Kuala Lumpur, 1958); George F. Hourani, *Arab Seafaring in the Indian Ocean in Ancient and Early Medieval Times* (Princeton, 1951); L. Rabinowitz, *Jewish Merchant Adventurers: A Study of the Radanites* (London, 1948); and Richard Hodges and David Whitehouse, *Mohammed, Charlemagne and the Origins of Europe: Archaeology and the Pirenne Thesis* (Ithaca, 1983).

2. For a spirited argument along similar lines, see Christopher I. Beckwith, *The Tibetan Empire in Central Asia* (Princeton, 1987), pp. 173–96.

3. D. G. E. Hall, *A History of South-East Asia*, 4th ed. (New York, 1981), pp. 47–73; George Coedès, *The Indianized States of Southeast Asia*, trans. S. B. Cowing (Honolulu, 1968), pp. 81–188. For Yijing's experience in Srivijaya, see the translation of his travel account: *A Record of the Buddhist Religion as Practised in India and the Malay Archipelago (A.D. 671–695)*, trans. J. Takakusu (Delhi, 1966), p. xxxiv.

4. See O. W. Wolters, *History, Culture, and Region in Southeast Asian Perspectives* (Singapore, 1982), especially pp. 56–68.

5. On Buddhism in central Asia, see Jan Nattier, "Buddhism in Central Asia: The State of the Field," unpublished conference paper, delivered before the American Academy of Religion, November 1988. On Dunhuang, see Aurel Stein, *On Ancient Central Asian Tracks* (London, 1933),

pp. 177–237; Zenryu Tsukamoto, "Historical Outlines of Buddhism in Tunhuang," in *Chinese Buddhist Texts from Tunhuang* (Kyoto, 1958), pp. 1–10; and *The Art Treasures of Dunhuang*, comp. Dunhuang Institute for Cultural Relics (New York, 1981).

6. On the Uighurs, see Colin Mackerras, *The Uighur Empire according to the T'ang Dynastic Histories* (Columbia, S.C., 1972); and Thomas J. Barfield, *The Perilous Frontier: Nomadic Empires and China* (Cambridge, Mass., 1989), pp. 131–63.

7. On Uighur culture, see especially James Hamilton, ed., *Manuscrits ouighurs du IXe–Xe siècle de Touen-Houang* (Paris, 1986), especially pp. 175–82; and Hans-J. Klimkeit, "Christians, Buddhists and Manichaeans in Medieval Central Asia," *Buddhist-Christian Studies* 1 (1981): 46–50.

8. Liu Xinru, *Ancient India and Ancient China: Trade and Religious Exchanges, A.D. 1–600* (Delhi, 1988), pp. 139–58; and Wang, *The Nanhai Trade*, pp. 46–61, 113–17.

9. Liu, *Ancient India and Ancient China*, pp. 139–58; Arthur F. Wright, *Buddhism in Chinese History* (Stanford, 1959), pp. 31–41.

10. Liu, *Ancient India and Ancient China*, pp. 167–73; Yang Xuanshi, *Memories of Loyang: Yang Hsüan-shih and the Lost Capital (493–534)*, trans. W. J. F. Jenner (Oxford, 1981), especially pp. 192–93, 198–99, 251. Yang's work has also been translated as *A Record of Buddhist Monasteries in Lo-yang*, trans. Y. T. Wang (Princeton, 1984); in that edition, see especially pp. 98–99, 109–10, 208.

11. The best study of early gentry Buddhism is that of E. Zürcher, *The Buddhist Conquest of China*, 2 vols. (Leiden, 1959–1972). See also Wright, *Buddhism in Chinese History*, pp. 42–54; and Tsukamoto Zenryu, *A History of Early Chinese Buddhism*, trans. L. Hurvitz, 2 vols. (Tokyo, 1985).

12. See Jenner's introduction to his translation of Yang, *Memories of Loyang*, pp. 16–37; also René Grousset, *The Empire of the Steppes: A History of Central Asia*, trans. N. Walford (New Brunswick, 1970), pp. 60–66.

13. See Arthur F. Wright, *The Sui Dynasty* (New York, 1978), pp. 126–38; and Stanley Weinstein, *Buddhism under the T'ang* (Cambridge, 1987).

14. Jacques Gernet, *Les aspects économiques du bouddhisme dans la société chinoise du Ve au Xe siècle* (Saigon, 1956), especially pp. 90–101; Kenneth K. S. Ch'en, *Buddhism in China: A Historical Survey* (Princeton, 1964), especially pp. 145–58.

15. On popular Buddhism, see Wright, *Buddhism in Chinese History*, pp. 72–75, 96–107; Edwin O. Reischauer, *Ennin's Travels in T'ang China* (New York, 1955), pp. 164–216; and Ennin, *Ennin's Diary: The Record of a Pilgrimage to China in Search of the Law*, trans. E. O. Reischauer (New York, 1955).

16. See translations of these travelers' accounts as follows: Faxian, *A Record of Buddhistic Kingdoms*, trans. J. Legge (Oxford, 1886); Yang, *Memories of Loyang*, pp. 255–71; Xuanzang, *Si-yu-ki: Buddhist Records of the Western World*, trans. S. Beal, 2 vols. (London, 1906); Yijing, *A Record of the Buddhist Religion*; and Yijing, *Chinese Monks in India*, trans. L. Lahiri (Delhi, 1986).

17. Yijing, *Chinese Monks in India*, pp. 75–76 (translation slightly edited here). For an alternate translation of this passage, see Yijing, *A Record of the Buddhist Religion*, p. xxvii.

18. Zürcher, *Buddhist Conquest of China*, 1:254–320.

19. See the translation of Han Yu's memorial in Reischauer, *Ennin's Travels*, pp. 221–24.

20. Weinstein, *Buddhism under the T'ang*, pp. 114–36. See also Ennin, *Ennin's Diary*, pp. 308–93; and Reischauer, *Ennin's Travels*, pp. 217–71.

21. Wright, *Buddhism in Chinese History*, pp. 86–127; Ch'en, *Buddhism in China*, pp. 471–86.

22. Wang, *The Nanhai Trade*.

23. For a fascinating study of these encounters, from which the following section draws much inspiration, see Edward H. Schafer, *The Vermilion Bird: T'ang Images of the South* (Berkeley, 1967).

24. Ibid., p. 21.

25. Ibid., pp. 42–44, 50, 59–60, 91, 100. The quotations occur on pp. 50 and 91.

26. Ibid., pp. 45–47, 56–69, 90–114.

27. For general discussions of this point, see Mary W. Helms, *Ulysses' Sail: An Ethnographic Odyssey of Power, Knowledge, and Geographical Distance* (Princeton, 1988), pp. 66–130; and Jane Schneider, "Was There a Pre-Capitalist World System?" *Peasant Studies* 6 (1977): 20–29.

28. For an impressive analysis, see Edward H. Schafer, *The Golden Peaches of Samarkand: A Study of T'ang Exotics* (Berkeley, 1963). The quotation comes from p. 28.

29. See two articles by Jan Nattier: "Buddhism in Central Asia"; and "The *Heart Sutra*: A Chinese Apocryphal Text?" *Journal of the International Association of Buddhist Studies* (forthcoming).

30. See, for example, Marshall G. S. Hodgson, *The Venture of Islam* (Chicago, 1974), vol. 1; and Ira M. Lapidus, *A History of Islamic Societies* (Cambridge, 1988). On the theme of conversion, see also Michael Gervers and Ramzi Jibran Bikhazi, eds., *Conversion and Continuity: Indigenous Christian Communities in Islamic Lands, Eighth to Eighteenth Centuries* (Toronto, 1990).

31. Bulliet, *The Camel and the Wheel*, pp. 87–110.

32. Hodges and Whitehouse, *Mohammed, Charlemagne and the Origins of Europe*, especially pp. 123–68.

33. Besides the passages quoted, see also 3:20, 16:82–83, 29:46, and 73:10–11, among many other similar teachings in the Qur'an.

34. Nehemia Levtzion, ed., *Conversion to Islam* (New York, 1979), especially Levtzion's introductory essay, "Toward a Comparative Study of Islamization," pp. 1–23. See also Georges C. Anawati, "Factors and Effects of Arabization and Islamization in Medieval Egypt and Syria," in *Islam and Cultural Change in the Middle Ages*, ed. Speros Vryonis (Wiesbaden, 1975), pp. 17–41.

35. See especially Daniel C. Dennett, *Conversion and the Poll Tax in Early Islam* (Cambridge, Mass., 1950).

36. Richard W. Bulliet, *Conversion to Islam in the Medieval Period* (Cambridge, Mass., 1979). See also Bulliet's essay, "Conversion Stories in Early Islam," in *Conversion and Continuity: Indigenous Christian Communities in Islamic Lands, Eighth to Eighteenth Centuries*, ed. Michael Gervers and Ramzi Jibran Bikhazi (Toronto, 1990), pp. 123–33.

37. See Ira M. Lapidus, "The Conversion of Egypt to Islam," *Israel Oriental Studies* 2 (1972): 248–62; and Gladys Frantz-Murphy, "Conversion in Early Islamic Egypt: The Economic Factor," in *Documents de l'Islam médiéval. Nouvelles perspectives de recherche*, ed. Yusuf Ragib (Cairo, 1991), pp. 11-17.

38. Alfred Bel, *La religion musulmane en Berbérie* (Paris, 1938). See also two articles by Tadaeusz Lewicki: "Prophètes antimusulmans chez les berbères médiévaux," *Boletín de la associación española de orientalistas* 3 (1967): 143–49; and "Survivances chez les berbères médiévaux d'ère musulmane de cultes anciens et de croyances païennes," *Folia orientalia* 8 (1967): 5–40.

39. Mary Boyce, *Zoroastrians: Their Religious Beliefs and Practices* (London, 1979), pp. 145–76.

40. The best study of Manichaeism is that of Samuel N. C. Lieu, *Manichaeism in the Later Roman Empire and Medieval China: A Historical Survey* (Manchester, 1985). On the later period, see especially pp. 178–264. See also Geo Widengren, *Mani and Manichaeism*, trans. C. Kessler (New York, 1965), pp. 117–34; and Otto Maenchen-Helfen, "Manichaeans in Siberia," in *Semitic and Oriental Studies*, ed. Walter J. Fischel (Berkeley, 1951), pp. 311–26.

41. On Uighur culture, see Mackerras, *The Uighur Empire*; Barfield, *The Perilous Frontier*, pp. 131–63; and Hamilton, *Manuscrits ouighurs*, pp. 175–82. On the Uighur city of Karabalghasun, see V. Minorsky, "Tamim Ibn Bahr's Journey to the Uighurs," *Bulletin of the School of Oriental and African Studies* 12 (1948): 275–305.

42. The only reliable guide to this development is Lieu, *Manichaeism*, pp. 178–264.

43. On the martyrs of Córdoba, see Norman Daniel, *The Arabs and*

Mediaeval Europe, 2d ed. (London, 1979), pp. 23–48; and especially the recent volume of Kenneth Baxter Wolf, *Christian Martyrs in Muslim Spain* (Cambridge, 1988). See also Jessica A. Coope, "Religious and Cultural Conversion to Islam in Ninth-Century Umayyad Córdoba," *Journal of World History* 4 (1993).

44. For some prominent examples, see Eleanor Duckett, *The Wandering Saints of the Early Middle Ages* (New York, 1964).

45. E. A. Thompson, *The Visigoths in the Time of Ulfila* (Oxford, 1966).

46. For a recent discussion of the Franks' conversion to Christianity, see Edward James, *The Franks* (Oxford, 1988), pp. 121–61. Gregory of Tours provided the classic account of Clovis's conversion; see his *History of the Franks*, trans. E. Brehaut (New York, 1916), 2:27–31, pp. 36–41. See also James, *The Franks*, pp. 121–23.

47. C. E. Stancliffe, "From Town to Country: The Christianization of the Touraine, 370–600," *Studies in Church History* 16 (1979): 43–59; Paul Fouracre, "The Work of Audoneus of Rouen and Eligius of Noyon in Extending Episcopal Influence from the Town to the Country in Seventh-Century Neustria," *Studies in Church History* 16 (1979): 77–91; and Johannes Geffcken, *The Last Days of Greco-Roman Paganism*, trans. S. MacCormack (Amsterdam, 1978), pp. 223–80.

48. Friedrich Heer, *Charlemagne and His World* (New York, 1975), pp. 119–36; Louis Halphen, *Charlemagne and the Carolingian Empire*, trans. G. de Nie (Amsterdam, 1977), pp. 47–51.

49. Fouracre, "The Work of Audoneus," p. 82. For a general discussion of the conversion of the Franks, see also James, *The Franks*, pp. 124–61.

50. On early Christian accommodation to pagan traditions: Geffcken, *Last Days of Greco-Roman Paganism*, pp. 281–304. For the period examined here, see Valerie I. J. Flint, *The Rise of Magic in Early Medieval Europe* (Princeton, 1991); and two articles by Karen L. Jolly: "Anglo-Saxon Charms in the Context of a Christian World View," *Journal of Medieval History* 11 (1985): 279–93; and "Magic, Miracle, and Popular Practice in the Early Medieval West: Anglo-Saxon England," in *Religion, Science, and Magic in Concert and in Conflict*, ed. Jacob Neusner, E. S. Frerichs, and Paul V. M. Flesher (New York, 1989), pp. 166–82. For Pope Gregory's policy, see Bede, *Bede's Ecclesiastical History of the English People*, ed. B. Colgrave and R. A. B. Mynors (Oxford, 1969), pp. 106–9.

51. J. P. Asmussen, "Christians in Iran," in *Cambridge History of Iran* (Cambridge, 1983) 3:2:924–48.

52. On Nestorians in central Asia, see G. W. Houston, "An Overview of Nestorians in Inner Asia," *Central Asiatic Journal* 24 (1980): 60–68; and A. Mingana, "The Early Spread of Christianity in Central Asia and

the Far East: A New Document," *Bulletin of the John Rylands Library* 9 (1925): 297–371. English translations of Nestorian documents are available in two works: A. C. Moule, *Christians in China before the Year 1550* (London, 1930); and P. Y. Saeki, *The Nestorian Documents and Relics in China*, 2d ed. (Tokyo, 1951). Saeki's work is relatively inaccessible, but includes documents that do not appear in Moule's collection. Notes will refer to both editions when possible.

53. The quotation (slightly edited here) comes from Saeki, *Nestorian Documents*, pp. 57–58. An alternative translation of the same document occurs in Moule, *Christians in China*, p. 65.

54. Saeki, *Nestorian Documents*, pp. 11–247; Moule, *Christians in China*, pp. 57–64. See the translation of the monument's inscription in Saeki, pp. 53–77; also in Moule, pp. 34–52.

55. Samuel N. C. Lieu, *The Religion of Light: An Introduction to the History of Manichaeism in China* (Hong Kong, 1979), p. 22.

56. Klimkeit, "Christians, Buddhist and Manichaeans"; also the same author's "Christian-Buddhist Encounter in Medieval Central Asia," in *The Cross and the Lotus*, ed. G. W. Houston (Delhi, 1985), pp. 9–24.

57. Saeki, *Nestorian Documents*, pp. 471–73; see also Moule, *Christians in China*, p. 70.

58. Al-Nadim, *The Fihrist of al-Nadim: A Tenth-Century Survey of Muslim Culture*, trans. B. Dodge, 2 vols. (New York, 1970) 2:836–37.

59. Saeki, *Nestorian Documents*, pp. 281–311.

60. For a similar argument, see Beckwith, *The Tibetan Empire in Central Asia*, pp. 173–96.

Chapter 4

1. Janet L. Abu-Lughod, *Before European Hegemony: The World System, A.D. 1250–1350* (New York, 1989); Philip D. Curtin, *Cross-Cultural Trade in World History* (New York, 1984), pp. 109–35; and the two recent volumes of K. N. Chaudhuri: *Trade and Civilisation in the Indian Ocean: An Economic History from the Rise of Islam to 1750* (Cambridge, 1985); and *Asia before Europe: Economy and Civilisation of the Indian Ocean from the Rise of Islam to 1750* (Cambridge, 1990).

2. Marco Polo, *The Book of Ser Marco Polo*, 3d ed., ed. Henry Yule and Henri Cordier, 2 vols. (London, 1929); Ibn Battuta, *The Travels of Ibn Battuta, A.D. 1325–1354*, trans. H. A. R. Gibb, 3 vols. to date (Cambridge, 1956–71). For Ibn Battuta's boast, see 2:451. For the recent calculations of his travels, see Ross E. Dunn, *The Adventures of Ibn Battuta* (Berkeley, 1989), p. 3.

3. Zhao Rugua, *Chu-fan-chi*, trans. F. Hirth and W. Rockhill (New York, 1966).

4. The best studies are those of S. M. Ikram, *Muslim Civilization in India* (New York, 1964); and Aziz Ahmad, *Studies in Islamic Culture in the Indian Environment* (Oxford, 1964).

5. Al-Biruni, *Alberuni's India*, trans. E. C. Sachau, 2 vols. (Delhi, 1964), especially 1:22–23, 110, 179–86.

6. William Theodore de Bary, ed., *Sources of Indian Tradition*, 2 vols. (New York, 1958), 1:355–57.

7. Ibn Battuta, *The Travels*, 3:763.

8. By far the best work on this subject is the exhaustive and brilliant analysis of Speros Vryonis, *The Decline of Medieval Hellenism in Asia Minor and the Process of Islamization from the Eleventh through the Fifteenth Century* (Berkeley, 1971). See also Claude Cahen, *Pre-Ottoman Turkey*, trans. J. Jones-Williams (New York, 1968).

9. Vryonis, *Decline of Medieval Hellenism*, p. 195.

10. Ibid., pp. 231–32.

11. Dunn, *The Adventures of Ibn Battuta*, pp. 229–37. The quotation occurs on p. 235.

12. Polo, *The Book of Ser Marco Polo*, 2:284.

13. See the somewhat speculative but well-reasoned work of M. C. Ricklefs, "Six Centuries of Islamization in Java," in *Conversion to Islam*, ed. Nehemia Levtzion (New York, 1979), pp. 100–128, especially 101–12. On the political culture of southeast Asia, see O. W. Wolters, *History, Culture, and Region in Southeast Asian Perspectives* (Singapore, 1982), especially pp. 1–15.

14. Derek Nurse and Thomas Spear, *The Swahili* (Philadelphia, 1985). See also the rich archeological study of Neville Chittick, *Kilwa: An Islamic Trading City on the East African Coast*, 2 vols. (Nairobi, 1974).

15. See Nehemia Levtzion, "Patterns of Islamization in West Africa," in his *Conversion to Islam*, pp. 207–16; and his *Ancient Ghana and Mali* (London, 1973). See also E. W. Bovill, *The Golden Trade of the Moors*, 2d ed. (London, 1968).

16. Dunn, *Adventures of Ibn Battuta*, pp. 290–309.

17. Kenneth K. S. Ch'en, *Buddhism in China: A Historical Survey* (Princeton, 1964), especially pp. 389–408.

18. Wolters, *History, Culture, and Region*, pp. 34–55.

19. George Coedès, *The Indianized States of Southeast Asia*, trans. S. B. Cowing (Honolulu, 1968), pp. 33–34, 188, 218–46; and D. G. E. Hall, *A History of South-East Asia*, 4th ed. (New York, 1981), pp. 74–104.

20. Hall, *History of South-East Asia*, pp. 105–50. For an analysis of Angkor's hydraulic system aided by aerial photography, see Bernard P.

Groslier, *Angkor et le Cambodge au XVIe siècle d'après les sources portu-gaises et espagnoles* (Paris, 1958), pp. 101–21. For a contemporary account of Angkor at its height, see Zhou Daguan, *The Customs of Cambodia*, trans. P. Pelliot and J. G. Paul (Bangkok, 1987).

21. Bernard P. Groslier, *Angkor: Art and Civilization*, trans. E. Smith (New York, 1966), p. 31.

22. Karl A. Wittfogel and Feng Chia-sheng, *History of Chinese Society: Liao (907–1125)* (Philadelphia, 1949). This work includes not only an analysis but also numerous documents in translation.

23. Wittfogel and Feng, *History of Chinese Society*, p. 265.

24. Jing-shen Tao, *The Jurchen in Twelfth-Century China: A Study of Sinicization* (Seattle, 1976).

25. On the Mongols in general, see the recent work of David Morgan, *The Mongols* (Oxford, 1986); and Luc Kwanten, *Imperial Nomads: A History of Central Asia, 500–1500* (Philadelphia, 1979). Though much criticized, Kwanten's work offers some useful insights concerning the relationship between central Asian nomads and their steppe environment.

26. For a French translation of the correspondence between Genghis and Chang Chun, see Edouard Chavannes, "Inscriptions et pièces de chancellerie chinoise de l'époque mongole," *T'oung Pao* 9 (1908): 297–308. For a contemporary account of Chang Chun's travels, see Li Zhichang, *The Travels of an Alchemist*, trans. A. Waley (London, 1931). The quotation comes from E. Bretschneider, *Mediaeval Researches from Eastern Asiatic Sources*, 2 vols. (New York, 1967), 1:37–39.

27. Morris Rossabi, *Khubilai Khan: His Life and Times* (Berkeley, 1988), pp. 37–43, 131–76.

28. Ibid., pp. 37–43, 142–46; and W. Heissig, *The Religions of Mongolia*, trans. G. Samuel (London, 1980).

29. On his career, see Igor de Rachewiltz, "Yeh-lü Ch'u-ts'ai (1189–1243): Buddhist Idealist and Confucian Statesman," in *Confucian Person-alities*, ed. A. F. Wright and D. Twitchett (Stanford, 1962), pp. 189–216.

30. Polo, *The Book of Ser Marco Polo*, 1:418.

31. On the Mongols in Persia and their conversion to Islam, see Morgan, *Mongols*, pp. 145–74.

32. E. A. Wallis Budge, trans., *The Monks of Kublai Khan, Emperor of China* (London, 1928), pp. 210–306. For an alternate translation: James A. Montgomery, trans., *The History of Yaballaha III, Nestorian Patri-arch, and of His Vicar Bar Sauma* (New York, 1927).

33. Polo, *The Book of Ser Marco Polo*, 1:263.

34. Chen Yüan, *Western and Central Asians in China under the Mongols: Their Transformation into Chinese*, trans. H. Ch'ien and L. Carring-ton Goodrich (Los Angeles, 1966). The quotation occurs on p. 252.

35. On this topic in general, see Chen, *Western and Central Asians in China*. L. Carrington Goodrich summarizes Chen's work in his article, "Westerners and Central Asians in Yuan China," in *Oriente poliano* (Rome, 1957), pp. 1–21.

36. Chen, *Western and Central Asians in China*, p. 132.

37. Ibid., pp. 48–49.

38. Ibid., pp. 98–110, 282–83. The quotation occurs on p. 110.

39. To mention only two works that represent a great deal of literature and basic research: Robert S. Lopez, *The Commercial Revolution of the Middle Ages* (Cambridge, 1976); and Lynn White, *Medieval Technology and Social Change* (Oxford, 1962). For a superb recent analysis that places Europe in the context of the broader Eurasian experience, see Abu-Lughod, *Before European Hegemony*.

40. For a recent survey of this topic, see J. R. S. Phillips, *The Medieval Expansion of Europe* (Oxford, 1988).

41. See especially Robert I. Burns, *Muslims, Christians, and Jews in the Crusader Kingdom of Valencia* (Cambridge, 1984); "Journey from Islam: Incipient Cultural Transition in the Conquered Kingdom of Valencia (1240–1280)," *Speculum* 35 (1960): 337–56; and "Renegades, Adventurers, and Sharp Businessmen: The Thirteenth-Century Spaniard in the Cause of Islam," *Catholic Historical Review* 58 (1972): 341–66. See also Angus MacKay, "Religion, Culture, and Ideology on the Late Medieval Castilian-Granadan Frontier," in *Medieval Frontier Societies*, ed. Robert Bartlett and Angus MacKay (Oxford, 1989), pp. 217–43.

42. See David S. H. Abulafia, "The End of Muslim Sicily," in *Muslims under Latin Rule, 1100–1300*, ed. James M. Powell (Princeton, 1990), pp. 103–33; and Benjamin Z. Kedar, *Crusade and Mission: European Approaches toward the Muslims* (Princeton, 1984), pp. 42–57.

43. Ibn Jubayr, *The Travels of Ibn Jubayr*, trans. R. J. C. Broadhurst (London, 1952), pp. 357–60.

44. Ibid., pp. 338–60, especially 340–43, 357–58. The quotation occurs on p. 342.

45. Kedar, *Crusade and Mission*, pp. 74–85. See also Kedar's "The Subjected Muslims of the Frankish Levant," in *Muslims under Latin Rule, 1100–1300*, ed. James M. Powell (Princeton, 1990), pp. 135–74.

46. Usamah Ibn Munqidh, *An Arab-Syrian Gentleman and Warrior in the Period of the Crusades: Memoirs of Usamah Ibn-Munqidh*, trans. P. K. Hitti (New York, 1929), p. 160.

47. T. W. Arnold, *The Preaching of Islam*, 2d ed. (London, 1913), pp. 89–96; and Norman Daniel, *The Arabs and Mediaeval Europe*, 2d ed. (London, 1979), pp. 195–232.

48. Fulcher of Chartres, *A History of the Expedition to Jerusalem, 1095–1127*, trans. F. R. Ryan, ed. H. S. Fink (New York, 1973), pp. 270–72.

49. Ibn Munqidh, *An Arab-Syrian Gentleman*, pp. 163–64, 169–70. The quotation occurs on p. 163.

50. Jacques de Vitry, *Lettres de Jacques de Vitry*, ed. R. B. C. Huygens (Leiden, 1960), pp. 79–97, especially 83–87.

51. The most important literature on this theme includes Jean Richard, *La papauté et les missions d'orient au moyen age* (Rome, 1977); and Igor de Rachewiltz, *Papal Envoys to the Great Khans* (Stanford, 1971). For a recent survey, see Phillips, *Medieval Expansion of Europe*, pp. 57–140. The most important collections of primary sources include A. van den Wyngaert, ed., *Sinica franciscana*, 3 vols. (Florence, 1929–36); Christopher Dawson, ed., *The Mongol Mission* (New York, 1955); and Henry Yule and Henri Cordier, eds., *Cathay and the Way Thither*, 2d ed., 4 vols. (London, 1913–16).

52. For an account of his mission, see Budge, *Monks of Kublai Khan*, and Montgomery, *History of Yaballah III*. See also the recent study by Morris Rossabi: *Voyager from Xanadu: Rabban Sauma, First Eastern Emissary to the West* (Berkeley, 1992).

53. See for example the second letter that John of Montecorvino wrote from Khanbaliq, in Dawson, *Mongol Mission*, pp. 224–27; Andrew of Perugia's report that he lived on an imperial stipend in Khanbaliq and Quanzhou, ibid., pp. 235–36; and the "Book of the Estate of the Great Caan," attributed to the Dominican John de Cora, in Yule and Cordier, *Cathay*, 3:100–3.

54. For some illustrations of the archeological remains, see P. Y. Saeki, ed., *The Nestorian Documents and Relics in China*, 2d ed. (Tokyo, 1951), especially pp. 429–39; and A. C. Moule, *Christians in China before the Year 1550* (London, 1930), pp. 78–93. Among Catholic reports, see especially John de Cora's "Book of the Estate of the Great Caan," 3:101–2.

55. See William's account of his experiences in Dawson, *Mongol Mission*, especially pp. 144–45, 173–80, 192.

56. Dawson, *Mongol Mission*, pp. 224–25; and John de Cora, "Book of the Estate of the Great Caan," 3:100–2.

57. Dawson, *Mongol Mission*, pp. 201, 206.

58. Ibid., pp. 236–37. The quotations occur on p. 237.

59. Francis J. Rouleau, "The Yangchow Latin Tombstone as a Landmark of Medieval Christianity in China," *Harvard Journal of Asiatic Studies* 17 (1954): 346–65. See also Rachewiltz, *Papal Envoys*, pp. 182, 203.

60. See John's two surviving letters and the letter of Brother Peregrine in Dawson, *Mongol Mission*, pp. 222–34.

61. See especially Chen, *Western and Central Asians in China*, pp. 53–57; also Rachewiltz, *Papal Envoys*, pp. 164–67.

62. Namio Egami, "Olon-Sume et la découverte de l'église catholique romaine de Jean de Montecorvino," *Journal asiatique* 240 (1952): 155–67.

For an earlier report, less systematic but quite engaging, see Owen Latti-more, "A Ruined Nestorian City in Inner Mongolia," in his *Studies in Frontier History* (London, 1962), pp. 221–40.

63. Frank W. Iklé, "The Conversion of the Alani by the Franciscan Missionaries in China in the Fourteenth Century," in *Papers in Honor of Professor Woodbridge Bingham*, ed. James B. Parsons (San Francisco, 1976), pp. 29–37.

64. Dawson, *Mongol Mission*, pp. 110, 179.

65. See John of Marignolli's own account of his mission in Henry Yule and Henri Cordier, eds., *Cathay and the Way Thither*, 2d ed., 4 vols. (London, 1913–16), 3:177–269; also Rachewiltz, *Papal Envoys*, pp. 187–204.

66. William H. McNeill, *Plagues and Peoples* (Garden City, 1976), pp. 149–98.

67. Abu-Lughod, *Before European Hegemony*, especially pp. 170–75, 183, 352–73.

Chapter 5

1. On the background and context of the Ming voyages, see Wang Gungwu, "Early Ming Relations with Southeast Asia: A Background Es-say," in *The Chinese World Order: Traditional China's Foreign Relations*, ed. John K. Fairbank (Cambridge, Mass., 1968), pp. 34–62. There is a large body of scholarly literature on the voyages themselves. See especially the following works: Joseph Needham *Science and Civilisation in China*, 6 vols. to date (Cambridge, 1954–), 4:3:486–553; J. J. L. Duyvendak, "The True Dates of the Chinese Maritime Expeditions in the Early Fifteenth Century," *T'oung Pao* 34 (1939): 341–412, and *China's Discovery of Africa* (London, 1949); Morris Rossabi, "Cheng Ho and Timur: Any Relation?" *Oriens extremus* 20 (1973): 129–36; and Jung-Pang Lo, "The Termination of the Early Ming Naval Expeditions," in *Papers in Honor of Professor Woodbridge Bingham*, ed. James B. Parsons (San Francisco, 1976), pp. 127–40. For a contemporary account of the voyages in English translation, see Ma Huan, *The Overall Survey of the Ocean's Shores*, trans. J. V. G. Mills (Cambridge, 1970).

2. Johann Schiltberger, *The Bondage and Travels of Johann Schilt-berger, a Native of Bavaria, in Europe, Asia, and Africa, 1396–1427*, trans. J. B. Telfer (London, 1879), especially pp. 74–75, 102.

3. For the experiences of Nikitin and Conti, see R. W. Major, ed., *India in the Fifteenth Century* (London, 1857).

4. Miguel de Epalza, *La Tuhfa. Autobiografía y polémica islámica de Abdallha al-Taryuman (fray Anselmo Turmeda)* (Rome, 1971).

5. On the early history of Melaka, see Kernial Singh Sandhu, *Early Malaysia* (Singapore, 1973), pp. 50–61; and especially C. W. Wake, "Melaka in the Fifteenth Century: Malay Historical Traditions and the Politics of Islamization," in *Melaka: The Transformation of a Malay Capital, c. 1400–1980*, ed. Kernial Singh Sandhu and Paul Wheatley, 2 vols. (Kuala Lumpur, 1983), 1:128–61. See also the early sixteenth-century account by Tomé Pires, *The Suma Oriental of Tomé Pires*, ed. and trans. A. Cortesão, 2 vols. (London, 1944), especially 2:229–89.

6. Richard Winstedt, *The Malays: A Cultural History*, rev. ed. (Singapore, 1981), pp. 35–38.

7. H. B. Johnson, ed., *From Reconquest to Empire: The Iberian Background to Latin American History* (New York, 1970).

8. On this theme see several excellent works: Charles Verlinden, *The Beginnings of Modern Colonization*, trans. Y. Freccero (Ithaca, 1970); Felipe Fernández-Armesto, *Before Columbus: Exploration and Colonisation from the Mediterranean to the Atlantic, 1229–1492* (London, 1987); and J. R. S. Phillips, *The Medieval Expansion of Europe* (Oxford, 1988), pp. 227–59.

9. Gomes Eannes de Azurara, *The Chronicle of the Discovery and Conquest of Guinea*, trans. C. R. Beazley and E. Prestage, 2 vols. (London, 1896–1899), especially 1:29, 79–86, and 2:201, 288. The quotation occurs at 1:81. See also G. R. Crone, ed., *The Voyages of Cadamosto* (London, 1937); and John William Blake, ed., *Europeans in West Africa, 1450–1560*, 2 vols. (London, 1942). For a somewhat different and richly detailed perspective on the encounter betweeen Portuguese and west Africans, see Ivana Elbl, "Cross-Cultural Trade and Diplomacy: Portuguese Relations with West Africa, 1441–1521," *Journal of World History* 3 (1992): 165–204.

10. Alonso de Espinosa, *The Guanches of Tenerife*, trans. C. Markham (London, 1907). The quotation occurs on pp. 90–91.

11. On the conquest of the Canaries, see Alfred W. Crosby, *Ecological Imperialism: The Biological Expansion of Europe, 900–1900* (New York, 1986), pp. 70–103; and John Mercer, *The Canary Islanders: Their Prehistory, Conquest, and Survival* (London, 1980).

12. Espinosa, *The Guanches*, pp. 45–78.

13. The accumulation of technological expertise in centers of high skills, followed by its diffusion to other lands, is a prominent theme in the works of William H. McNeill. See especially *The Rise of the West* (Chicago, 1963); and *"The Rise of the West* after Twenty-Five Years," *Journal of World History* 1 (1990): 1–21.

14. William H. McNeill, *Plagues and Peoples* (Garden City, 1976), pp. 1–76.

BIBLIOGRAPHY

Abulafia, David S. H. "The End of Muslim Sicily." In *Muslims under Latin Rule, 1100–1300*, edited by James M. Powell, pp. 103–33. Princeton, 1990.

Abu-Lughod, Janet L. *Before European Hegemony: The World System, A.D. 1250–1350*. New York, 1989.

Adshead, S. A. M. *China in World History*. London, 1988.

Ahmad, Aziz. *Studies in Islamic Culture in the Indian Environment*. Oxford, 1964.

Al-Biruni. *Alberuni's India*. Translated by E. C. Sachau. 2 vols. Delhi, 1964.

Al-Nadim. *The Fihrist of al-Nadim: A Tenth-Century Survey of Muslim Culture*. Translated by B. Dodge. 2 vols. New York, 1970.

Al-Qur'an: A Contemporary Translation. Translated by A. Ali. Princeton, 1988.

Anawati, Georges. "Factors and Effects of Arabization and Islamization in Medieval Egypt and Syria." In *Islam and Cultural Change in the Middle Ages*. Edited by Speros Vryonis, pp. 17–41. Wiesbaden, 1975.

Arnold, T. W. *The Preaching of Islam*. 2d ed. London, 1913.

Asmussen, J. P. "Christians in Iran." In *Cambridge History of Iran*, 3:2: 924–48. 6 vols. Cambridge, 1983.

Azurara, Gomes Eannes de. *The Chronicle of the Discovery and Conquest of Guinea*. Translated by C. R. Beazley and E. Prestage. 2 vols. London, 1896–1899.

Bachrach, Bernard S. *Early Medieval Jewish Policy in Western Europe*. Minneapolis, 1977.

_____. *A History of the Alans in the West*. Minneapolis, 1973.

Barfield, Thomas J. *The Perilous Frontier: Nomadic Empires and China*. Cambridge, Mass., 1989.

Note: Apart from works cited in the notes, this bibliography also includes many other items pertinent to the study of pre-modern cultural traditions and particularly to the study of their encounters.

Barth, Fredrik, ed. *Ethnic Groups and Boundaries*. Boston, 1969.

Beckwith, Christopher I. *The Tibetan Empire in Central Asia*. Princeton, 1987.

Bede. *Bede's Ecclesiastical History of the English People*. Edited by B. Colgrave and R. A. B. Mynors. Oxford, 1969.

Bel, Alfred. *La religion musulmane en Berbérie*. Paris, 1938.

Blake, John William, ed. *Europeans in West Africa, 1450–1560*. 2 vols. London, 1942.

Bovill, E. W. *The Golden Trade of the Moors*. 2d ed. London, 1968.

Boyce, Mary. *Zoroastrians: Their Religious Beliefs and Practices*. London, 1979.

Bretschneider, E. *Mediaeval Researches from Eastern Asiatic Sources*. 2 vols. New York, 1967.

Budge, E. A. Wallis, trans. *The Monks of Kublai Khan, Emperor of China*. London, 1928.

Bulliet, Richard W. *The Camel and the Wheel*. Cambridge, Mass., 1975.

_____. "Conversion Stories in Early Islam." In *Conversion and Continuity: Indigenous Christian Communities in Islamic Lands, Eighth to Eighteenth Centuries*, edited by Michael Gervers and Ramzi Jibran Bikhazi, pp. 123–33. Toronto, 1990.

_____. *Conversion to Islam in the Medieval Period*. Cambridge, Mass., 1979.

Burns, Robert I. "Journey from Islam: Incipient Cultural Transition in the Conquered Kingdom of Valencia (1240–1280)." *Speculum* 35 (1960): 337–56.

_____. *Muslims, Christians, and Jews in the Crusader Kingdom of Valencia*. Cambridge, 1984.

_____. "Renegades, Adventurers, and Sharp Businessmen: The Thirteenth-Century Spaniard in the Cause of Islam." *Catholic Historical Review* 58 (1972): 341–66.

Cahen, Claude. *Pre-Ottoman Turkey*. Translated by J. Jones-Williams. New York, 1968.

Cartier, Michel. "Barbarians through Chinese Eyes: The Emergence of an Anthropological Approach to Ethnic Differences." *Comparative Civilizations Review* 6 (1982): 1–14.

Casson, Lionel, ed. and trans. *The "Periplus Maris Erythraei"*. Princeton, 1989.

Chau Ju-kua. *See* Zhau Rugua.

Chaudhuri, K. N. *Asia before Europe: Economy and Civilisation of the Indian Ocean from the Rise of Islam to 1750*. Cambridge, 1990.

_____. *Trade and Civilisation in the Indian Ocean: An Economic History from the Rise of Islam to 1750*. Cambridge, 1985.

Chavannes, Edouard. "Inscriptions et pièces de chancellerie chinoise de l'époque mongole." *T'oung Pao* 9 (1908): 297–428.

Chavannes, Edouard, and Paul Pelliot. "Un traité manichéen retrouvé en Chine." *Journal asiatique* 10th series 18 (1911): 499–617; 11th series 1 (1913): 99–199, 261–394.

Ch'en, Kenneth K. S. *Buddhism in China: A Historical Survey*. Princeton, 1964.

Ch'en Yüan. *Western and Central Asians in China under the Mongols: Their Transformation into Chinese*. Translated by H. Ch'ien and L. Carrington Goodrich. Los Angeles, 1966.

Chittick, Neville. *Kilwa: An Islamic Trading City on the East African Coast*. 2 vols. Nairobi, 1974.

Chittick, H. Neville, and Robert I. Rotberg, eds. *East Africa and the Orient: Cultural Syntheses in Pre-Colonial Times*. New York, 1975.

Chou Ta-kuan. *See* Zhou Daguan.

Chuvin, Pierre. *A Chronicle of the Last Pagans*. Translated by B. A. Archer. Cambridge, Mass., 1990.

Coedès, George. *The Indianized States of Southeast Asia*. Translated by S. B. Cowing. Honolulu, 1968.

Coope, Jessica A. "Religious and Cultural Conversion to Islam in Ninth-Century Umayyad Córdoba," *Journal of World History* 4 (1993).

Creel, H. G. "The Role of the Horse in Chinese History." *American Historical Review* 70 (1965): 647–72.

Crone, G. R., ed. *The Voyages of Cadamosto*. London, 1937.

Crosby, Alfred W. *Ecological Imperialism: The Biological Expansion of Europe*. New York, 1986.

Cumont, Franz. *The Mysteries of Mithra*. Translated by T. J. McCormack. New York, 1956.

Curtin, Philip D. *Cross-Cultural Trade in World History*. New York, 1984.

Daniel, Norman. *The Arabs and Mediaeval Europe*. 2d ed. London, 1979.

Dawson, Christopher, ed. *The Mongol Mission*. New York, 1955.

de Bary, William Theodore, ed. *Sources of Indian Tradition*. 2 vols. New York, 1958.

Dennett, Daniel C. *Conversion and the Poll Tax in Early Islam*. Cambridge, Mass., 1950.

Dols, Michael W. *The Black Death in the Middle East*. Princeton, 1977.

Donner, Fred McGraw. *The Early Islamic Conquests*. Princeton, 1981.

Duckett, Eleanor. *The Wandering Saints of the Early Middle Ages*. New York, 1964.

Dunhuang Institute for Cultural Relics. *The Art Treasures of Dunhuang*. New York, 1981.

Dunlop, D. M. *History of the Jewish Khazars*. Princeton, 1954.

Dunn, Ross E. *The Adventures of Ibn Battuta: A Muslim Traveler of the Fourteenth Century*. London, 1986.

Duyvendak, J. J. L. *China's Discovery of Africa*. London, 1949.

————. "The True Dates of the Chinese Maritime Expeditions in the Early Fifteenth Century." *T'oung Pao* 34 (1939): 341–412.

Egami, Namio. "Olon-Sume et la découverte de l'église catholique romaine de Jean de Montecorvino." *Journal asiatique* 240 (1952): 155–67.

Elbl, Ivana. "Cross-Cultural Trade and Diplomacy: Portuguese Relations with West Africa, 1441–1521." *Journal of World History* 3 (1992): 165–204.

Elias, Norbert. *The History of Manners*. Translated by E. Jephcott. New York, 1978.

————. *Power and Civility*. Translated by E. Jephcott. New York, 1982.

Elvin, Mark. *The Pattern of the Chinese Past*. Stanford, 1973.

Emmerick, R. E. "Buddhism among Iranian Peoples." In *Cambridge History of Iran*, 3:2:949–64. 6 vols. Cambridge, 1983.

Ennin. *Ennin's Diary: The Record of a Pilgrimage to China in Search of the Law*. Translated by E. O. Reischauer. New York, 1955.

Epalza, Miguel de. *La Tuhfa. Autobiografía y polémica islámica contra el cristianismo de Abdallha al-Taryuman (fray Anselmo Turmeda)*. Rome, 1971.

Espinosa, Alonso de. *The Guanches of Tenerife*. Translated by C. Markham. London, 1907.

Fa-hsien. *See* Faxian.

Faxian. *A Record of Buddhistic Kingdoms*. Translated by James Legge. Oxford, 1886.

Fernández-Armesto, Felipe. *Before Columbus: Exploration and Colonisation from the Mediterranean to the Atlantic, 1229–1492*. London, 1987.

Filesi, Teobaldo. *China and Africa in the Middle Ages*. Translated by D. L. Morison. London, 1972.

Fisher, Humphrey J. "Conversion Reconsidered: Some Historical Aspects of Religious Conversion in Black Africa." *Africa* 43 (1973): 27–40.

Flint, Valerie I. J. *The Rise of Magic in Early Medieval Europe*. Princeton, 1991.

Fouracre, Paul. "The Work of Audoneus of Rouen and Eligius of Noyon in Extending Episcopal Influence from the Town to the Country in Seventh-Century Neustria." *Studies in Church History* 16 (1979): 77–91.

Frank, Andre Gunder. "The Thirteenth-Century World System: A Review Essay." *Journal of World History* 1 (1990): 249–56.

_____. "A Plea for World System History." *Journal of World History* 2 (1991): 1–28.

Frantz-Murphy, Gladys. "Conversion in Early Islamic Egypt: The Economic Factor." In *Documents de l'Islam médiéval. Nouvelles perspectives de recherche*, edited by Yusuf Ragib, pp. 11–17. Cairo, 1991.

Frend, W. H. C. "Some Cultural Links between India and the West in the Early Christian Centuries." *Theoria to Theory* 2 (1968): 306–11.

Fulcher of Chartres. *A History of the Expedition to Jerusalem, 1095–1127.* Translated by F. R. Ryan. Edited by H. S. Fink. New York, 1973.

Geertz, Clifford. *Islam Observed: Religious Development in Morocco and Indonesia.* Chicago, 1968.

Geffcken, Johannes. *The Last Days of Greco-Roman Paganism.* Translated by S. MacCormack. Amsterdam, 1978.

Gernet, Jacques. *Les aspects économiques du bouddhisme dans la société chinoise du Vᵉ au Xᵉ siècle.* Saigon, 1956.

Gervers, Michael, and Ramzi Jibran Bikhazi, eds. *Conversion and Continuity: Indigenous Christian Communities in Islamic Lands, Eighth to Eighteenth Centuries.* Toronto, 1990.

Glick, Thomas F. *Islamic and Christian Spain in the Early Middle Ages.* Princeton, 1979.

Goitein, S. D., ed. *Letters of Medieval Jewish Traders.* Princeton, 1973.

_____. *A Mediterranean Society.* 5 vols. Berkeley, 1967–88.

Gokhale, B. G. *Asoka Maurya.* New York, 1966.

Goodrich, L. Carrington. "Westerners and Central Asians in Yuan China," in *Oriente poliano*, pp. 1–21. Rome, 1957.

Grant, Frederick C., ed. *Hellenistic Religions: The Age of Syncretism.* Indianapolis, 1953.

Gregory of Tours. *History of the Franks.* Translated by E. Brehaut. New York, 1916.

Groslier, Bernard P. *Angkor: Art and Civilization.* Translated by E. Smith. New York, 1966.

_____. *Angkor et le Cambodge au XVIᵉ siècle d'après les sources portugaises et espagnoles.* Paris, 1958.

Grousset, René. *The Empire of the Steppes: A History of Central Asia.* Translated by N. Walford. New Brunswick, 1970.

Gumilev, L. N. *Searches for an Imaginary Kingdom: The Legend of the Kingdom of Prester John.* Translated by R. E. F. Smith. Cambridge, 1987.

Hall, D. G. E. *A History of South-East Asia*. 4th ed. New York, 1981.

Halphen, Louis. *Charlemagne and the Carolingian Empire*. Translated by G. de Nie. Amsterdam, 1977.

Hamilton, James, ed. *Manuscrits ouighurs du IXe-Xe siècle de Touen-Houang*. Paris, 1986.

Harden, Donald. *The Phoenicians*. New York, 1962.

Hay, Denys. *Europe: The Emergence of an Idea*. Rev. ed. Edinburgh, 1968.

Heer, Friedrich. *Charlemagne and His World*. New York, 1975.

Heissig, W. *A Lost Civilization: The Mongols Rediscovered*. Translated by D. J. S. Thomson. London, 1966.

_____. *The Religions of Mongolia*. Translated by G. Samuel. London, 1980.

Heitzman, James. "Early Buddhism, Trade and Empire." In *Studies in the Archaeology and Palaeoanthropology of South Asia*, edited by Kenneth A. R. Kennedy and Gregory L. Possehl, pp. 121–37. New Delhi, 1984.

_____. *The Origin and Spread of Buddhist Monastic Institutions in South Asia, 500 B.C.–300 A.D.* Philadelphia, 1980.

Helms, Mary W. *Ulysses' Sail: An Ethnographic Odyssey of Power, Knowledge, and Geographical Distance*. Princeton, 1988.

Herskovits, Melville J. *Acculturation*. Gloucester, Mass., 1958.

Heyerdahl, Thor. *Early Man and the Ocean*. London, 1978.

Ho, Ping-ti. *The Cradle of the East*. Hong Kong, 1975.

Hodges, Richard, and David Whitehouse. *Mohammed, Charlemagne and the Origins of Europe: Archaeology and the Pirenne Thesis*. Ithaca, 1983.

Hodgson, Marshall G. S. "Hemispheric Interregional History as an Approach to World History." *Cahiers d'histoire mondiale* 1 (1954): 715–23.

_____. *The Venture of Islam*. 3 vols. Chicago, 1974.

Horton, Robin. "African Conversion." *Africa* 41 (1971): 85–108.

_____. "On the Rationality of Conversion." *Africa* 45 (1975) 219–35, 373–99.

Hourani, George F. *Arab Seafaring in the Indian Ocean in Ancient and Early Medieval Times*. Princeton, 1951.

Houston, G. W. "An Overview of Nestorians in Inner Asia." *Central Asiatic Journal* 24 (1980): 60–68.

Hsüan Tsang. *See* Xuanzang.

Hudson, G. F. *Europe and China*. Boston, 1961.

Ibn Battuta. *The Travels of Ibn Battuta, A.D. 1325–1354*. Translated by H. A. R. Gibb. 3 vols. Cambridge, 1956–1971.

Ibn Jubayr. *The Travels of Ibn Jubayr*. Translated by R. J. C. Broadhurst. London, 1952.

Ibn Munqidh, Usamah. *An Arab-Syrian Gentleman and Warrior in the Period of the Crusades: Memoirs of Usamah Ibn-Munqidh*. Translated by Philip K. Hitti. New York, 1929.

I-ching. *See* Yijing.

Iklé, Frank W. "The Conversion of the Alani by the Franciscan Missionaries in China in the Fourteenth Century." In *Papers in Honor of Professor Woodbridge Bingham*, edited by B. Parsons, pp. 29–37. San Francisco, 1976.

Ikram, S. M. *Muslim Civilization in India*. New York, 1964.

Jagchid, Sechin, and Van Jay Symons. *Peace, War, and Trade along the Great Wall*. Bloomington, 1989.

James, Edward. *The Franks*. Oxford, 1988.

Jaspers, Karl. *The Origin and Goal of History*. Translated by M. Bullock. New Haven, 1953.

Johnson, H. B., ed. *From Reconquest to Empire: The Iberian Background to Latin American History*. New York, 1970.

Jolly, Karen Louise. "Anglo-Saxon Charms in the Context of a Christian World View." *Journal of Medieval History* 11 (1985): 279–93.

_____. "Magic, Miracles, and Popular Practice in the Early Medieval West: Anglo-Saxon England." In *Religion, Science, and Magic in Concert and in Conflict*, edited by Jacob Neusner, E. S. Frerichs, and Paul V. M. Flesher, pp. 166–82. New York, 1989.

Jones, W. R. "The Image of the Barbarian in Medieval Europe." *Comparative Studies in Society and History* 13 (1971): 376–407.

Kedar, Benjamin Z. *Crusade and Mission: European Approaches toward the Muslims*. Princeton, 1984.

_____. "The Subjected Muslims of the Frankish Levant." In *Muslims under Latin Rule, 1100–1300*, edited by James M. Powell, pp. 135–74. Princeton, 1990.

Klimkeit, Hans-J. "Christian-Buddhist Encounter in Medieval Central Asia." In *The Cross and the Lotus*, edited by G. W. Houston, pp. 9–24. Delhi, 1985.

_____. "Christians, Buddhists and Manichaeans in Medieval Central Asia." *Buddhist-Christian Studies* 1 (1981): 46–50.

Koshelenko, G. "The Beginnings of Buddhism in Margiana." *Acta antiqua* 14 (1966): 175–83.

Kuan, Huan. *Discourses on Salt and Iron*. Translated by E. M. Gale. Leiden, 1931.

Kwanten, Luc. *Imperial Nomads: A History of Central Asia, 500–1500*. Philadelphia, 1979.

210 *Bibliography*

Lamotte, E. *History of Indian Buddhism.* Translated by S. Webb-Boin. Louvain, 1988.

Landon, Kenneth Perry. *Southeast Asia: Crossroad of Religion.* Chicago, 1949.

Lapidus, Ira M. "The Conversion of Egypt to Islam." *Israel Oriental Studies* 2 (1972): 248–62.

———. *A History of Islamic Societies.* Cambridge, 1988.

Latourette, Kenneth Scott. *A History of the Expansion of Christianity.* 7 vols. New York, 1937–1945.

Lattimore, Owen. *Inner Asian Frontiers of China.* 2d ed. New York, 1951.

———. "A Ruined Nestorian City in Inner Mongolia." In *Studies in Frontier History,* pp. 221–40. London, 1962.

León-Portilla, Miguel. "El processo de acculturación de los chichimecas de Xólotl." *Estudios de cultura nahuatl* 7 (1968): 59–86.

Levtzion, Nehemia. *Ancient Ghana and Mali.* London, 1973.

———. *Conversion to Islam.* New York, 1979.

———. "Patterns of Islamization in West Africa." In *Conversion to Islam,* edited by Levtzion, pp. 207–16. New York, 1979.

———. "Toward a Comparative Study of Islamization." In *Conversion to Islam,* edited by Levtzion, pp. 1–23. New York, 1979.

Lewicki, Tadaeusz. "Prophètes antimusulmans chez les berbères médiévaux." *Boletín de la associación española de orientalistas* 3 (1967): 143–49.

———. "Survivances chez les berbères médiévaux d'ère musulmane de cultes anciens et de croyances païennes." *Folia orientalia* 8 (1967): 5–40.

Lewis, Archibald R. *Nomads and Crusaders, A.D. 1000–1368.* Bloomington, 1988.

Li Chih-ch'ang. *See* Li Zhichang.

Li Zhichang. *The Travels of an Alchemist.* Translated by A. Waley. London, 1931.

Lieu, Samuel N. C. *Manichaeism in the Later Roman Empire and Medieval China: A Historical Survey.* Manchester, 1985.

———. *The Religion of Light: An Introduction to the History of Manichaeism in China.* Hong Kong, 1979.

Liu Xinru. *Ancient India and Ancient China: Trade and Religious Exchanges, A.D. 1–600.* Delhi, 1988.

Lo, Jung-Pang. "The Termination of the Early Ming Naval Expeditions." In *Papers in Honor of Professor Woodbridge Bingham,* edited by James B. Parsons, pp. 127–40. San Francisco, 1976.

Lopez, Robert S. *The Commercial Revolution of the Middle Ages.* Cambridge, 1976.

Ma Huan. *The Overall Survey of the Ocean's Shores*. Translated by J. V. G. Mills. Cambridge, 1970.

Maalouf, Amin. *The Crusades through Arab Eyes*. Translated by J. Rothschild. London, 1984.

MacKay, Angus. "Religion, Culture, and Ideology on the Late Medieval Castilian-Granadan Frontier." In *Medieval Frontier Societies*, edited by Robert Bartlett and Angus MacKay, pp. 217–43. Oxford, 1989.

Mackerras, Colin, ed. and trans. *The Uighur Empire according to the T'ang Dynastic Histories*. Columbia, S.C., 1972.

MacMullen, Ramsay. *Christianizing the Roman Empire (A.D. 100–400)*. New Haven, 1984.

Maenchen-Helfen, Otto. "Manichaeans in Siberia." In *Semitic and Oriental Studies*, edited by Walter J. Fischel, pp. 311–26. Berkeley, 1951.

_____. *The World of the Huns*. Berkeley, 1973.

Major, R. W., ed. *India in the Fifteenth Century*. London, 1857.

Majumdar, R. C., ed. *The Classical Accounts of India*. Calcutta, 1981.

Marvazi, S. *Sharaf al-Zaman Tahir Marvazi on China, the Turks and India*. Translated by V. Minorsky. London, 1942.

McNeill, William H. "The Eccentricity of Wheels, or Eurasian Transportation in Historical Perspective." *American Historical Review* 92 (1987): 1111–26.

_____. *Plagues and Peoples*. Garden City, 1976.

_____. *The Rise of the West*. Chicago, 1963.

_____. "*The Rise of the West* after Twenty-Five Years." *Journal of World History* 1 (1990): 1–21.

Mercer, John. *The Canary Islanders: Their Prehistory, Conquest, and Survival*. London, 1980.

Mingana, A. "The Early Spread of Christianity in Central Asia and the Far East: A New Document." *Bulletin of the John Rylands Library* 9 (1925): 297–371.

Minorsky, V. "Tamim Ibn Bahr's Journey to the Uyghurs." *Bulletin of the School of Oriental and African Studies* 12 (1948): 275–305.

Miyakawa, Hisayuki. "The Confucianization of South China." In *The Confucian Persuasion*, edited by Arthur F. Wright, pp. 21–46. Stanford, 1960.

Montgomery, James A., trans. *The History of Yaballaha III, Nestorian Patriarch, and of His Vicar Bar Sauma*. New York, 1927.

Morgan, David. *The Mongols*. Oxford, 1986.

Morony, Michael G. "The Age of Conversions: A Reassessment." In *Conversion and Continuity: Indigenous Christian Communities in Is-*

lamic Lands, Eighth to Eighteenth Centuries, edited by Michael Gervers and Ramzi Jibran Bikhazi, pp. 135–50. Toronto, 1990.

———. *Iraq after the Muslim Conquest*. Princeton, 1984.

Moscati, Sabatino. *The World of the Phoenicians*. Translated by A. Hamilton. New York, 1965.

Moule, A. C. *Christians in China before the Year 1550*. London, 1930.

Nattier, Jan. "The *Heart Sutra*: A Chinese Apocryphal Text?" *Journal of the International Association of Buddhist Studies*, forthcoming.

———. "Buddhism in Central Asia: The State of the Field." Unpublished conference paper delivered before the American Academy of Religion, November 1988.

Needham, Joseph. *Science and Civilisation in China*. 6 vols. to date. Cambridge, 1954–.

Neill, Stephen. *A History of Christianity in India: The Beginnings to A.D. 1707*. Cambridge, 1984.

Nock, Arthur Darby. *Conversion: The Old and the New in Religion from Alexander the Great to Augustine of Hippo*. Oxford, 1933.

Noonan, Thomas S. "What Does Historical Numismatics Suggest about the History of Khazaria in the Ninth Century?" *Archivum eurasiae medii aevi* 3 (1983): 265–81.

Nurse, Derek, and Thomas Spear. *The Swahili*. Philadelphia, 1985.

Pagels, Elaine. *Adam, Eve, and the Serpent*. New York, 1988.

Panikkar, K. M. *India and China: A Study of Cultural Relations*. Bombay, 1957.

———. *India and the Indian Ocean: An Essay on the Influence of Sea Power in Indian History*. 2d ed. London, 1951.

———. *Lectures on India's Contact with the World in the Pre-British Period*. Nagpur, 1964.

Peel, J. D. Y. "Conversion and Tradition in Two African Societies." *Past and Present* 77 (1977): 108–41.

Pelliot, Paul. "Chrétiens d'Asie centrale et d'extreme orient," *T'oung Pao* 15 (1914): 623–44.

Phillips, J. R. S. *The Medieval Expansion of Europe*. Oxford, 1988.

Pires, Tomé. *The Suma Oriental of Tomé Pires*. 2 vols. Edited and translated by A. Cortesão. London, 1944.

Polo, Marco. *The Book of Ser Marco Polo*. 3d ed. 2 vols. Edited and translated by Henry Yule and Henri Cordier. London, 1929.

———. *The Description of the World*. 2 vols. Edited and translated by A. C. Moule and Paul Pelliot. London, 1938.

Powell, James M., ed. *Muslims under Latin Rule, 1100–1300*. Princeton, 1990.

Rabinowitz, L. *Jewish Merchant Adventurers: A Study of the Radanites.* London, 1948.

Rachewiltz, Igor de. *Papal Envoys to the Great Khans.* Stanford, 1971.

――――. "Yeh-lü Ch'u-ts'ai (1189–1243): Buddhist Idealist and Confucian Statesman." In *Confucian Personalities*, edited by A. F. Wright and D. Twitchett, pp. 189–216. Stanford, 1962.

Raschke, Manfred G. "New Studies in Roman Commerce with the East." In *Aufstieg und Niedergang der römischen Welt*, edited by H. Temporini and W. Haase, 2:9:2, pp. 604–1361. 2 vols. Berlin, 1978.

Ratnagar, Shereen. *Encounters: The Westerly Trade of the Harappa Civilization.* Delhi, 1981.

Reischauer, Edwin O. *Ennin's Travels in T'ang China.* New York, 1955.

Richard, J. "Essor et déclin de l'église catholique de Chine au XIVᵉ siècle." *Bulletin de la société des missions étrangères*, 2d series 134 (1960): 285–95.

――――. "Les missionaires latins dans l'Inde au XIVᵉ siècle." *Studi veneziani* 12 (1970): 231–42.

――――. "The Mongols and the Franks." *Journal of Asian History* 3 (1969): 45–57.

――――. *La papauté et les missions d'orient au moyen age (XIIIᵉ–XVᵉ siècles).* Rome, 1977.

Richards, D. S., ed. *Islam and the Trade of Asia.* Philadelphia, 1970.

Ricklefs, M. C. "Six Centuries of Islamization in Java." In *Conversion to Islam*, edited by Nehemia Levtzion, pp. 100–128. New York, 1979.

Rossabi, Morris. "Cheng Ho and Timur: Any Relation?" *Oriens extremus* 20 (1973): 129–36.

――――. *Khubilai Khan: His Life and Times.* Berkeley, 1988.

――――. *Voyager from Xanadu: Rabban Sauma, First Eastern Emissary to the West.* Berkeley, 1992.

Rouleau, Francis J. "The Yangchow Latin Tombstone as a Landmark of Medieval Christianity in China." *Harvard Journal of Asiatic Studies* 17 (1954): 346–65.

Rouse, Irving. *Migrations in Prehistory: Inferring Population Movement from Cultural Remains.* New Haven, 1986.

Rousselle, Aline. "From Sanctuary to Miracle-Worker: Healing in Fourth-Century Gaul." In *Ritual, Religion, and the Sacred*, edited by Robert Forster and Orest Ranum, pp. 95–127. Baltimore, 1982.

Saeki, P. Y. *The Nestorian Documents and Relics in China.* 2d ed. Tokyo, 1951.

Sandhu, Kernial Singh. *Early Malaysia.* Singapore, 1973.

Sandhu, Kernial Singh, and Paul Wheatley, "The Historical Context." In

　　　Melaka: The Transformation of a Malay Capital, c. 1400–1980, edited by Kernial Singh Sandhu and Paul Wheatley, 1:3–69. 2 vols. Kuala Lumpur, 1983.

Saunders, J. J. *Muslims and Mongols*. Christchurch, 1977.

Schafer, Edward H. *The Golden Peaches of Samarkand: A Study of T'ang Exotics*. Berkeley, 1963.

————. *The Vermilion Bird: T'ang Images of the South*. Berkeley, 1967.

Schiltberger, Johann. *The Bondage and Travels of Johann Schiltberger, a Native of Bavaria, in Europe, Asia, and Africa, 1396–1427*. Translated by J. Telfer. London, 1879.

Schneider, Jane. "Was There a Pre-Capitalist World System?" *Peasant Studies* 6 (1977): 20–29.

Scott, David A. "Christian Responses to Buddhism in Pre-Medieval Times." *Numen* 32 (1985): 88–100.

————. "Medieval Christian Responses to Buddhism." *Journal of Religious History* 15 (1988): 165–84.

Sedlar, Jean W. *India and the Greek World: A Study in the Transmission of Culture*. Totowa, 1980.

Sima Qian. *Records of the Grand Historian of China*. 2 vols. Translated by B. Watson. New York, 1961.

Simkin, C. G. F. *The Traditional Trade of Asia*. London, 1968.

Sinor, Denis. "Central Eurasia." In *Orientalism and History*, edited by Denis Sinor, pp. 93–119. 2d ed. Bloomington, 1970.

Southern, R. W. *Western Views of Islam in the Middle Ages*. Cambridge, Mass., 1962.

Speidel, Michael P. *Mithras-Orion: Greek Hero and Roman Army God*. Leiden, 1980.

Ssu-ma Ch'ien. *See* Sima Qian.

Stancliffe, C. E. "From Town to Country: The Christianization of the Touraine, 370–600." *Studies in Church History* 16 (1979): 43–59.

Stein, Aurel. *On Ancient Central Asian Tracks*. London, 1933.

Tao, Jing-shen. *The Jurchen in Twelfth-Century China: A Study of Sinicization*. Seattle, 1976.

Tarn, W. W. *Hellenistic Civilisation*. 3d ed. New York, 1961.

Teggart, Frederick J. *Rome and China: A Study of Correlations in Historical Events*. Berkeley, 1939.

Thapar, Romila. *Asoka and the Decline of the Mauryas*. Oxford, 1961.

————. "The Image of the Barbarian in Early India." *Comparative Studies in Society and History* 13 (1971): 408–36.

Thompson, E. A. *The Visigoths in the Time of Ulfila*. Oxford, 1966.

Tibbetts, G. R. *Arab Navigation in the Indian Ocean before the Coming of the Portuguese*. London, 1971.

Toussaint, Auguste. *History of the Indian Ocean*. Translated by J. Guicharnaud. Chicago, 1966.

Trimingham, J. Spencer. *The Influence of Islam upon Africa*. 2d ed. London, 1980.

Tsukamoto, Zenryu. "Historical Outlines of Buddhism in Tunhuang." In *Chinese Buddhist Texts from Tunhuang*, pp. 1–10. Kyoto, 1958.

––––––. *A History of Early Chinese Buddhism*. Translated by L. Hurvitz. 2 vols. Tokyo, 1985.

Ulansey, David. *The Origins of the Mithraic Mysteries*. New York, 1989.

Verlinden, Charles. *The Beginnings of Modern Colonization*. Trans. by Y. Freccero. Ithaca, 1970.

Vitry, Jacques de. *Lettres de Jacques de Vitry*. Edited by R. B. C. Huygens. Leiden, 1960.

Vryonis, Speros. *The Decline of Medieval Hellenism in Asia Minor and the Process of Islamization from the Eleventh through the Fifteenth Century*. Berkeley, 1971.

––––––, ed. *Islam and Cultural Change in the Middle Ages*. Wiesbaden, 1975.

Wake, C. W. "Melaka in the Fifteenth Century: Malay Historical Traditions and the Politics of Islamization." In *Melaka: The Transformation of a Malay Capital, c. 1400–1980*, edited by Kernial Singh Sandhu and Paul Wheatley, 1:128–61. 2 vols. Kuala Lumpur, 1983.

Wang Gungwu. "Early Ming Relations with Southeast Asia: A Background Essay." In *The Chinese World Order: Traditional China's Foreign Relations*, edited by John K. Fairbank, pp. 34–62. Cambridge, Mass., 1968.

––––––. *The Nanhai Trade: A Study of the Early History of Chinese Trade in the South China Sea*. Kuala Lumpur, 1958.

Weinstein, Stanley. *Buddhism under the T'ang*. Cambridge, 1987.

Wheatley, Paul. *The Golden Khersonese*. Kuala Lumpur, 1961.

White, Lynn. *Medieval Technology and Social Change*. Oxford, 1962.

––––––. "Tibet, India, and Malaya as Sources of Western Medieval Technology." *American Historical Review* 65 (1960): 515–26.

Widengren, Geo. *Mani and Manichaeism*. Translated by C. Kessler. New York, 1965.

Winstedt, Richard. *The Malays: A Cultural History*. Rev. ed. Singapore, 1981.

Wittfogel, Karl, and Feng Chia-sheng. *History of Chinese Society: Liao (907–1125)*. Philadelphia, 1949.

Wolf, Kenneth Baxter. *Christian Martyrs in Muslim Spain*. Cambridge, 1988.

Wolters, O. W. *History, Culture, and Region in Southeast Asian Perspectives.* Singapore, 1982.

Wright, Arthur F. *Buddhism in Chinese History.* Stanford, 1959.

——. "Fo-t'u-teng: A Biography." *Harvard Journal of Asiatic Studies* 11 (1948): 321–71.

——. *The Sui Dynasty.* New York, 1978.

Wyngaert, A. van den, ed. *Sinica franciscana.* 3 vols. Florence, 1929–36.

Xuanzang. *Si-yu-ki: Buddhist Records of the Western World.* Translated by Samuel Beal. 2 vols. London, 1906.

Yang Hsüan-chih. *See* Yang Xuanshi.

Yang Xuanshi. *Memories of Loyang: Yang Hsüan-chih and the Lost Capital (493–534).* Translated by W. J. F. Jenner. Oxford, 1981.

——. *A Record of Buddhist Monasteries in Lo-yang.* Translated by Yi-t'ung Wang. Princeton, 1984.

Yijing. *Chinese Monks in India.* Trans. by L. Lahiri. Delhi, 1986.

——. *A Record of the Buddhist Religion as Practised in India and the Malay Archipelago (A.D. 671–695).* Translated by J. Takakusu. Delhi, 1966.

Yü, Ying-shih. "Han Foreign Relations." In *The Cambridge History of China*, edited by Denis Twitchett and Michael Loewe, 1:377–462. 15 vols. Cambridge, 1987.

——. *Trade and Expansion in Han China.* Berkeley, 1967.

Yule, Henry, and Henri Cordier, eds. *Cathay and the Way Thither.* 2d ed. 4 vols. London, 1913–16.

Zaehner, R. C. *The Dawn and Twilight of Zoroastrianism.* London, 1961.

Zhau Rugua. *Chu-fan-chi.* Translated by F. Hirth and W. Rockhill. New York, 1966.

Zhou Daguan. *The Customs of Cambodia.* Translated by P. Pelliot and J. G. Paul. Bangkok, 1987.

Zürcher, E. *The Buddhist Conquest of China.* 2 vols. Leiden, 1959–1972.

INDEX

Abbasid empire, 68, 95
Achaemenid empire, 53, 55
Ahura Mazda, 55
al-Biruni, 119
al-Nadim, 108
Alans, 158, 161–62
Alexander the Great, 29, 46, 53, 54
Almohads, 94, 98
Almoravids, 98
Alopen, 106
Alvarus, Paulus, 99
An Lushan, 74, 96
Andrew of Perugia, 160
Angkor, 134–35
Anton the Guanche, 180–81
Arghun Ilkhan, 157
Asoka, 44–46, 92
Augustine of Canterbury, 101, 104
Augustine of Hippo, 7, 57, 63
axial age, 24–25, 33
Azurara, Gomes Eannes de, 178–79

Bactria, 53, 54
barbarian, concept of, 23–24
Benedict the Pole, 156
Berbers, 94
bhakti movement, 119–21
boddhisatvas, 76, 80, 102
Book of Daniel, 55–56
Boucher, Guillaume, 157
Bracciolini, Poggio, 171
Brother Peregrine, 161
bubonic plague, 27, 65, 162, 163–64, 182
Buddha, 7, 17, 44, 47, 52, 53, 54, 56, 77, 80, 82–83, 142
Buddhism, 16, 43–53, 65, 75, 92, 98, 107, 139, 140, 141–42, 143, 144, 147–48, 174, 175: Chan sect, 80, 133;

Hinayana, 76–77, 89; in central Asia, 47–49, 73–75, 89, 146; in China, 17, 49–51, 75–84, 132–33; in Persia, 46–47; in southeast Asia, 51–53, 72–73, 86–87, 133–35; Lamaist, 142, 158; Mahayana, 47, 56, 76–77, 89; Pure Land sect, 80, 133; Sarvastivada, 89; Tantric, 134, 142
Bukka, 121–22
Byzantine empire, 67

Cadamosto, 178
Candragupta Maurya, 46
Carolingian empire, 68
Celestine, pope, 105
Chang Chun, 140
Charlemagne, 18, 103
Chen Yüan, 161
Chichimecs, 25–26
Christianity, 55, 65, 92, 100–109, 151–52; Arian, 100, 102; Celtic, 101–102; in central Asia and China, 105–9, 156–63; in Europe, 101–5; in the Middle East, 105–6, 152–55; in the Roman empire, 16–17, 60–64; Nestorian, 14, 16, 75, 83, 89, 100, 101, 105–9, 141, 144, 158–60, 161, 162
Clotilda, 102
Clovis, 102
Confucianism, 35–36, 65, 82, 133, 138, 139, 140, 141, 142–43, 146–48, 161
Confucius, 80
Constantine, 12, 61, 62, 63–64, 92, 100
Conti, Niccolò, 171
conversion, 6–7; by assimilation, 13–15, 17, 26, 40, 98, 101, 106, 109, 139, 145–49, 153–55, 179; cross-cultural, 6–15, 18, 19; induced by pressure, 11–13, 14–15, 17, 62, 63–64, 68, 91,

217